LIFELONG EDUCATION AND THE TRAINING OF TEACHERS

Developing a Curriculum for Teacher Education
on the Basis of the Principles of
Lifelong Education

LIFELONG EDUCATION
AND THE
TRAINING OF TEACHERS

Developing a Curriculum for Teacher Education
on the Basis of the Principles of
Lifelong Education

by

A.J. CROPLEY
University of Regina and Unesco Institute for Education

and

R.H. DAVE
International Institute for Educational Planning

UNESCO INSTITUTE FOR EDUCATION, HAMBURG
and
PERGAMON PRESS
OXFORD · NEW YORK · TORONTO · SYDNEY · PARIS · FRANKFURT

43414

U.K.	Pergamon Press Ltd., Headington Hill Hall, Oxford OX3 0BW, England
U.S.A.	Pergamon Press Inc., Maxwell House, Fairview Park, Elmsford, New York 10523, U.S.A.
CANADA	Pergamon of Canada Ltd., 75 The East Mall, Toronto, Ontario, Canada
AUSTRALIA	Pergamon Press (Aust.) Pty. Ltd., 19a Boundary Street, Rushcutters Bay, N.S.W. 2011, Australia
FRANCE	Pergamon Press SARL, 24 rue des Ecoles, 75240 Paris, Cedex 05, France
FEDERAL REPUBLIC OF GERMANY	Pergamon Press GmbH, 6242 Kronberg-Taunus, Pferdstrasse 1, Federal Republic of Germany

First edition 1978

British Library Cataloguing in Publication Data

Cropley, Arthur John
Lifelong education and the training of teachers.
- (Advance studies in lifelong education; vol. 5).
1. Teachers, Training of 2. Continuing education
I. Title II. Dave, R H III. Unesco. Institute
for Education IV. Series
370'.71   LB1731   78-40002
ISBN 0-08-022987-5 Hardcover (Pergamon)
ISBN 0-08-023008-3 Flexicover (Pergamon)
ISBN 92-820-1015-5 Hardcover (UIE)
ISBN 92-820-1016-3 Flexicover (UIE)

In order to make this volume available as economically and as rapidly as possible the author's typescript has been reproduced in its original form. This method unfortunately has its typographical limitations but it is hoped that they in no way distract the reader.

"The UNESCO Institute for Education, Hamburg, is a legally independent entity. While the programmes of the Institute are established along the lines laid down by the General Conference of UNESCO, the publications of the Institute are issued under its sole responsibility; UNESCO is not responsible for their content.
   The points of view, selection of facts and opinions expressed are those of the author and do not necessarily coincide with official positions of the UNESCO Institute for Education, Hamburg."

The designations employed and the presentation of the material in this publication do not imply the expression of any opinion whatsoever on the part of the UNESCO Secretariat concerning the legal status of any country or territory, or of its authorities, or concerning the delimitations of the frontiers of any country or territory.

*Printed in Great Britain by William Clowes & Sons Limited
London, Beccles and Colchester*

ABOUT THE AUTHORS

CROPLEY, Arthur J. (Australia). Studied at universities of Adelaide and Alberta, and is now Professor of Psychology at the University of Regina, in Canada. During 1977 and 1978 he was on leave and worked at the Unesco Institute for Education in Hamburg. He has taught in Australia, England and Canada. Among his publications are *Creativity; Immigrants and Society* and *Lifelong Education: A Psychological Analysis.*

DAVE, Ravindra H. (India). Studied at universities of Bombay, Gujerat and Chicago. In 1976 joined the International Institute for Educational Planning (Paris), after completing four years as Technical Director at the Unesco Institute for Education, Hamburg. His previous experience included the post of Dean of Educational Development, National Council of Educational Research and Training, New Delhi; he directed the first Asian Curriculum Research Project. His publications include *Lifelong Education and School Curriculum; Reflections on Lifelong Education,* and *Foundations of Lifelong Education.*

CONTENTS

vii

43414

Contents

Contents

        INSTITUTIONAL IMPLICATIONS OF THE STUDY   186
        The role of lifelong education in
            guiding change   186
        The inevitability of institutional
            change   186
        The structure of changes   187
            Large- versus small-scale change   187
            Duration of change   188
            Need for a special course   188
            Time factor   188
            Implications for costs   189
            Relations with other institutions   189
            Preparatory steps   190
        Necessary pre-conditions   191
            Autonomy   191
            Readiness for change   191
            The role of the college's size   192

        EFFECTS ON INSTRUCTORS   192
            Instructors' workload   193
            Instructors' motivation   193
            Need for insight   194

        EFFECTS OF LIFELONG EDUCATION ON STUDENTS 194
            High level of pre-existing knowledge   194
            Greater amenability of students   195
            Central role of affective factors   195
            The avalanche effect   196
            Build-up of motivation   196
            Acceptance of self-evaluation   196
            Effects on morale   197
            Orientation to the external world   197

        IMPLICATIONS FOR PRACTICE TEACHING   197
            Broader concept of practice teaching   198
            Acceptance by students   198
            Need for preparation   198
            Integrated experiences   198
        Effects of school factors   199
            Inertia in the system   199
            Patterns of reinforcement in schools   200
            Role of key personnel   200
            Effects on pupils   201

Contents

LIST OF TABLES AND FIGURES

Page

xvii

FOREWORD

The constantly recurring demands, whenever educational
change takes place, for reconsideration both of the role of
teachers and of the nature of their training are already commonplace in educational literature. They are based on two im-
plicit assumptions which, although critically examined from
time to time and apparently controverted, have never been deci-
sively rejected. The first is that teachers are an important
factor mediating the effects of educational services, institutions and systems. The second is that the influence of teachers on the future personal, social and productive lives of pupils reflects, to a great extent, the professional training
they have received. It seems logical, therefore, that with the
adoption of a comprehensive and global approach to educational
innovation such as that resulting from the principles of lifelong education, the teacher's role and training should be the
objects of reconsideration and analysis.

To a certain extent, statements about teachers' roles and
training which are made in the perspective of lifelong education overlap with existing statements repeatedly made in the
past without reference to lifelong education. Among these may
be cited as instances discussion of the participative role of
teachers in the preparation and implementation of educational
reforms, particularly at the instructional level, or of the new
curricular content and methodology resulting from developments
in the various subject areas and from the emergence of new
kinds of educational technology.

Despite this, the principles of lifelong education have
implications of their own for the role assigned to the personnel responsible for the various stages and phases of the lifelong education process, and the expectations society has of
these people, as well as for the conception, organization and
implementation of their training. These implications may be
theoretically deduced, but their outcomes, feasibility, pre-

conditions and spin-off effects can only be assessed through experimentation and observation.

Within its current research programme, focussed on innovation in the substantive aspects of school level education (curriculum, evaluation, teacher education) as dictated by the principles of lifelong education, the Unesco Institute for Education has entered several avenues of work on teacher training. Following a preliminary theoretical study of the inter-relationship between lifelong education and the role of teachers, a review was made of the international literature on teacher training and of current trends in the area, developmental work was carried out, and an analysis of on-going related experiences was conducted.

The present report represents the outcome of a co-operative project in which selected teacher training institutions from different countries experimented with curricular and institutional modifications corresponding with the principles of lifelong education. Although based on the national findings submitted by the six research teams, this report is neither the simple juxtaposition of those findings nor their synthesis. Following a comparative methodology of its own, it identifies elements of knowledge not apparent when each of the reports is examined in isolation.

This study would not have been possible without the co-operation of the six participating institutions, their staff and students. They have given the benefit of their knowledge and skills, as well as considerable time and resources to ensure the success of this work. Whatever has been achieved is largely to their credit.

I would like to express my gratitude for the contributions made by a large number of specialists from all over the world who, through their experience, knowledge, advice and criticisms facilitated the progress of this project in the various stages from its conception to the preparation of the present volume.

Particular appreciation is due to the authors of the report, A.J. Cropley and R.H. Dave, who have not only guided and directed the project from its first stages, but have also succeeded in making an original contribution to the area of teacher education.

M.D. Carelli,
Director,
Unesco Institute for Education

INTRODUCTION

The Unesco Institute for Education is involved in a long term study of lifelong education and its implications for school level education. The programme includes both theoretical and empirical investigations. In the course of planning the various projects to be undertaken, it was realized that curriculum changes in the light of lifelong education could not be achieved without teachers who accepted their value, and who possessed the necessary attitudes, motives and skills. Consequently, it was concluded that appropriate changes in the content and methods of teacher training were needed. For this reason, it was decided to undertake a study of teacher training within the context of lifelong education.

The project was conceptualized as having two basic elements, the first theoretical, the second empirical. The theoretical part would specify the implications of lifelong education for teachers and teacher training. The empirical part would consist of actual implementation of practices consistent with lifelong education in teacher training institutions. The present text addresses itself to both of these tasks. Its first three chapters contain a description of lifelong education as it is understood by the present authors, along with specification of what this principle, as it has been defined here, implies for teacher training. The last six chapters contain a description and analysis of a project in which changes were introduced in six teacher training institutions.

The objective of the empirical part of the project was to design and implement a number of workable changes in the participating teacher-training institutions, and to evaluate the results. In this way it was hoped to show that the principle of lifelong education could be given concrete forms and put into practice in teacher training. Changes were to be made in the content of courses, in teaching and learning methods, in the institutions' internal organization, and in practice teaching, although not all of the institutions were expected to be able to make changes in all areas. Evaluation of the procedures was to be carried out where possible, although it was recognized from the start that formal evaluations might not be conducted in all cases, and that much of the evaluative material would be in the nature of qualitative judgments, subjective impressions and the like.

The project was co-ordinated by the Institute. It was international in scope, including six teacher-training institutions from five different countries in Asia, Southeast Asia, Eastern Europe and Western Europe. Thus it permitted application of the principles of lifelong education to a wide variety of social and political settings, and to institutions with different traditions, roles, and responsibilities. In this sense, the project was comprehensive in scope. It was hoped to demonstrate that the principles of lifelong education are not confined to a single socio-political setting. However, as a result of the variety of institutions involved it was not possible to develop a single experimental design to be followed by all of them. This meant that there was great variability in the changes made, the degree to which each institution was affected by the project, the kinds of evaluation carried out, and so on. Consequently, there was no attempt to determine, for example, which institution had been most successful in implementing lifelong education, which procedures worked best, or which setting was most favourable to the adoption of lifelong education. Nonetheless, as will become apparent later, some generalizations were possible. They are reported where appropriate.

Each institution was asked to make changes in such aspects as courses, methods, practice teaching and administrative procedures, according to what was feasible in view of the particular conditions prevailing within the institution. The rationale for these changes was to be lifelong education. Subsequently, each institution prepared a report on what had been done and how it had worked out, and transmitted its report to the Institute. After a final plenary meeting in Hamburg of the people who had directed the project in each institution, a cross-national report was prepared. The present book contains the final version of that report.

The report includes a theoretical introduction to the ideas encompassed by the term "lifelong education". It also outlines the changes introduced in the various participating

institutions, although this description is selective on the
basis of the needs of the present document. The text then summarizes findings from the various local projects, again in a
selective way, and finally develops a number of generalizations
which could serve as guidelines for teachers, administrators,
planners, teacher educators and researchers interested in further developing or in implementing the principles of lifelong
education in teacher training.

A number of appendices list details of the personnel in
each of the institutions who were involved, and indicate the
nature of the content of each of the local reports forming the
basis of the present report. There is also a selected bibliog-
raphy containing titles concerned with the basic idea of lifelong education, with innovation and application of the principles to teacher training, and with problems and issues in curricular innovation. It is hoped that these materials will make
it possible for those who are interested to examine more deeply
the work done in the present project, as well as the whole general question of application of the principles of lifelong education to teacher training.

Many people made important contributions to the conduct of
the study described in the present volume. First and foremost,
of course were the governing councils, directors, staff and students of the institutions which participated in the project,
and especially the local project leaders and those who directly
assisted them in designing, carrying out and reporting the work
at the local level. We gratefully acknowledge the contribution
of these people, some of whose names are listed in Appendix B.
When the first draft of the present report had been completed,
several scholars gave of their time to read and criticize the
original document. These people included D. Buckley, P. Cook,
J. Lynch and W. Van Vliet. There is no doubt that they contributed greatly to a much improved final document, and we are very
grateful to them. The tables and figures in the report were
prepared by G. Silz.

At the institutional level, R.H. Dave transferred to the
International Institute for Educational Planning prior to the
finalization of the present report. We are grateful to H. Weiler,
Director of that Institute, for permitting us to work together
in Paris during the final stages of preparing the document. The
participation in the project of A.J. Cropley was made possible
by a total of 2 1/2 years of leave from the University of Regina,
and we express our gratitude to that institution for its generous
help.

The main institutional contribution, however, was that of the Unesco Institute for Education in Hamburg. Many people at the Institute gave valuable help which is acknowledged with gratitude here. Ursula Giere and Johanna Kesavan made professional contributions in their roles as librarian and editorial assistant respectively, Louise Ortmann and Louise Silz were towers of strength in carrying out clerical and secretarial aspects of the project with exceptional skill and cheerfulness, and K. Robinson and P. Sachsenmeier contributed greatly with technical advice, and with carrying out the administrative aspects of the production and publication of the present document. Finally, we must not neglect to mention our gratitude to M.D. Carelli, Director of the Unesco Institute for Education, for his role in the conduct of the project.

CHAPTER 1

LIFELONG EDUCATION

RATIONALE AND PURPOSE OF THE BOOK

The traditional view of education is that it takes place mainly in schools and that it occurs during childhood. However, according to many educational writers this point of view is now obsolete. What is said to be particularly important in contemporary life is that people be able to adjust effectively to rapid and pervasive change, which is already occurring and is likely to continue for a considerable time. Schools are thus seen as no longer capable of providing most of the learning experiences people need. Furthermore, learning is also seen as necessary throughout each person's lifetime. What is therefore said to be needed is provision for systematic and purposeful learning in a variety of settings and at all ages. Such learning is said to need a special kind of educational system -- one involving *lifelong education*.

Of course education is not the only factor to be relied upon in coping with societal problems such as those arising from rapid change, nor is education capable of providing solutions on its own. It is merely part of the complex of economic, social and political influences which operate in any society. Nonetheless, it has an important contribution to make, provided that progressive changes in society go hand in hand with it.

The kernel of lifelong education is not new. It has been seen in classical writings such as those of Brahmin philosophers, in the writings of Solon and other Greek writers, and in the Koran. In more modern times, it has been advocated by Comenius and other early educational reformers such as Matthew Arnold. In recent times, the actual term "lifelong education" appeared in English educational writings more than 50 years ago,

1

while the main ideas of lifelong education in the contemporary
form were spelled out immediately after the Second World War
(see for example Jacks, 1946). Nonetheless, there may well be
special aspects of present-day life giving a new urgency to the
need for lifelong education, and establishing a climate in which
its acceptance may at last become widespread.

The present book is the final report of a project involving six teacher-training institutions in five different countries. In each institution an attempt was made to modify teacher training in ways consistent with the principles of lifelong education. Subsequently each institution prepared a report of what had been done there. These reports were then discussed at a meeting of the research teams concerned, and eventually a final report containing what might be called a cross-
analysis of the six local reports was prepared. The present
book is the final, cross-national report. Its first three chapters contain a theoretical introduction to the project. They
include a review of the basic ideas referred to as "lifelong
education", a discussion of the implications of these ideas for
the role of teachers, and an outline of what this implies for
teacher training. The subsequent chapters describe the steps
in the execution of the project, the nature of the changes introduced in the various participating institutions, and the outcomes of the changes. Finally, the last two chapters evaluate
the general feasibility and usefulness of the changes which
were carried out.

THE CHALLENGE OF CHANGE

The particular feature of contemporary life said to be establishing the new, more urgent need for lifelong education is
the phenomenon of rapid change. As McClusky (1974, p. 101)
put it, "continuous change requires continuous learning". Change
is taking the form of a "scientific-technological revolution"
and of associated socio-cultural changes (Agoston, 1975; Batyshev, 1972). Of course, civilization has seen sweeping change
before, for example in Europe at the time of the industrial revolution. However, two features of the present cycle of change
distinguish it from earlier phases. The first is the rapidity
with which it is occurring. In the past, change has always been
slow relative to the life expectancy of a single human being,
so that people could adapt themselves to conditions which re-
mained more or less fixed during their lifetimes (Knowles,
1975a). However, the present set of changes is occurring with-

in periods shorter than an individual lifespan, so that people
now living have seen, or will see, the world around them change
to a marked degree. The second feature of the contemporary cycle of change is that many of the developments have assumed
global proportions, and have been diffused across national and
regional boundaries with a speed never seen before (Dave, 1976).
The result is that change has become ubiquitous both geographically and also in the sense that it now pervades all aspects of
life. To some extent this has been made possible by some of
the changes themselves; for instance, developments in communications technology have contributed to wider and more rapid distribution of information about other areas of change, so that
change is as it were self-fuelling, and may even have become
self-sustaining.

The forms and effects of change are not identical in all
societies. On the contrary, change manifests itself in a variety of ways, depending upon the kind of society involved. Less-
developed nations, for example, may be more affected by changes
in world needs for primary products, by the need for increased
technology, and by the effects of newly-adopted modes of production on traditional societal structures. In more highly-
developed socialist countries, on the other hand, or in more-
developed capitalist societies, somewhat different patterns of
change and of reaction to change may be expected. Thus, it is
difficult to make generalizations about the phenomenon of change
without the risk of being too sweeping. There is also a problem that, even where it is agreed that change is having effects
in a particular area, the extent of these effects and the ability of different societies to control or avoid them differs according to the political and economic organization of the society and similar factors. Thus, the general remarks concerning
the areas and effects of change which follow have differing degrees of applicability to differing societies, and are often
largely threats or potentials, pitfalls to be avoided, or even
directions or trends, rather than universal realities.

Scientific-technological change

In the scientific-technological world, changes have been
seen in transport, communications, agriculture, medicine, and
all fields of science. Changes have been seen in the availability of and demand for consumer goods, and in the organization of the means of their production and distribution. The
transformation of industry as a result of widespread automation

is fast becoming a reality in many countries. To take other examples, computer processing of diagnostic data in medicine is finding increasing acceptance, extensive gains are being made in the technological and engineering problem of harnessing solar energy, and so on. Who could have predicted in the nineteenth century that some people then alive would live through the progression from the achievements of the Wright Brothers at Kitty-hawk to the commencement of regular crossings of the Atlantic at speeds faster than sound? These kinds of change in the scientific-technological domain are altering the meaning of work, leisure, health, distance, and many more.

Sociocultural change

Associated with the changes arising from the scientific-technological revolution are many sociocultural changes, including a change in the role of the family. In the past, the family was one of society's main educative agencies, especially in the areas of values, morals and social attitudes. However, as Coleman (1972) has pointed out, in some societies it is now coming to play a decreasing role. In technologically-developed capitalist societies, for example, children are exposed to socializing influences such as peers, TV and sports heroes, pop music stars and similar models, which compete with parents and often offer conflicting or contradictory sets of standards and values. Further changes in the role of the family may be expected in all societies as a result of factors like increasing urbanization, increasing technological growth and increasing complexity of life (Aujaleu, 1973). In some societies, the effects are potentially disastrous, with the possibility of a "collapse of values" (p. 25).

Other sociocultural changes affecting most societies, although in different ways according to factors like cultural traditions, speed and extent of technological development, and political leadership, include the changing social role of adolescents (Hicter, 1972), the changing relationship of workers to their work, to their fellow workers and to their bosses (Kupisiewicz, 1972), and in some wealthier nations, the problem of increased leisure. In many societies there is now increasing participation by the citizenry in the political lives of their local communities or of their nation (Lengrand, 1970). Sex stereotypes are also undergoing rapid change in both more-traditional and also in conformist societies, with increasing numbers of women playing vocational and social roles closed to

them in the past. In some wealthy nations in particular, there
is even decreasing emphasis on the whole idea of people as
breadwinners. Consequently, today's children may in the future
have to play social roles that differ from those accepted in
contemporary society. This suggests that they will need early
experience in playing a variety of such roles (Coles, 1972).

THE NEGATIVE CONSEQUENCES OF CHANGE

Change is not necessarily something to be viewed with
alarm. Indeed, without change there would clearly be no progress. However, when change occurs with excessive speed, and
simultaneously affects a wide range of basic values and life-
ways, it may have serious negative effects. Not only do these
possible effects involve vocational problems such as the obsolescence of job skills, but they may also include a threat to
psychological well-being (Suchodolski, 1976a). In such a situation, it is necessary to identify the potentially negative
consequences of change, and to try to develop ways of dealing
with them. A number of areas in which they may occur have already been identified by writers on lifelong education. They
are sometimes described in dramatic terms which, while possibly
exaggerated, serve to emphasize that some observers are deeply
concerned. The second necessary step, as far as education is
concerned, is to evaluate the capacity of existing systems to
cope with or avoid these consequences. Finally, there is need
for a constructive response to the possibility that change will
become destructive and harmful, so that alternatives can be
found which will avoid the problems and potential problems that
have been identified. The sections immediately following address themselves to the first step.

The threat of obsolescence

In the vocational world new jobs are appearing which did
not exist a few years ago, and old jobs which have existed for
many years are disappearing. In agriculture, for example, the
small, hand-worked farm is becoming obsolete, and many rural
people are experiencing the disruptions resulting from a shift
to the cities and the need to gain employment in industry. In
the factories new technologies are eliminating old jobs and
creating new ones. In the professions, knowledge and skill are
changing rapidly, so that the possibility of getting out of
date is always present. As a result of these kinds of change,

old skills, crafts and knowledge are rapidly becoming obsolete or irrelevant, so that people may have to change their job skills several times in a lifetime (Ulmer, 1974). Wroczyński (1973) reported that knowledge in some fields is doubling every 8-10 years, while Dubin (1974) has estimated that the knowledge gained in some university courses in engineering is already obsolete five years after students have graduated! For these kinds of reason, it is impossible, during the course of 10 to 20 years of initial schooling, to provide the young with a set of vocational skills which will serve them throughout their lives (McClusky, 1974). As a consequence for today's workers and for the children who will become tomorrow's workers, there is a genuine possibility of vocational obsolescence.

Psychological threats

When changes in work and social relations occur too quickly and are too sweeping, people can no longer make sense out of their interactions with their environments, they can no longer feel confident about their understanding of who they are and where they belong in the world. An inner state of uncertainty may be experienced, they become alienated (Suchodolski, 1976b), and individuality is threatened (Cropley, 1976; Dumazedier, 1972). At the same time, there is increasing concentration on the cognitive functions needed for functioning in a complex technology. There is a danger that in some societies this will lead to decreasing emphasis on the affective processes through which people express feelings and emotions. A closely-related effect of increasing technology and urbanization is the growth of materialistic values at the expense of the spiritual and aesthetic (Suchodolski, 1976b). As a result, contemporary people may find that their way of life is less and less capable of satisfying their emotional and aesthetic needs (De'Ath, 1976). These potential deprivations combine to produce the risk of alienation; society is threatening to become a "spiritual desert" (Suchodolski, 1976b, p. 82).

Threats to society

Change is also altering the social structures through which people relate to each other, such as work, family, friendship groups, and others of this kind. These are being rapidly transformed by the effects of technology. Workers are becoming more and more remote from their labour and from a sense of community with their fellow practitioners as a result, for example,

of the disappearance of the craftsman and the tiller of the
soil. Large urban residential conglomerates are also emerging,
with a further serious reduction in the quality of contacts between people (De'Ath, 1976). The family too is sometimes break-
ing down as a primary source of social life, and also of ethical
and cultural values. The result in some societies is the progressive destruction of the complex network of relations between
people based on respect, trust and close mutual interdependence.
These are being replaced by hostility, suspicion and even fear.
A further effect of urbanization, the spread of mass-produced
goods, and similar factors, is that many people nowadays live
more and more in artificial or "built" environments. Such environments are increasingly fragile and vulnerable, and depend,
among other things, on the smooth running of machines, the efficiency of complex systems of supply, the availability of vast
quantities of non-renewable resources, and the poisoning of the
ecosystem with waste products. Thus, social systems based on
technology can generate high levels of "survival pathology"
(De'Ath, 1976), posing the threat of destruction of human society, in the physical as well as the psychological sense.

DEFECTS IN TRADITIONAL EDUCATION

The negative consequences of change just described are not
inevitable. For example, they could be reduced or avoided if
people were equipped to carry out new learning in the face of
change, and thus to acquire new skills and knowledge when they
were needed, tolerate uncertainty, and resist alienation (Cropley, 1976). However, education as it currently exists is said
to have shortcomings which reduce its ability to prepare people
for productive and fulfilled lives in the face of the challenges
that have been described. These are discussed below.

Restriction of education to childhood

Education has traditionally been conceptualized as something that goes on during childhood, in order to provide children with the skills they will need in the future. As a result
the child has been seen as "a mere receptacle or 'stockpot' of
knowledge" (Silva, 1973, p. 43), absorbing information whose
value lies in the adult life to come. Education has thus been
regarded as "the influence exercised by adult generations on
the young" (Durkheim, 1961), and as best administered during
childhood, from about the age of 6 to 16, to 18 or even to 25,

despite the fact that there is some doubt that this period
really is the best time for learning (Rohwer, 1971). Consequently, conventional educational organization fails to meet
the needs of adults, and also neglects the very young in the
"pre-school" phase.

Excessive emphasis on knowledge of facts

If it is accepted that the primary purpose of education is
preparing children for making a living as adults, it follows
logically that its main emphasis should be on imparting knowledge likely to prove useful in later life. As a result, a
strong tendency has developed for schooling to concentrate on
cognitive processes such as knowing, reasoning, recalling, and
similar capacities, at the expense of affective factors such as
feeling, willing, hoping, fearing, and the like. Even within
the cognitive domain, emphasis has been placed on knowledge and
logical reasoning, to the detriment of skills such as identifying problems, locating resources, digging out information, evaluating, planning, and so on. This detracts greatly from education's potential for helping people to cope with the problems
of uncertainty and alienation that have been mentioned.

Pre-eminence of schooling

The views just mentioned give rise to the notion that education is something that goes on in schools only, under the
supervision of experts (i.e., professional teachers). As Suchodolski (1972) has shown, this view is of relatively recent
origin. At one time learning was carried out mainly in real-
life settings such as on-the-job, and was frequently of an informal or even unconscious kind. However, with the need for
skilled people able to understand and carry out the relatively
complex processes of emerging technology, on-the-job learning
has become inadequate and the idea has arisen that education
requires a special environment centering on schools. These
schools came to be "good, difficult and required many years of
attendance" (p. 142). Consequently, other educative experiences
and other potential sources of educative learning have been neglected in conventional education systems.

Dissociation of education and life

As a result of the factors already outlined, the process

of education and that of living one's life are seen as two separate and distinct sets of circumstances. Life is thought to
begin only when education has ended. The young learn, but
adults are thought to be too busy to spend time learning. This
means that connections between schooling and real life are regarded as more or less fortuitous. It also means that life itself is not seen as an educative experience. Finally, it means
that continued education is not regarded as a natural and normal way to deal with problems of life.

THE ALTERNATIVE: LIFELONG EDUCATION

One approach recently proposed as the master principle for
education, and said to be capable of dealing with the kinds of
problems that have been outlined, is that of *lifelong education*
(e.g., Faure, 1972). A major difficulty with the use of this
concept, however, has been its lack of clarity. As, for example Cropley (1974) and Duke (1976) have pointed out, it has
tended to be used by educational writers in a variety of ways,
and to be modified in order to fit each writer's notions of
what an ideal educational system would be like. As a result,
many different educational practices have been justified on the
grounds that they involve application of the ideas of lifelong
education, regardless of whether or not there is an obvious
connection. Nonetheless, review of writings in the area suggests that there is a coherent concept of lifelong education,
even though this may not be apparent from examination of any
single source. For the purposes of the present report, lifelong education is defined here in terms of three major characteristics which are outlined below. It may conveniently be
referred to by the label "lifelong education" because this is
its most prominent concrete feature, but the adjective "lifelong" does not, on its own, provide a comprehensive definition,
as will be seen shortly.

Vertical integration – Education throughout life

Lifelong education is based on the view that learning occurs throughout life as a normal and natural process, in much
the same way as physical and personal development continue.
According to proponents of lifelong education, this fact should
be formally recognized by educational theorists, and deliberate
attempts made to foster systematic and purposeful learning
from earliest years to old age. Systematic educative experi-

ences should therefore be available to people throughout their lives, whether for the purpose of remedying earlier educational defects, acquiring new skills, upgrading themselves vocationally, increasing their understanding of the world, developing their personalities, or for other purposes. Thus, the first broad principle of lifelong education is that it should be an integrated and co-ordinated process going on throughout life. As Bengtsson (1975, p. 7) puts it:

> It was deemed necessary to start gradually to change the present uninterrupted educational system from a concentrated education for the individual between 7 and 25 years of age, towards a system that would be available for an individual over his entire life cycle...

This notion is the first fundamental principle of lifelong education, and involves what may be called its "vertical integration" (Dave, 1973). It has been seen by some writers as implying that schools will cease to exist. However, a basic belief underlying the present project is that acceptance of lifelong education would give more emphasis to the importance of education in childhood and youth, not less. Thus, it is anticipated that schools will continue to function, although as will become more apparent from later sections, their methods and principles may change.

Horizontal integration - linking education and life

At one time life itself was one of the main sources of education. Social skills were largely learned through day-to-day interactions with other people, and vocational skills were mainly acquired by working with more skilled people on the job, observing them in action, taking advice from them, practising under their supervision, and so on. However, such systems of education have become impossibly inefficient, as a result of the increasing complexity of work and life (Suchodolski, 1972). The result has been emergence of the specialists in education and specialized places of education already discussed in an earlier section, and the consequent disuse of the learning resources of the community itself and of the experiences of normal life.

This state of affairs is now a matter of particular concern, because everyday life is so much affected by the kinds of change already outlined. The matters of making a living, being a member of a social group, sharing in recreational facilities, contributing to cultural life, and so on, require new learning almost constantly. Everyday life demands new learning, not simply the reapplication of old learning. Furthermore, the circumstances of life have themselves become the source of important knowledge, since it is here that the new knowledge is emerging. As a result, learning needs to be recognized as something which is closely linked with day-to-day living. The fact of the matter is that there are millions of teachers in industry, business, unions, churches, community service organizations, political parties and many similar aspects of non-school life. At the same time, the community contains many educative agencies such as museums, zoos, art galleries, churches, community centres, and similar agencies. In fact (Hiemstra, 1974, p. 35),

> ...most people, organizations, and agencies in
> a community have a potential...capacity for be-
> ing part of the educational process.

The basic problem, however, is that this educational potential often goes unacknowledged and unrecognized (Delker, 1974). What is needed, then, is to identify, recognize and improve the persons, processes, structures and agencies in each culture which have this educational potential, and thus to link education and life. Achieving such a linkage is the second major principle of lifelong education, the principle of "horizontal integration" (Dave, 1973). Again, as was mentioned in connection with vertical integration, this principle suggests an altered role for schools, which are seen as part of a complex educative network, not as the only sources of education. However, it does not necessarily imply their abolition.

Pre-requisites for learning - The means of lifelong education

Even if educational facilities were widely available to people of all ages, and the required degree of integration of education and life had been achieved, this would involve merely provision of the *opportunity* for lifelong education. It still could not be put into effect without the presence of appropriate skills and dispositions in the people who were to be the users of the system. Thus, it also requires what Dave (1973) called *educability*, along with the necessary *motives, values* and *attitudes*. Educability involves possession of appropriate learning skills such as the ability to set oneself learning tasks, to make use of the facilities available for carrying them out, and to judge whether or not results meet the needs of the sit-

uation. The second set of factors includes appropriate levels
of motivation, positive attitudes towards continued learning,
self definition of oneself as a learner, belief in one's own
ability to learn, and similar properties. If these two sets of
factors were sufficiently developed, people could be described
as "autodidactic" (Dumazedier and Gisors, 1973, p. 19).

   Educability. Lifelong education emphasizes the importance
of acquiring general thinking skills based on a grasp of the
structure of knowledge and on familiarity with its languages
and logics. This process is often referred to as "learning to
learn". Included in the learning skills making up educability
are self-directed learning (the ability to set one's own goals
and to pursue them through learning activities), and self-learning (the ability to learn by oneself, for example as a result
of mastery of knowledge-getting skills like reading). Educability also includes familiarity with learning aids (such as
libraries), and familiarity with technological aids to learning
(such as films, tapes, programmed materials, and similar devices). However, learning does not go on in isolation. On the
contrary, an important aspect of educability is the capacity to
learn with other people and from others, for example by learning in a group or learning from another student. Basically,
educability can be thought of as involving (a) learning to
learn, (b) learning to share knowledge, (c) learning to evaluate oneself, (d) learning to improve.

   Motivation and self-image. The second broad pre-requisite
for lifelong education is the possession of attitudes, values
and motives as a result of which people believe that learning
is a good thing and wish to continue learning. People are capable of learning at all ages (Cropley, 1976), but if they really are to learn there is a need for motivation, especially motivation to seek new knowledge and new skills. A second aspect
of psychological preparedness for lifelong learning is the necessity that people see themselves as learners and regard learning as something which is relevant to their lives. They need a
self-image of themselves as lifelong learners. Taken together,
motivation and self-image imply continuing flexibility and curiosity, and exuberance in the face of the new instead of fear of
it. This involves what Suchodolski (1976b) called "inward
youthfulness". What this means is that, among other things,
people will have to take responsibility for making decisions
and choosing among conflicting alternatives, helping to "build"
themselves instead of being built by other people's structuring
of their environments (Janne, 1976).

Characteristics of a lifelong education system

The guiding goals or ideals for education just described have implications for the structures and systems through which educational services would be delivered. Dave (1973, 1975) has developed a list of 20 "concept characteristics" which he felt summarized the main ideas of lifelong education. Taken in conjunction with other summaries such as those of Cropley (1974) and Lengrand (1970), this list has been consolidated into five major characteristics. For the present purposes, this list defines a policy for organizing educational systems in terms of lifelong education, in order to implement the three principles already specified.

Totality. Lifelong education covers the entire lifespan of the individual, includes all levels of education including pre-primary, primary, secondary, post-secondary, adult, and so on, and encompasses all forms of education including formal, school-based learning, non-formal learning that goes on in non-institutionalized settings, and informal learning which occurs in many different settings. It thus recognizes existing learning systems in a society, even when they do not conform to the conventional European-North American model of formal schooling. It also recognizes the importance of learning experiences occurring in the very young, prior to the time at which formal schooling commences, as well, of course, as stressing the importance of all the agencies through which adults learn.

Integration. All educative agencies are seen by writers in the area of lifelong education as inter-related and inter-connected. The home, for example is the earliest place of learning and should be seen as part of a network of learning systems. In the same way, the community is a major source of educative experiences throughout life. The work-place too is an important educative agency. Finally, schools, universities and other formal institutions of education are also part of the integrated learning system that includes home and community. However, they should not be regarded as enjoying a monopoly in educating people, nor as existing in isolation from other agencies.

Flexibility. The principles of lifelong education imply a dynamic approach to education. For example, it would allow adaptation of learning materials to changing needs, and adoption of new media as they become available. It would also be flexible in that it would allow alternative patterns of education, and diversity in content, in learning tools, in techniques of learning and in the timing of learning. Finally, it would not suppose that an individual is committed to a single life path as a result of educational decisions taken in childhood, but would permit change, for example through new learning carried out after the period of conventional schooling had ended.

Democratization. Lifelong education would make it possible for people of differing patterns of intellectual development, interests and motivation to benefit from education. Its aim is to provide educative experiences as and when people feel the need for them, and when the people concerned are appropriately motivated. Lifelong education would also permit education to have a corrective function, making up for shortcomings in earlier education. Finally, lifelong education is seen as something for everybody, with relevance to the lives of all people in a society. For these reasons, it may be said to be democratic rather than elitist in nature.

Self-fulfilment. The ultimate goal of lifelong education would be to improve each individual's quality of life. In order to achieve this, it would have to help people to adapt to change and to give full vent to their innovative capacities. In a similar way, it seeks a society whose adaptive and innovative functions are maximized through the self-confidence and vigor of its members. This would require people who could cope with the political and social pressures of the times, who could express their emotions, and who could find personal fulfilment partly in cooperating with other people.

THE PRACTICABILITY OF LIFELONG EDUCATION

It has been argued that existing educational systems are not completely capable of coping with the conditions of contemporary life that have already been outlined. Lifelong education has been proposed as an essential element in society's response to the new needs and challenges. In view of this claim, some examination of the practical feasibility of lifelong education seems to be appropriate at this point. Evidence, for example, that the basic principles were consistent with knowledge about human capacities would strengthen the confidence with which it could be applied. For this reason, review of the practicability of lifelong education is called for.

The ability to learn throughout life

It has often been noticed that children learn with speed and apparent ease, whereas adults seem to find learning harder and take longer to master school-like learning tasks. At the same time, the kinds of things learned by infants and very young children are often denigrated, involving as they do things that older children and adults can do with ease (e.g., walking, talking and similar capacities). These observations have led to the emergence of what McClusky (1974) called a "myth" that childhood is the best time for learning. Other writers (see Cropley, 1976 for a review) have reinforced this notion by reporting that 75% of all learning is done in early childhood, that nothing much is learned after 40, that creativity normally occurs in early adulthood, and similar ideas. Data on intelligence test scores at different ages and similar studies have also reinforced the belief, summed up in the popular saying "You can't teach an old dog new tricks", that worthwhile learning occurs primarily in middle and late childhood, adolescence, and early adulthood.

However, there is now increasing evidence, both from research studies (see Cropley, 1976), and also from practical observation (see Tough, 1971), that adults are perfectly capable of learning even formal, school-like material, such as the grammar of a foreign language, until very advanced ages. In fact, Schaie (1974) identified a second "myth" in the area of age and learning ability: the view that adults cannot learn. Changes in learning ability, or even declines, undoubtedly occur (Horn and Donaldson, 1976). However, it is now quite clear that adults not only *can* learn, but that many of them actually *do* learn, even in old age. In terms of the question of whether people can learn other than between the ages of 6 and 15, then, there is strong evidence that the capacity for lifelong education exists. In this sense, the concept is feasible.

The skills and the will to learn

However, the mere existence of a capacity for lifelong education does not on its own establish its feasibility. Lifelong education would require considerable change in societal attitudes and values in the area of education. For example, it involves a continuing movement towards not only the democratization of education but also the democratization of society (Kirpal, 1976). In some ways, its implementation would be a political event of great significance. Furthermore, education systems themselves are highly resistant to change, so that the problem arises of inertia or resistance in the system. The provision of further opportunities for lifelong education on a widespread scale could thus be seen as largely an administrative, organizational or political problem, requiring what Dave (1976, p. 362) called "the political will".

Even granted the will, however, the question remains of whether, given the opportunity for lifelong education and the intellectual capacity for it, people possess the abilities or skills needed to engage in lifelong learning, the desire to carry on a process of lifelong education, and the necessary attitudes, self-concepts and values that would lead to regarding both the entire lifetime and also the events of life itself as educative experiences. It is apparent that the necessary learning skills are often lacking. Teachers, for example, will also be aware that intrinsic motivation, self-evaluation, and similar properties are often difficult to foster in their pupils. Similarly, it is apparent that many people define education as something that goes on strictly in schools, and that they regard themselves as incapable of learning once they have left school. A good example of this is to be found in the problem Cropley (1976) cited of workers in the USA who were offered retraining courses when their previous job skills became obsolete. Few of them completed the courses of training, largely because they felt humiliated and embarrassed at going back to a formal learning situation, something which they defined as fit only for children and degrading for adults. Wlodarski (1976) referred to a similar stigmatization of adult education in Poland.

Thus, the issue of motivation and possession of appropriate skills for lifelong education is an important one in assessing its real-life feasibility. At present, the necessary motives and skills are probably lacking in many people. This raises the question of the strategy to be pursued in implementing lifelong education. Broadly speaking, it could be attempted through focusing on the learning systems, or else on the learners. As Duke (1976) has pointed out, the institutional approach is fraught with difficulties. It is all very well to adopt lifelong education as an institutional principle, but its true implementation would only be possible if it were accepted by the individuals involved. Furthermore, attempts to impose lifelong education through changes in the system not only smack of authoritarianism, but raise the spectre of lifelong education participated in through coercion or even fear, rather than out of curiosity and interest (Dauber, Fritsch, Liegle, Sachs,

Scheilke and Spiekermann, 1975). Thus, an approach is called
for in which the primary focus is on encouraging people to seek
lifelong education. Changes in the system would then have the
primary purpose of supporting people in their lifelong learning,
not of compelling or requiring it.

Suchodolski (1976b) has made an interesting and hopeful
point in this connection. He pointed out that motives and
skills are not only pre-conditions for lifelong education (i.e.,
factors to be taken into account in weighing the question of
whether it is feasible or not), but that they are also outcomes
that will be realized if lifelong education is established.
This means that the pre-conditions for lifelong education will
be created as results of movements towards its adoption. As a
result, the more that lifelong education is implemented, the
easier will be its further implementation, because the earlier
attempts at implementation will help to provide the pre-conditions necessary for it to be fully adopted. This means that
the more attempts are made to adopt lifelong education, the
more feasible does its adoption become, because of what Suchodolski (p. 75) referred to as an "avalanche" effect.

Communication systems

Lifelong education would require that systematic learning
go on in many places at many times. It would also require
mechanisms permitting integration of information from many
sources such as family, work, culture and school, along with
the linking of information from past and present. Thus, it
would have to be freed from confinement to schools and from
restrictions in time. It would also require ready transfer of
information among, for example, people engaged in group learning, while individual access to sources of knowledge such as
books and up-to-date information about the society would be
necessary. On the other hand, it is important to bear in mind
at this point that learning is only partly under the control of
stimuli such as the information presented by a mass medium.
For example, practice which is "correct" (it resembles the desired end-product), and which is rewarded in some way, is also
important. Consequently, there would also be need for goal-
setting, feedback and evaluation of outcomes. For these reasons, the feasibility of lifelong education would be greatly
increased by the availability of complex systems of communication, information transfer, and feedback. Fortunately, most
human societies already possess one very well-developed system

of this kind -- language. Because of the complex manipulation
of abstract symbols which it permits, language serves a major
purpose in communication. However, it is not the only system
of information transfer available to human beings. They also
possess "extra-linguistic" modes of communication (De'Ath, 1976,
p. 273), which could be used to make it more efficient. This
seems likely to be particularly the case in less-developed countries, because many of them lack a single, common language.

In view of the need of lifelong education for techniques
for transmitting information over and above the face-to-face
verbal contact of the traditional classroom, the mass media assume considerable importance in assessing its practicability.
They permit the distribution of information on a very widespread
basis, and eliminate the need for all students to be together in
classrooms as they are currently known. Furthermore, some media
permit communication through alternative modes, such as vision.
In developing countries, because of language problems, this
could prove to be a major advantage. Through the mass media,
information can be presented in a highly abstract form to widely diffused audiences, but still can be linked to everyday life.
The mass media make it possible to use informal learning processes and sources of information that are not physically at-
tainable, to represent the past, and to depict images of the
future. Finally, the media permit contact with sources of
learning that are geographically remote, such as other societies. Thus, they are of great importance in achieving certain
aspects of vertical and horizontal integration and, in this respect, are a major element in assuring the feasibility of lifelong education.

LIFELONG EDUCATION AND THE SCHOOL

In earlier sections the terms "lifelong education" and
"lifelong learning" have been used more or less interchangeably.
However, although the two processes are closely related they
are not the same, and a distinction needs to be drawn. In general, learning may be conceptualized as a process resulting in
changes in an individual's knowledge, skills, beliefs, attitudes, values and similar properties, as a result of experience.
Normally, learning is only known to have occurred when it manifests itself in behaviour, although the exact relationship of
learning and behaviour is a matter of debate. Education on the
other hand, is concerned with the events in life which bring
about learning. It involves the system which modifies the spontaneous and natural process of learning.

A further important distinction is that between education and schooling. In some sections of this report the two terms may be used as though they mean the same. However, where this occurs, it is purely for ease of reference. Schooling involves conscious teaching/learning processes deliberately designed for modifying behaviour. This is regulated according to goals and purposes specified by curricula, and using methods agreed upon by professional educators. Schooling is thus a special case of education, not a definition of it. In the context of the present report, lifelong learning is thus the hoped-for process, lifelong education the system which it is thought will foster and encourage that process, and schooling one part of the system (although an important one, and of major interest in this book).

The systems through which learning occurs

Coombs (1973) has developed a valuable conceptualization of the way in which the processes just discussed (learning, education and schooling) are fostered by the learning structures of society. He first distinguishes between "formal education" and "non-formal education". The former refers to the structured set of organized educational institutions including primary schools, high schools, universities, other institutions offering professional and technical training, and the whole range of educational organizations involved in full-time training. Schools are, of course, the best known examples of the system of formal education. Non-formal education, by contrast, refers to less highly organized educational activities which go on outside the formal system that has just been described. Although it involves structures deliberately constructed to promote learning, non-formal education need not be identified with schools at all, is often voluntary and part-time in participation, may be ungraded and loosely organized, and is frequently concerned with immediate and practical goals. Finally, Coombs refers to "in-formal education". It involves the whole system of learning through day-to-day experiences in an unstructured, spontaneous manner, and may not have any specific conscious or systematic educational organization.

Independent existence of lifelong education

It has been argued in earlier sections that learning is already a lifelong process. Small children, for example, master the fundamentals of the mother tongue during the first three

years or so of life. They also learn the toilet habits of their
society during the same period, and many of the social customs
such as the basis of "good" manners, the elementary forms for
interacting with other people, and so on. At the time of commencing school they can usually speak well, observe the sleep-
ing, waking and eating cycles of their societies, eliminate
bodily wastes in socially-acceptable ways, follow basic dress
habits, observe the more superficial forms of conventional sex
roles, and many more. Similarly, after the termination of
schooling people learn how to play the roles of adults, how to
participate in community affairs, how to be spouses and parents,
and similar achievements. They also adjust more or less continuously to changing roles, rights and responsibilities as
they grow older, become richer or poorer, experience sicknesses,
and so on. Finally, they may acquire new job skills, assume
different roles in the work setting, or make similar changes,
in most cases with an acceptable degree of success. Thus, it
is quite clear that life itself is a dynamic process in which
constant learning takes place. There is no need to talk about
lifelong learning as a new phenomenon, nor to advocate changes
in life to make lifelong learning possible, for it already
exists.

Lifelong education and lifelong learning

The important question for the present sections is that of
the connection between lifelong learning and lifelong education.
The purpose of lifelong education is that of influencing the
process of lifelong learning which already exists. The goal is
not that of making lifelong learning occur; that already happens. What is needed is an education system which is capable
of aiding, guiding, systematizing and accelerating the process
of lifelong learning, in order to improve its efficiency, increase its extent, provide it with goals and purposes, and make
it more capable of meeting the needs of the individual.

Implications for schooling

The goal just spelled out has major implications for the
ways in which schools function. Indeed, it implies the need
for changes of many kinds, some of which are discussed below.

Role of the school. Some writers have suggested that the
introduction of lifelong education would be marked by the dis-
solution of schools. However, this view has been specifically

rejected by Agoston (1975) and Hiemstra (1974). As the latter
writer put it, with the implementation of lifelong education,

> ...schools do not become irrelevant and pro-
> fesstional teachers do not become outmoded...
> they are given new opportunities to meet the
> needs of people (p. 35).

Thus, acceptance of lifelong education would not imply the
abolition of schools, but the modification of their purposes as
they accepted the "new opportunities" just mentioned. Schools
will need to become agencies in which the foundation for lifelong education is laid. This means that they will need to equip
their pupils with the attitudes and interests, motives and abilities necessary for carrying on a lifetime of systematic learning (Wolczyk, 1976).

Content and structure of curriculum. This image of the
role of schools has major implications for curriculum. It is
seen by Delker (1974) as involving four main ideas. The first
is that all adults will need an effective core education, so
that they will possess the knowledge and skills needed for a
lifetime of learning. The second is that schools will have to
offer multiple learning opportunities, and will have to be
closely linked to learning systems lying outside them, such as
the home, work, social life and leisure. The third point
stresses that schools will also need to offer opportunities for
multiple education experiences, through systematizing and organizing the learning opportunities that are available. Finally, lifelong education implies that all people will have
equitable access to learning facilities.

A report by the Swedish Ministry of Education (1972) has
stated these implications in terms somewhat more specific and
more directly related to classroom practice. Lifelong education will involve a shift in emphasis away from transmission of
fixed knowledge to the imparting of fundamental skills, above
all learning to learn. This is seen as requiring that there be
less emphasis in school curriculum on specialization, and that
general and specialist education move closer to each other. It
also implies more emphasis on communication skills, on the mass
media and on interacting with peer groups. Finally, lifelong
education will involve more individualized learning, more individual contacts between teachers and pupils, and more individual and group work through projects, investigations, and the
like.

Skager and Dave (1977) have extended the kinds of statement just made, and have developed a series of criteria for
judging how well school curricula conform to the idea of lifelong education. Detailed reproduction of the examples they
give of the day-to-day realization of lifelong education in
school curricula is beyond the scope of the present section.
However, they stated in general terms the properties that curricula should possess if they are to be oriented towards lifelong education, and the list below is based on their summary.
Curricula should

1. regard learning processes as continuous, oc-
    curring from early childhood to late adulthood

2. be viewed in the context of concurrent learn-
    ing processes going on in the home, community,
    places of work, etc.

3. recognize the importance of the essential uni-
    ty of knowledge and the interrelationship be-
    tween different subjects of study

4. recognize that the school is one of the chief
    agencies for providing basic education within
    the framework of lifelong education

5. emphasize autodidactics, including development
    of readiness for further learning and cultiva-
    tion of learning attitudes appropriate to the
    needs of a changing society

6. take into account the need for establishing
    and renewing a progressive value system by in-
    dividuals, so that they can take responsibility
    for their own continuous growth throughout life

7. provide historical as well as contemporary per-
    spectives of life and help understand divergent
    value systems

Implications for teachers and teacher training

Realization of curricular changes such as those just outlined could not be achieved in a vacuum in which, for example,
curriculum planners and educational administrators laid down
prescriptions concerning how schooling was to be carried on and
expected teachers to put these prescriptions into effect. The
concept of lifelong education has implications for the role of
teachers in the classroom and the kinds of skills they should

possess, and probably could not be achieved without teachers
who possessed the necessary attitudes and abilities. On the
other hand, it is also necessary to ask seriously whether teachers as we presently know them are absolutely necessary, especially in the context of lifelong education. At the very least,
as is emphasized in Chapter 2, a drastically changed conceptualization of the teacher's role is called for. The fact that
many educational systems are presently scarcely able to bear
the expense of providing teachers to support a conventional
school system also suggests that it is probably necessary to
visualize the possibility of other definitions of who is a
teacher (see Chapter 2), what constitutes teaching, what duties
may be reasonably required from professional teachers, and similar questions. An extended discussion of some of these issues
is to be found in a recent Unesco paper (1976).

In suggesting new roles, skills and attitudes for teachers,
lifelong education has implications for the kinds of training
that teachers should receive. For example, teachers who were
unaware of the existence of important sources of learning outside the classroom could hardly be expected to foster horizontal integration of learning. The present report focuses on this
whole area. It is concerned with the implications of lifelong
education for the behaviour of teachers, and, above all, with
its implications for teacher training. The book is essentially
the report of a project aimed at deriving more operational definitions of lifelong education's implications for teachers' behaviour in the classroom, specifying what these statements suggest about teacher training, and attempting to put some of these
ideas into effect in a number of teacher training institutions.

STRUCTURE OF THE REPORT

The report may be conceptualized as having three main sections. The first of these is essentially theoretical. It contains an introduction to the principle of lifelong education, a
discussion of its implications for the role of the teacher, and
a review of what this means for teacher training. The present
chapter has already introduced the concept and spelled out some
of its main features. Chapter 2 takes up the matter of what
lifelong education implies for the role of the teacher in the
classroom, and Chapter 3 discusses the implications of the first
two chapters for the training of teachers. These three chapters
thus lay down the theoretical basis out of which arose the procedures adopted in the empirical part of the report.

The second section describes the teacher training institutions which participated in the project, and then outlines the changes that were made in these institutions in response to the theoretical considerations spelled out in the first section. Chapter 4 is thus concerned with information about the teachers colleges and about the steps involved in the planning and execution of the empirical part of the project. Chapter 5 describes in summary form the changes in the theoretical aspects of teacher training that were made in the colleges. Chapter 6 is concerned with changes in practice-teaching activities, and Chapter 7 with changes in the institutions themselves in such areas as methods of instruction, internal organization, evaluation procedures, and similar aspects.

The third broad section of the report concentrates on findings. In presenting these findings, Chapter 8 outlines the main results of the quantitative and qualitative evaluations that were carried out by the investigators in the individual colleges, and Chapter 9 integrates and summarizes the findings that emerged from the different aspects of the project as it was variously implemented in the colleges.

SUMMARY

Rapid change in contemporary society has created the need for a new conceptualization of education. Since the events and processes of everyday life, such as earning a living, interacting with other people, participating in cultural life, and so on, are directly affected by change, and are the area in which new knowledge is to be applied, educative learning needs to be closely associated with the structures and processes of day-to-day life. These include work, leisure, social groups, recreation, political and cultural activities, and others of this kind. Secondly, since change is likely to continue and to affect the entire lifetimes of most people, adaptive learning will also have to be carried on throughout the lifespan. As a result, there is need for an educational system which fosters systematic and purposeful learning both in close relationship to ordinary life, and also throughout the lives of individual people. Such a system has recently been advocated as the master concept for future educational development in all societies. It is referred to as "lifelong education".

The major characteristics of lifelong education are that it is "horizontally integrated", that it is "vertically inte-

grated", and that it fosters the "personal pre-requisites" for
lifelong learning. It involves an educational system which is
comprehensive, flexible, and democratic, and which emphasizes
self-fulfilment of each individual person.

Such a system is feasible in terms of human learning capacity and the necessary technological base. However, it would
require possession of special learning skills and of appropriate attitudes, values, motives and self-image. As a result,
schools would assume new functions in which they fostered the
development of such skills and personal properties. Curriculum
would be affected, both in terms of content and of teaching and
learning procedures, with emphasis on fostering skill in the
acquisition of knowledge, recognition of the relationship of
school learning to real life, expectation that learning would
be continued throughout life, and so on. School would thus
have an important role in preparing pupils to become purposeful
and systematic lifelong learners. This in turn implies new
roles for teachers, and hence for the training of teachers, as
will be shown in Chapters 2 and 3.

CHAPTER 2

LIFELONG EDUCATION AND
THE TEACHER

WHO IS A TEACHER?

The principles of lifelong education, as they were defined in the previous chapter, raise important questions about the role of teachers. Of these, perhaps the most fundamental is the question of just who is a teacher. Conventional beliefs about education include the idea that learning requires the services of specialists, who know things that children ought to learn and have special training in how to teach them. It is also supposed that these experts are the only people who possess this knowledge. The experts are, of course, professional teachers. However, one of the ideas now being questioned by proponents of lifelong education is this narrow conceptualization of who is a teacher. It is increasingly being emphasized, for instance, that not all worthwhile teaching is done by persons specifically trained, licensed and paid to teach, but that other teachers exist in society.

Teachers in everyday life

Most societies contain large numbers of people who are not professional teachers, but who do a great deal of teaching, possibly without even being aware of it. Some of them are part of the non-formal educational system that has already been mentioned in Chapter 1, while others are part of the educational system constituted by the processes and events of life itself, even if such educative experiences are seldom given due recognition. Both children and adults are thus surrounded by "teachers". What is needed in the lifelong education context is to acknowledge, support and strengthen the contribution of these teachers, even though they may not be trained or paid to teach.

27

One large group of people who function as teachers but often without recognition, and who frequently work quite separately from schools, includes librarians, experts in zoos, museums and the like (ornithologists, archeologists, etc.), education officers in professional associations, training personnel in unions, factories or the armed forces, social workers, family counsellors, and many more. Doctors, dentists, lawyers, pharmacists and other professionals are also coming to be included in this group. All the people mentioned to date normally have special qualifications with fairly specific educational implications. In addition, however, there is a second major group of often unacknowledged teachers. Despite the fact that these people often have no formal or professional qualifications at all, they do most of the educating that some people experience. This group consists of those who know how to do things which are important in life -- the practitioners. When they pass on their knowledge and skills, they function as "life educators" (Unesco, 1976, p. 3). They include parents, peers, siblings, work-mates, friends, tradesmen, and many more.

Teaching networks in life

This informal, non-professional, often unconscious teaching that is a part of life itself involves networks of peer-to-peer learning and cross-age learning. Probably the most extensive example of the former is seen in the social relationships people develop as they form groups with similar interests, background, education and other such properties. In these groups, norms and expectations, skills, standards and techniques are communicated and even enforced. This is true of peer-age learning both among children and among adults. Other examples already mentioned include learning and teaching in the place of work, among colleagues and co-workers in societies, unions and the like, in clubs and organizations, and in all settings where people learn from their peers. However, learning is not confined to people of similar age. Cross-age learning outside the formal education system is also common, as older and younger people learn from each other. In its archetypal form such learning takes place within the family, where parents and to a lesser extent older siblings act as teachers of young children. Indeed, it may be argued that as much learning typically goes on in the family setting as in formal settings, or indeed in all other informal settings combined, although the influence of the family is now said to be declining in some societies.

At the same time, as has already been pointed out, it is normal and natural for everybody to continue to learn throughout life. (Lifelong education does not cause lifelong learning it merely facilitates it.) Every person is thus also a learner, again not only in formal and non-formal education settings, but in all of life. It could thus be said that all people can be conceptualized as being both teachers and learners, as a result of their participation in the learning and teaching networks of which life is composed.

Concentration on professional teachers

This point of view certainly expands the notion of who is a teacher, in fact to the ultimate degree possible. However, even laying stress upon the educative functions of all people does not mean that, in a lifelong education system, there will cease to be people who have special responsibility for teaching (i.e., professional teachers). On the contrary, the position adopted here is that there will continue to be an important role for teachers, although recognizing that they are simply part of a network. The important point at this stage is to specify the roles, purposes and functions of professional teachers, the people whom society specifically identifies as teachers, and to whom it assigns responsibility for carrying out the conscious, deliberate and structured aspects of education. For this reason, the balance of the chapter concentrates upon professional teachers.

NEW ROLES AND RESPONSIBILITIES FOR TEACHERS

Teachers have traditionnally been conceptualized as authoritative sources of knowledge, keepers of order, and judges of outcomes. It is this image of their role which is specifically challenged by lifelong education. The lifelong education curriculum, as it was spelled out in Chapter 1, indicates that the responsibilities of teachers as well as the kinds of skills, knowledge and attitudes they will be expected to promote in their pupils will be greatly changed from the familiar tasks of deciding what children ought to know, presenting a set of experiences aimed at transmitting this information to them, and ascertaining how well they have carried out the assigned learning tasks. The present section is concerned with this changed role of the professional teacher.

The teacher and knowledge

The key feature of the knowledge oriented aspect of a lifelong education curriculum is that it will be concerned with the structures and forms of knowledge. The aim of such a curriculum will be mastery of the process of acquiring knowledge rather than of particular segments of it (Lynch, 1977). The role of the teacher will thus be that of fostering mastery of the general principles of knowledge in pupils, rather than formally presenting information to be digested according to some externally determined schedule. Such a role will also require that teachers develop in pupils skill at locating information as and when it is needed and using it for particular purposes, rather than storing up knowledge thought likely to be useful in the future.

It is worth reemphasizing at this point that such an approach is not meant to imply that there will be no demands made upon pupils except the gratification of their own whims. For example, it has already been emphasized in the comments on lifelong education and school curriculum in Chapter 1 that basic learning and communicating skills will have to be mastered by people who hope to carry on a process of lifelong education. Self-evaluation, planning and purposefulness, and the ability to improve have also been emphasized as important lifelong education skills, so that it is clear that mere superficial self-gratification is not envisaged by writers in the area. Similarly, emphasis on fostering educability rather than knowledge of facts is not meant to imply that there is no place at all for factual content; it is difficult, for example, to see how a foreign language could be mastered without learning its vocabulary. What is important here is that lifelong education aims at giving renewed due emphasis to educability skills, thus seeking a better balance between processes which may presently be over-emphasized (factual learning, etc.) and those which may not receive enough systematic attention (educability).

It is also important to notice that the teacher is not seen as a spectator who will stand by as pupils act out their own impulses. On the contrary, a central and major role is still envisaged for teachers, and a systematic and genuine learning task is still seen as required of the pupil. However, the relation of these two agents to each other is seen as changed, along with their relationship to knowledge and the mechanisms through which it is created, disseminated and evaluated. Pupils, for example, will need to know "how?" and "where?" as much as "what?" (Lynch,

1977). Teachers will need to be effective in stimulating learning by organizing experiences that will not only permit learning but that will encourage and guide it. They will be "facilitators of learning" (Knowles, 1975b, p. 235). This role of
the teacher has been depicted in a striking manner by Lynch
(1977) as that of a "knowledge broker" whose task is to arouse
interest in the clients (the pupils) and then bring them into
contact with the resources available (the knowledge), leaving
the question of what then happens to the two parties concerned.

The teacher is thus seen as a "leader" (Hicter, 1972, p.
309) or "educational consultant" (Council of Europe, 1968, p.
53), rather than as a "purveyor of facts" (IBE, 1975, p. 15).
The teacher will guide and co-ordinate knowledge rather than
present it in pre-digested packages, functioning as a "specialist in learning methods" (Frese, 1972, p. 11), "co-ordinator of
learning activities" (Dave, 1973, p. 44), "learning project
consultant" (Hiemstra, 1974, p. 39), "orchestrator of learning"
(IBE, 1975, p. 5), or "resource guide" (Lynch, 1977, p. 46).
The expectation is that teachers will energize or activate
learning in pupils, and guide them to necessary resources, as
well as helping them to develop the ability to find, choose and
evaluate knowledge for themselves.

The teacher and pupil growth

The teacher's task is to "plan, guide and evaluate the progress of each individual pupil" (Ministry of Education, 1972,
p. 61). However, this process of diagnosis and planning involves more than simply assessment of academic achievement. It
includes understanding of personality, social and cultural background, and similar traits, with the goal of becoming "an effective mediator between the young person and the confusion of
the environment" (IBE, 1975, p. 15). This requires a highly
individualized education responsive to each pupil's particular
pattern of capacities, inclinations, motivations, aspirations
and needs. Teaching will thus have a strong orientation to the
future, with the aim of promoting change for the better (IBE,
1975). Its broad purpose is to "generate lifelong learning in
others" (Lynch, 1977, p. 43).

Thus, teachers have a special role to play, as a result of
which they will have to be capable of assessing the needs and
capacities of their pupils and subsequently structuring learning experiences in accordance with their diagnosis of the situa-

tion. This process will involve fostering and maximizing the
personal growth and self-fulfilment of pupils. Such a goal may
make it necessary for teachers to learn to co-operate more extensively with other professions such as social work, psychology or medicine, so that they become members of a team whose
major task is to facilitate the realization of potential. In
addition, it may require a broader set of roles for teachers,
in which they sometimes function as social workers, sometimes
as counsellors, sometimes as diagnosticians, and sometimes in
other roles.

Relationships with pupils

The role of teachers is seen as changing to that of animators and facilitators of learning processes largely initiated
by pupils and pursued for purposes important to the learners
rather than the teachers. They are also seen as guides, consultants and diagnosticians engaged in the maximization of pupils' potentials and the fostering of their personal fulfilment.
This suggests that there will be substantial changes in the
teacher's relationship with pupils. For example, it would be
expected to be closer and more personal than is typically the
case today. Furthermore, a co-operative relationship would be
sought in which pupils and teacher perceived each other as working together, rather than a coercive relationship based on power and compulsion. In its most thoroughgoing form, this relationship might sometimes require that teachers learned from
their pupils, some of whom would for example, be expected to be
more knowledgable than their teachers about a particular piece
of information that they had pursued in detail (even if with
the teacher's advice and guidance). Thus, the teacher might become not only a colleague and advisor, but even a fellow learner or, as Dave (1973) put it a "co-learner" (p. 44).

This would require "the skills of individual counselling"
of students (Lynch, 1977, p. 46). It would also require
the capacity to communicate with them in terms that were mean-
ingful and cogent by their standards. However, this would presumably not mean simply the adoption of the jargon of school-
children and adolescents by teachers, since the capacity for
communication is one of the fundamental skills which schools
will need to impart to pupils. It would also require awareness
on the part of teachers of the day-to-day life of their pupils,
even where the social origins of the pupils differed sharply
from those of most teachers. In any case, the fundamental re-

lationship of pupils and teachers is seen as being that of fellow workers, colleagues, and co-learners engaged upon a joint learning venture, even though one participant (the teacher) would continue to be recognized as having special knowledge and skills, and a responsibility for putting them at the service of the other (the pupils).

Mastery of learning and teaching skills

In facilitating or energizing learning in pupils, teachers would need more than a close personal relationship with them, of course. One of the broad skills implied by the role of the teacher as learning consultant or resource guide is mastery of the techniques and skills through which knowledge is obtained. Lifelong education teachers, then, are conceptualized as persons who possess the ability to utilize a wide variety of learning activities, such as group learning and self-directed learning, and to make use of varied techniques, such as research projects and many more. They would be flexible and resourceful in designing learning experiences, and would seek innovative and more effective methods at all times. Such teachers would also be skilled at locating information and at helping others to find it when they needed it.

An important lifelong education learning skill in this area is concerned with the ability to comprehend the structures and forms of knowledge, and to deal in a confident and interested way with the systems and structures through which new knowledge comes into existence. Furthermore, it is important to be able to raise questions concerning the function of knowledge in society, and to ask whether particular knowledge is dangerous or likely to lead to more harm than good. In other words, an important lifelong education skill in the area of learning is that of assessing and legitimating knowledge (Lynch, 1977), and thus of distinguishing between worthwhile and trivial knowledge. Learning should, in fact, be carried on with discrimination, purpose and judgment. Related to this is the maintenance of a questioning and inquiring frame of mind in which the new is constantly sought, although with a distinction drawn between the merely different and the important or worthwhile, and with a basic acceptance of the broad canons of society, so that the search for the new does not become merely anarchy or the pursuit of the cheap and trivial.

This emphasis on the importance of judgment as a learning

skill raises the matter of evaluation. The lifelong education teacher will transmit to pupils the capacity not only to question knowledge and society's use of it, but also to subject their own goals to a process of evaluation. A key skill in lifelong education is the ability to set one's own goals, evaluate the legitimacy of the goals, assess the extent to which they have been realized, and plan the necessary remedial steps when they have not. Thus, skill in self-criticism and in the adoption of new measures when old ones fail, what Dave (1973) has referred to as "learning to improve", is a major lifelong education skill.

Lifelong education teachers also need to be aware of sources of knowledge outside the classroom, and to recognize the validity of such alternative sources (Lynch, 1977). Associated with this familiarity with non-classroom sources of information, teachers will need skill in directing pupils to where the learning resources of the community are located, and the ability to recognize the educational components of non-school experiences. These out-of-the-classroom sources include places where knowledge is stored with a deliberate educational intent, such as in libraries, museums, zoos and the like, and also organizations and structures which are not usually labelled as educative, such as factories and places of recreation. Finally, they include not only places and organizations, but a great number of people who have a legitimate but often unrecognized role to play as learning resources, so that the lifelong education teacher should also possess skill in making use of such people's knowledge and expertise.

Some learning experiences are not available to direct observation. Most of the information in libraries, for example, is stored in books. A major task for teachers is the communicating of information in forms that are readily comprehensible to pupils, even when it is information about information. Thus, the lifelong education teacher will need particular skill in communication. This will also require skill in alternatives to formal, verbal communication, for example, through the use of media such as TV, films, slide and transparency projectors, charts and diagrams, and many similar devices.

The new roles and responsibilities of teachers, in the context of lifelong education have been strikingly stated in a report of the International Bureau of Education (IBE, 1975) in the following way:

> (Lifelong education imposes)...upon the teach-
> er the duty of accepting, organizing and co-
> ordinating the educational potential of ele-
> ments foreign to the traditional school -- the
> various media of communication, cultural and
> artistic activities in the community, the spe-
> cialized knowledge of professionals in various
> fields, and the practical wisdom and experience
> of workers in industry, crafts and agriculture
> (p. 15).

Personal qualities of teachers

Like other workers, teachers in a world of rapid change
will be faced with the problem that their own skills will periodically become obsolete. As a result, they will have to be
willing to accept change in their own lives, and to up-date
themselves as the need arises. Thus, the first implication of
lifelong education for teachers is that they will have to engage in a personal programme of lifelong learning. It will be
incumbent upon them to adapt and adjust continually to the processes of change (Dave, 1973). This will require a high degree
of personal stability and a secure self-concept, if uncertainty
and anxiety are to be avoided. A further problem for teachers
lies in the fact that they play a dual role in that they are
responsible both for preserving their society's way of life and
helping children to adjust to it, and also for being at the
forefront of change. The role of preserver of the status quo
must be rejected, but at the same time a high level of responsibility is also called for. As a result, teachers will need
enough individuality to resist social pressures or passing fads,
while remaining highly responsive to the need for adjustment to
change (Lynch, 1977).

The role spelled out in the previous paragraph calls for a
high level of educability in teachers themselves; educability
becomes not only a goal for teachers to develop in their pupils,
but a personal goal as well. This means that they will need to
be willing to change themselves as they "feel the future". It
requires an inquiring attitude and a research orientation
(Lynch, 1977). In addition, it requires that teachers be able
to evaluate both themselves and the knowledge to which they are
exposed, in order to assess their own learning needs and to
make responsible choices among the competing alternatives available. In this respect, teachers could become models, from whom

pupils could learn the skills of educability by direct observation of the teachers' personal examples. This programme of personal updating would be seen in the professional sphere in willingness to try new methods and procedures, to subscribe to professional journals and similar periodicals in order to get new ideas, and to participate in such activities as refresher courses.

Finally, lifelong education would require that teachers were skilled in linking what goes on in schools with life itself. Thus, they would be expected to be aware of the community, both as a source of learning experiences and as the real world to which school is integrated and for which it exists. They would recognize the importance of the family, peers and other community agencies in the education of the individual. They would also be aware of the responsibility of schools to the community, would be able to assess the needs of the community and, more important, would be able to work with parents, citizens and community leaders. Consequently, teachers will need the ability to play many roles in addition to the traditional role of knowledge expert. They will need to be able to function as social workers, family visitors, vocational guidance experts, contributors to other teachers' lifelong learning, experts in communications, and to assume many other roles. Again, a strong sense of who and what they are is implied, so that they can accept as equals engaged in a joint project representatives of the non-school learning agencies in the community, other professionals, and so on.

CHARACTERISTICS OF THE TEACHER AS A LIFELONG LEARNER

It has already been pointed out that teachers will need a number of special personal properties, of which one is the capacity to engage in a process of lifelong learning themselves, both in order to offer a model of lifelong learning for their pupils and also to cope with their own periodical obsolescence. At this point, the characteristics of the teacher as a lifelong learner require more detailed explication. One of the documents produced during the course of the present project (see Chapter 4 for details of the way in which the project was implemented) was a set of "Minutes" of a meeting of the participating institutions held in Hamburg in late 1973. This meeting discussed the characteristics of the lifelong education teacher in some detail. One of the items involved was a presentation

by R.H. Dave, in which he summarized the main properties of the
lifelong education teacher as a lifelong learner. This list
forms the basis of the discussion which follows.

Knowledge of lifelong education

Lifelong education teachers would be expected to be aware
of the need for lifelong education, and of its potential to
achieve significant changes in educational practice. They
would also be familiar with the characteristics of lifelong education, the arguments for its adoption, the problems it aims
at overcoming, and its significance for classroom practice. As
a result, they would be expected to perceive education in a
perspective both broader and also longer, covering horizontal
and vertical integration of different stages, forms, structures
and methods of learning. They would also be expected to have
internalized the implications of lifelong education for their
own personal, social and professional lives, and to practise
lifelong education as a means of improving the quality of their
own lives. Finally, they would spread information about lifelong education, both by exposition and by personal example,
among pupils, colleagues, family members, friends, and others.

The teacher's role

Teachers would act as co-learners among their pupils, and
would thus promote participatory learning, co-operative studies,
inter-learning, inter-generational learning, and similar learning strategies. This would be extended to their own learning,
in which they would practise self-directed learning, and assume
the responsibility for self-initiated and self-directed in-service education. They would also act as animators of learning
in their own families and in the community, as appropriate occasions arose. For example, they would be active among colleagues, and would participate in professional organizations
both for their own growth and also to promote the growth of
others. For these reasons, the teachers would be up-to-date in
pedagogical and academic aspects of their professional work,
would be enlightened members both of the profession and also of
society, and would share their enlightenment with others.

In the classroom, lifelong education teachers would function as co-ordinators and facilitators of learning, with a view
to developing educability among their pupils and helping them
to become lifelong learners. Being adaptive and innovative,

they would accept alternative structures, processes and means
for learning. They would also be flexible about the ages at
which learning occurs, and would promote not only communication
among peers, but also across generations. In their own lives
they would move smoothly from one stage to another, possessing
an articulated and integrated view of professional development
as a result of which, for example, they would see pre-service
and in-service teacher education as aspects of the same extended
learning process.

Integration of school and community

Lifelong education teachers would be strongly aware that
the role of the school and other educational institutions, although of major significance, is still much more restricted
than has been traditionally thought to be the case. They would
also be aware of the important roles of the home, the place of
work, mass media, social activities, religious organizations,
political events, and many others, as educational structures
and processes of great importance. As a result, they would integrate their own learning experiences by linking formal studies
with out-of-school, real-life experiences, and would seek to
foster such integration in the learning experiences of their
pupils. This would require that teachers be familiar with
learning resources outside the school, and that they utilized
them in the optimal manner. This would include utilizing agencies such as their own places of work, their homes, and the community for their own concurrent learning, as well as making
best use of the opportunities for recurrent learning within the
formal structure of professional training.

Attitudes towards formal curricula

Lifelong education teachers would regard formal education
structures as part of a wider life curriculum, existing in society as a whole. Consequently, they would perceive the role
of schools as being the development of basic educability, out
of which a lifetime of learning would arise. For this reason,
they would emphasize the structure, processes and key concepts
of disciplines of study, not their specific facts. Similarly,
they would prefer self-evaluation and evaluation aimed at improving, rather than external evaluation aimed at assessing the
relative presence or absence of certain specified skills or
pieces of information. They would thus seek to identify their
own strengths and weaknesses in order to promote further per-

sonal growth and development.

RELATIONSHIP WITH REMAINING CHAPTERS

The discussion of the implications of the theory of life-long education for the role of the teacher has been couched in abstract and general terms. Three tasks remain. The first is to specify what teacher training would have to be like in order to produce teachers of the kind described here. This is done in Chapter 3. The second is to develop practical activities, based on these general principles and guidelines, which can be implemented in real-life teacher-training institutions. This was attempted by the teams of workers from the institutions participating in the project. What they did is described in Chapters 5, 6 and 7. The final task is that of evaluating what was done, and indicating what implications this has for other institutions concerned with the pre-service education of teachers. This was attempted throughout the empirical sections of the book, and in Chapter 8 and 9 in particular.

SUMMARY

One implication of lifelong education is that the idea of who is a teacher needs to be greatly broadened to include acknowledgement of people who are important sources of information, but are not professional teachers. This requires recognition of the contributions both of people with special formal training but no specific teaching role, and also of people whose teaching function arises from their activities in everyday life. Nonetheless, the emphasis of the present report is on professional teachers. They will play new roles in a lifelong education-oriented system, for example becoming learning guides and resource persons rather than infallible authorities. They will be expected to foster in pupils the skills and values of educability, which will include the capacity for self-learning and self-evaluation, as well as positive attitudes to learning, desire for continued learning, and self-image as a learner. This altered role will change relationships with pupils. It will also require special personal properties in teachers, including willingness to accept change, recognition of the need to update themselves periodically, and the personal capacity for lifelong learning. It will thus necessitate the development of special knowledge, skills and attitudes in teachers. Consequently, changes will be needed in the ways in which potential teachers are trained; some of these are discussed in the next chapter.

CHAPTER 3

LIFELONG EDUCATION AND THE
TRAINING OF TEACHERS

Lifelong education implies new roles and functions for teachers, and thus requires that they possess special knowledge, attitudes, and skills. According to Knowles (1975b), the necessary properties can be fostered by appropriate patterns of teacher education, but this requires changes in the ways in which teachers are trained (Hiemstra, 1974). Basically these changes would be aimed at developing appropriate knowledge on the one hand, and the necessary skills on the other. What this means is that teacher training appropriate to lifelong education would aim at fostering knowledge of lifelong education and understanding of its implications, and also the capacities, motives, attitudes and values needed to put it into effect. The present chapter is concerned with spelling out some of the main features of such a system of teacher training.

CONCEPTS IN TEACHER EDUCATION

Applicability of lifelong education

Teacher education has many aspects. For example it may be considered in terms of its temporal organization, and thus divided very broadly into training occurring before the commencement of actual service as a teacher, and training occurring after teaching service has commenced. These two phases of teacher training are often referred to as "pre-service training" and "in-service training" respectively. Where in-service training occurs, the ways in which it is organized may also vary. Thus, it may be recurrent in nature, with periods of teaching service alternating with periods of further training, or it may take other forms. Another distinction which also applies to teacher training is that between formal, non-formal and informal sys-

41

tems of education, since it may occur in all three kinds of
settings. It may also be considered from the point of view of
content, for example by distinguishing between general education, training in special disciplines, professional education
and induction into the practical skills of teaching.

Lifelong education has implications for all of these phases
and aspects of teacher training. Indeed, to some extent it implies that the distinctions are unnecessary. Through the stress
it places on the linking of school-like learning and the learning that goes on in life itself, for example, it emphasizes the
importance of informal learning systems in the preparation of
teachers. Similarly, in stressing the essential unity of knowledge (i.e., its horizontal integration), lifelong education implies that general, professional and academic training will have
a common core or base, and will be conceptualized as at most
different aspects of the same unity. Finally, it has implications for the relationships between pre-service and in-service
training, as will be shown below.

Continuity of teacher training

The need for continuous learning on the part of teachers
has been strongly emphasized by Bär and Slomma (1973), who described it as "one of the necessities of life" (p. 41) if teachers are to keep up to date. James (1972), too, criticized the
existing "overdependence on initial training" (p. 1), and
stressed the need for teachers to engage in continued learning.
He saw this continued learning as the third element in a three
cycle process, involving "personal education" (the acquisition
of a body of knowledge such as mathematics or history) as the
first phase, "pre-service training and induction" as the second,
and "in-service training" as the last. Of the three, in-service
training was seen as the most important. James pointed out that
teachers now have to be experts in areas as diverse as using
libraries, career advising, personal counselling, working with
deprived children, teaching children with emotional disorders,
and teaching children from minority-culture family backgrounds.
Thus, not only is continuous learning necessary for teachers
because of the need to keep their skills and knowledge up to
date (Bär and Slomma, 1973), but also because they may have to
acquire new skills in unforeseen areas, after the conclusion of
their initial training.

It is clear from these examples that in-service training

is not necessarily conceptualized as falling within the domain
of teachers colleges. Indeed, James criticized what he regarded
as excessive dependence upon them. According to him, there is
a need for new organizational structures through which in-service training can be offered, including both what he called
"professional centres" (p. 14), and also use of schools themselves as places in which teachers continue to learn. Bär and
Slomma (1973) too emphasized the importance of schools (teachers' places of work) as the scene of further training. In the
German Democratic Republic for instance, teachers may engage in
continuing learning in existing institutions such as universities, through private study with the aid of manuals and specially prepared paedagogical literature, and in the schools themselves. Bär and Slomma give as an example of this latter kind
of in-service training, a situation in which several teachers
attend a class taught by a colleague, and then engage in an
evaluative discussion in the school staff room.

Emphasis in lifelong education on the interpretation and
continuity of learning and on its linkage with real life suggests that recurrent patterns of in-service training will be
replaced by what may be called "concurrent" in-service training.
The essential idea in this context is that further training
will not require interruption of the normal work of teachers
and their removal from their places of work, but that it will
be something which occurs simultaneously with work and, indeed,
that the place of work will be a major source of continuing
learning. In-service training will thus go on all the time. At
the same time, the boundary between pre-service and in-service
training will be broken down, with the former simply being seen
as one part of a process which continues in a normal and natural way. One of the major tasks of pre-service training will
thus become that of facilitating continuous, concurrent learning, by providing the knowledge, skills and attitudes needed
for continuing learning to occur.

Concentration on pre-service training

The division of teacher training into discrete segments,
especially in terms of the time at which it occurs in a teacher's career (i.e., pre-service or in-service), is thus an artificial distinction, from the point of view of lifelong education. Indeed, recent trends in teacher training suggest that
this has already been recognized to some extent. Courses have
been integrated, entry has been made available to people other

than new graduates from high school, in-service programmes have been developed more extensively, and other similar changes have appeared. Nonetheless, organizational bases, curriculum content, teaching and learning processes, and the like, have largely continued to follow traditional lines, despite some moves in directions consistent with lifelong education, with or without any conscious awareness of the principle. Thus, for practical purposes, it is necessary to deal with teacher training in a relatively segmented way, differentiating between pre-service and in-service training, between professional and academic training, and so on. This division is followed in the present report out of practical necessity. Of particular importance is the fact that the report is concerned almost exclusively with pre-service training, and with teacher-training institutions engaged to an overwhelming extent in initial training.

IMPLICATIONS FOR TEACHER TRAINING CURRICULUM

Curriculum content and structure

One major aspect of curriculum is the information which is transmitted, and the ways in which it is structured and organized. These kinds of considerations are discussed in the present section.

Knowledge about lifelong education. A teachers college curriculum oriented in the direction of lifelong education would include a course or courses concerned with information about lifelong education. This would include the history of the concept, the reasons why it is now receiving emphasis, the problems in modern life that it is said to be capable of alleviating, the advantages it possesses over traditional systems, and similar information. It would also include details of what is now understood by the term "lifelong education". The purpose of this aspect of curriculum would be to help students become aware of the need for lifelong education and to understand its characteristics, in the hope that they would subsequently adopt it in their teaching practices, their learning processes, and indeed in their own daily lives.

It is not suggested, however, that mere knowledge about the "facts" of lifelong education is a sufficient introduction to the area to achieve these latter goals. In particular, opportunities for personal experience of lifelong learning activities would probably be of great importance. This is why changes in teaching and learning styles, college organization, and teaching practice are also advocated.

The structure of curriculum. One of the aims of a life-long education-oriented approach would be to help students become aware of the inter-relatedness of the many areas of learning, and of the implications of this fact for curriculum. Consequently, the curriculum would introduce a broad central core of information aimed at building a broad grasp of the organization of knowledge and of the ways in which it is created, validated, located and used. This would include knowledge of self, of culture and society, of the means and forms of production, and of the environment (Lynch, 1977). The effect of such content would be to bring about a move away from greater specialization in favour of development of a broad core of cross-disciplinary studies. This would reverse the present trend in teacher training towards maximization of focus on fostering specialist skills and associated minimization of effort in the area of professional training. As the 35th Session of the International Conference on Education put it (IBE, 1975, p. 16):

> Teacher education must prepare the teacher to assume responsibility for integrating knowledge -- that acquired outside the school as well as that which was formally taught -- for the social integration of the individual into the community and for the integration of students into the world of work.

Learning skills

A further aspect of teacher training in the light of life-long education would be its emphasis on fostering special learning skills of the kind loosely grouped together under the heading "learning to learn" (see Chapter 1). This means that there would be heavy emphasis on the development of a wide range of basic skills and abilities, and recognition that there are many ways of learning and communicating (see Cropley, 1976 for a discussion of "learning styles" in different people). The curriculum would, for example, introduce students to different kinds of learning strategies, and would emphasize their equal legitimacy. In a similar manner, it would involve exposure of students to a variety of methods, and to the use of different kinds of aids to learning. In general, the aim would be to develop respect for different ways of teaching and learning, and the capacity both to learn in differing ways and also to foster learning in others through a variety of forms and techniques.

Teaching and learning methodology

A further important aspect of teacher training concerns the methods and techniques that are employed in communicating content material. This aspect of teacher training curriculum is discussed in the present section, from the point of view of lifelong education.

Variety of methods. The learning and teaching methods employed in a lifelong education curriculum would go well beyond traditional procedures, such as formal lectures, in which selected information is presented in pre-arranged portions and students are subsequently examined to determine to what extent they have mastered the desired material. For example there would be heavy emphasis on variety in methods, with lectures supplemented by project work, independent discovery through research programmes, student responsibility for locating information for themselves both in traditional sources such as libraries and also through other sources such as places of learning in the community (zoos, museums, community centres and the like), student-led seminars and tutorials, formal presentations by students themselves, and similar activities.

Thus, there would be a conscious and systematic effort to develop individual knowledge-related skills in students, and to promote inquiring attitudes. There would also be emphasis on fostering the kind of learning processes often neglected in traditional programmes, such as learning without a teacher by using the many other sources of knowledge that have already been mentioned (self-learning) and by setting one's own learning goals and planning the ways in which they are to be achieved (self-directed learning). The role of other people as aids to learning would also be emphasized through the fostering of learning in which students learned from each other through a process of sharing knowledge (inter-learning), or through a process of learning together (group-learning). In the process of learning with others, students would gain valuable experience of sharing knowledge as users rather than as possessing it as authorities, an experience which would be expected to facilitate acquisition of the co-learner role envisaged in earlier sections. These kind of learning processes would require that students be highly skilled in obtaining information from many sources of knowledge, most usually through the use of language, and in communicating with other learners, again through the use of language. Thus they imply highly developed communication skills.

Learning from real life. The lifelong education curriculum for teacher training would emphasize that there is a substantial body of human and material resources for learning available outside the college, or even outside traditional sources, and would encourage students to make use of these resources. For example, in addition to the sources of information in the community that have already been mentioned, students should be aware of the pool of expertise represented by people with special knowledge and skills. Almost everybody has the potential to function as a teacher in at least one respect, and is therefore a potential source of information. An example taken from one of the institutions involved in the present project is that of an illiterate old man whose job was spreading fertilizer, in the form of human waste, on the fields. Although he had never thought of himself in that way, and had not been regarded in this way by students, he was an expert on the agricultural methods and problems of his region, and, when introduced into the college as a teacher, was able to teach students a great deal about their own society.

A second aspect of the linking of curricular methods with real life involves the development of a body of theory which relates closely to the kind of things teachers actually do in the classroom. This would require that teaching processes de-emphasize simulation and other abstractions from real life, and seek ways to help students "live" the role of the teacher during their pre-service training (Lynch, 1977). This could be done, for example, through opportunities for co-operative learning with other students, through opportunities for team work with other experts, through practical experiences in the community, and similar activities. Students could also be given opportunities for taking decisions and accepting responsibility for them, as they would normally have to do when they were on the job, and for assisting other learners or helping with learning problems.

Evaluation processes

Some recent educational theories and practices have denigrated the notion of evaluation. For example, it has been said that the use of evaluation leads to a situation in which learners are motivated primarily by the desire to get good marks with the result that subject matter, methods and materials are all modified by teachers in order to help them do this. The question of external versus internal motivation raised by this argument is one of considerable interest in the context of lifelong education, as will shortly become apparent. However, the position adopted in the present project recognizes the importance of evaluation, and indeed, emphasizes its role in systematic and purposeful learning. Nonetheless, there are a number of implications for evaluation, and hence for teacher training, in the theory of lifelong education. These are discussed below.

Formative evaluation. One major emphasis in lifelong education is that the purpose of evaluation is to provide constructive information to learners, so that they can assess the extent to which they are achieving the goals they have set themselves, and can take appropriate corrective steps where necessary. In this sense, evaluation serves a diagnostic, corrective and guiding purpose; its use may be described as "formative" (Dave, 1973). This function of evaluation can be distinguished from its use as a device for ascertaining the extent to which externally-imposed tasks have been completed, targets have been met, required levels of competence reached, and so on. The purpose of this second kind of evaluation is not that of guiding and diagnosing, but of assessing and judging. In this approach negative feedback is not a guide to how to do better, but an indication of inadequancy or failure. Evaluation used in this way is referred to as "summative" in nature. There is of course an important place for summative evaluation, for example, where specifiable key skills are needed for licensing purposes. However, lifelong education re-emphasizes the importance of formative evaluation.

Continuous evaluation. A second important notion is that evaluation should occur continuously during the learning process, not just at convenient points such as at the end of the institution's academic year. Continuous evaluation would improve the formative role of evaluation, by allowing an on-going process of feedback, diagnosis and corrective action. Modes and techniques of evaluation other than formal written tests of the traditional kind and other traditional methods are also called for in a lifelong education-oriented system. These might include evaluation through observation of behaviours in actual learning settings, assessment of the extent of transfer of new learning to relevant real-life situations, and so on. Such evaluation might involve the use of check lists, feed-back

from colleagues, assessments by users (such as pupils), and
similar alternative ways of evaluating learning and personal
growth.

   Loci of evaluation. An important question in lifelong education is who would carry out evaluations in a teacher institution oriented according to its principles. The first persons
involved would be the learners themselves; self-evaluation would
be a norm in lifelong education-oriented institutions. However,
in addition, other sources of evaluation would be important.
Lecturers and other instructional staff would, of course, have
a role to play in their capacity as learning consultants, knowledge brokers, and similar roles. Other important sources of
evaluative information would be fellow students, colleagues,
and even pupils in schools where practice teaching was done.
Similarly, evaluation would be carried out individually and also on a group basis, as students learned from instructors,
alone, and in groups.

   Evaluation of the institution. Discussion of evaluation
to this point has been concerned with evaluation of learners.
This is what Skager (1978) called "L-Evaluation". However, as
he pointed out, it is also possible to evaluate the environment
in which learning occurs (in this case, the teachers college itself), in order to assess its suitability as a place of learning. This is what he called "C-Evaluation". Thus, a teacher-
training institution seeking to function in a way consistent
with the principles of lifelong education would engage in a
continuous process of formative self-evaluation, in addition to
seeking to foster such a process in its students. It would also offer opportunities for instructors and students to participate in the process of E-Evaluation, both in individual and
group settings. In this way, self-evaluation would become a
norm not only for students and instructors, but for the institution itself.

IMPLICATIONS FOR TEACHING PRACTICE

   In most teachers colleges, learning experiences include
opportunities for practical activities in which students assume
the role they will play once they have successfully completed
their training, that of teachers. These experiences do not always involve real pupils in real schools, as simulation, microteaching and similar expedients sometimes take the place of
such contacts. Nonetheless, it is almost universal to find

some kind of organized practical experiences as part of teacher training, and these activities are often referred to as "practice teaching". Thus, any set of statements about the role of teachers and the kind of skills and attitudes they should possess would have implications for the practice-teaching aspect of teacher training. As would be expected, therefore, the introduction of lifelong education as a principle guiding teacher training implies not only changes in curriculum and in teaching and learning procedures, but also changes in such areas as organization of practice teaching, the classroom methods that students are encouraged to emphasize, and even the kind of activities which are seen as constituting practice teaching.

Linking theory and practice

It has already been pointed out that the content of curriculum should include the development of a body of knowledge that is closely linked with the real-life things that teachers actually do when they are engaged in the practice of their profession. Teaching practice offers a major opportunity for making such a link, and particularly for making the link explicit, so that students can see the relationship between what they hear in the lecture theatre and what teachers do in the classroom. Thus, teaching practice offers opportunities for turning theoretical insights into actual behaviours in the classroom (Lynch, 1977). For this reason, it is important that students have opportunities, not only for practice teaching, but for experiences of a kind which make it possible for them to function as lifelong learning-oriented teachers, to link schooling and life, to foster many kinds of learning skills, to present information through a variety of modes, to carry out formative evaluation, and to practise other aspects of the lifelong education teacher's role.

Living the role of the teacher

A second major aspect of practice teaching is that it provides an opportunity for students to find out what it feels like to be a teacher. They need, therefore, a chance to live the teacher's role. This would include, not only opportunities for putting the theory of lifelong education into practice, but the opportunity of experiencing some of the processes in their own lives. For example, practice teaching would give them the opportunity of sharing knowledge. It would also make it possible for them to have actual experience of the process of "fil-

tering down" information (Lynch, 1977). At the same time, practice teaching should help students to develop and practise appropriate inter-personal skills, to energize learning in pupils,
and so on.

Recognition of a broader range of activities

In view of the great emphasis placed on the linking of
schooling and life, and the desire of lifelong education theorists to foster the incorporation of educative experiences found
in everyday life into the formal experiences normally regarded
as part of education, it would be anticipated that practice
teaching in a lifelong education context would stress, during
students' theoretical and practical preparation for a career in
teaching, experiences with learning agencies found in the everyday life of the society. This implies that a wide range of activities would come to be regarded as constituting practice
teaching, including experiences outside the formal educational
system. Such activities could include work in youth centres,
work in clubs and associations, activities in sports organizations, experiences in church groups or political parties, work
with apprentices in factories, social work with special socio-
economic groups, and similar activities.

The role of simulated teaching experiences

These kinds of conclusion raise the question of the role
of substitute experiences for practice teaching, such as microteaching. De-emphasis of simulation and the call for opportunities for relatively sustained experiences with real learning
agencies in real life (most notably in schools, but not in
schools alone), suggests that substitute experiences for actual
contacts with school-age learners would not be highly evaluated.
However, it is clear that the practical realities of life may
make it impossible for teaching practice to conform to the ideal
specified here, so that simulation procedures may have to suf-
fice in some teacher-training institutions. At the same time,
it seems likely that techniques such as micro-teaching still
have a valuable part to play in training students in the practical skills of teaching. For example, they can be used for
demonstrating specific skills and for giving students practice
in those skills. They can also be used, in conjunction with a
process of continuous, formative evaluation, for remedial purposes. Thus, although they would not ideally constitute the
only form of practice teaching, simulation methods look to have

a valuable role to play, especially when they are used in conjunction with real-life experiences.

IMPLICATIONS FOR STRUCTURES AND ORGANIZATION

In addition to the content of courses, the ways in which
teaching and learning are carried out, and the kind of practical
experiences which are available, teacher-training institutions
can also influence their students through the way in which the
institutions themselves are structured and organized, the kind
of staff they employ, and similar factors. Consequently, the
development of lifelong education-oriented teachers also has
implications for things like staffing, administration, internal
governance, and similar aspects of teacher training. Some of
them are discussed in following paragraphs.

Support for varied ways of learning

Lifelong education-oriented teacher-training institutions
would place great emphasis on self-learning and self-directed
learning, as has already been pointed out. This means that they
would have to provide adequate support services for such learning, in the form of library facilities, information retrieval
systems such as microfilm readers, and the like. Similarly, in
fostering group-learning and inter-learning, and in developing
students who adopted these kinds of technique in their classroom practices, there would be a need for appropriate media,
workshop facilities, and other such support services. Support
for non-traditional kinds of learning, especially under the
learners' own control, could also be provided by flexibility in
such organizational features as timetables and schedules of
activities, which could be arranged in such a way as to make it
possible for learners to spend time on their own or to come together into groups, to meet learning facilitators within the
college (instructors) in conditions conductive to free inter-
change of ideas, and by similar factors. Thus, scheduling of
classes, provision of appropriate meeting rooms, and other arrangements of this kind would be affected by a commitment to
lifelong education, and would be capable of providing important
support for a lifelong education-oriented learning atmosphere.

Links with the community

The importance of close links between institutions engaged

in formal education and the community have already been emphasized. This implies that teachers colleges would relate their
programmes not only to other educative agencies in formal and
non-formal education, but also to those in the informal area.
Thus, they would, in the first instance, be expected to establish close relations with schools and other educational institutions, but in addition they would maintain links with learning
sources within the community, even when these sources were not
usually recognized as educative in nature. This would require
opportunities for students to co-operate with people who were
not formal educators, as well as involvement in learning processes and programmes to be found in the events of everyday life
itself. The colleges might, for example, give students time to
work in the community, or even give credit for experiences outside the college, such as work experience in factories, commerce
or media, involvement in social work, appropriate participation
in recreational activities, or similar aspects of real life.

Provision of in-service training

The emphasis in the present report has already been stated
as being pre-service teacher training. Nonetheless, this is not
meant to imply that pre-service training and in-service training
do not have a good deal in common. In particular, one way in
which articulation of real life and the learning that goes on
within a teacher-training institution could be achieved would
be through development of the college as a source of in-service
training. This could be offered not only to practising teachers, but also to other professions, and to all those who have
an educative function in society (parents, clergymen, factory
supervisors, lawyers, senior tradesmen and many others). A
flourishing in-service training function would also help to foster lifelong education attitudes in student teachers, by demonstrating that in-service training is practicable and, if linked
with appropriate recognition of in-service training, by showing
its value to the individual practising it.

To turn to the more specific goals of in-service training,
its major concrete purpose would be to equip teachers with up-
dated knowledge, new attitudes and novel techniques, and with
the skills needed for adopting new roles. In doing this, it
would aim, among other things, at updating the knowledge and
renewing the competence of serving teachers, thus permitting
them to keep up with the development of the profession and the
new needs of pupils, at offering the opportunity to acquire in-

creased professional competence to those whose initial training had left them inadequately prepared, at enhancing the qualifications of those who originally entered the profession with lower formal qualifications, and at providing refresher training to people returning to teaching after an absence from it (IBE, 1975). Increased interest in in-service training would thus be expected among teacher-training institutions committed to the principles of lifelong education.

Qualities of instructors

The final element in a teacher training institution which needs to be considered is the staff of the college. To a great extent, what has been said about the role of the teacher applies to these people too, for they are in somewhat the same relationship to students in teachers colleges as are teachers to pupils in schools. As Anderson (1974) has pointed out, the instructors are important models for students. Where staff adopt innovations, students will follow. Thus, instructors would themselves be expected to be thoroughly aware of the concept of lifelong education and of its implications. They would also be expected to be capable of using many forms of learning, of presenting information in many ways, and of themselves engaging in self-learning, group-learning, and the like, as well as of functioning as learning-facilitators rather than as simply sources of authoritative information. Thus, an institution committed to lifelong education would be expected to seek staff who were lifelong learners themselves, with the skills and attitudes that this implies. Where staff did not possess the necessary knowledge and skills, the college would be expected to provide them with appropriate opportunities for in-service training aimed at acquainting them with lifelong education and all its implications. Thus, at least in the initial phases, a lifelong education-oriented institution might be heavily involved in a programme of staff development.

Staff members would also be expected to be skilled at relating learning in the college to the life of the community, and knowledgeable about such things as the problems of real life, the role of education in national development plans, and similar variables. One way which this kind of expertise might be fostered would be for teacher-training institutions to encourage their staff members to spend time working in real-life settings, especially in schools of course, but also in other settings having an educative function or potential. This might

be achieved by the establishment of schemes for exchanges of
staff among teacher-training and other institutions, or conversely by inviting persons in the community with special skills
and knowledge into the colleges to act as learning resources.
Staff members could also be recruited from among people with
appropriate knowledge and skills, for example those who had already had one career in industry or professions and who now
wished to enter teacher training. It could also be done by
greater use of part-time instructors, who could spend the balance of their time in some other profession or trade, or working in industry, in the home, in the community, or elsewhere.

BALANCE OF THE REPORT

To this point, an attempt has been made to introduce the
concept of lifelong education, to spell out the role of the
teacher as it is implied by the theory of lifelong education,
and to suggest some of the features of a system of teacher
training aimed at producing teachers who were capable of playing the role described for them. The remaining chapters of
the text involve a clear switch in content and emphasis. They
are concerned with the way in which some of the implications of
lifelong education for teacher training were actually implemented in working teachers colleges. Thus they contain information about the institutions (Chapter 4), details of the various procedures adopted in the different colleges (Chapters 5,
6 and 7), some evaluation of the effects of these changes (Chapter 8), and a summary of the main conclusions resulting from
the tryout of the innovations (Chapter 9).

SUMMARY

One of the effects of lifelong education on teacher training would be to emphasize that acquiring teaching skill is a
lifelong process. As a result, the division between pre-service and in-service training would become much less clear-cut
than at present. For example, schools themselves might become
not only places of work for teachers, but also places in which
they consciously carried on a process of continuing learning.
The present project concentrated on training occurring prior to
the commencement of duties as a teacher. Such training would
be re-oriented, in order to foster lifelong learning in the
teacher trainees themselves, and to build up their skills in
fostering lifelong learning in pupils.

In order to achieve these goals there would need to be curricular changes in teacher training institutions involving not only the content of courses, but also the ways in which teaching and learning were carried out. Teaching practice would also be affected, not only because of a change in the kinds of classroom activities emphasized, but because of factors like changes in relationships with co-operating schools, or even changes in the kinds of activities regarded as constituting practice teaching.

Changes would also be expected in the administration and organization of the teacher-training institutions themselves. For example, time-tabling would have to permit different kinds of learning activities, facilities for individual and group learning would be needed, relationships with agencies outside the institution would be changed and staff attitudes and values would need to be favourable to lifelong education. The following chapters describe attempts in six teacher-training institutions to make some of the necessary changes.

CHAPTER 4

BACKGROUND AND PROCEDURES
OF THE EMPIRICAL PROJECT

RATIONALE AND SIGNIFICANCE OF THE STUDY

Earlier chapters have developed the argument that there are new goals for teacher education. What is needed at this point are empirical projects which implement practical changes and subsequently evaluate their effects. The applied part of the present project was concerned with such a study. The first step was identification of the area to be studied (lifelong education), and the particular aspect of that area on which there was to be concentration (in this case, the implications of the concept of lifelong education for school-level education). When this degree of delimitation had been achieved, it was realized that if curricular reforms in terms of lifelong education were introduced in schools without preparing teachers for their new role, the innovations would have little chance of success. As a result, it was thought desirable to undertake a study concerned with the education of teachers, recognizing that a curricular reform such as lifelong education would be unlikely to be accepted unless there were some degree of teacher preparedness for it. (Of course, the reverse is also true; changes in teacher training without changes in school curriculum are unlikely to be successful. What is apparently needed is a simultaneous thrust in the areas of teacher training and curriculum. Indeed, a study on the evaluation of curriculum in terms of lifelong education was commenced as a sister project to the present one. This project is the subject of a separate report.)

Subsequently, six teacher training institutions were selected to participate in the project. One of the criteria for selection was willingness to take part, an important criterion in view of the fact that the UIE was not able to provide funds to support work carried on at the local level, and had to rely

57

heavily on the enthusiasm and dedication of people in the participating institutions. A second criterion was the desire to achieve a wide variety in the patterns of school organization, teacher preparation and socio-political orientation covered by the participating institutions. For this reason the project was cross-national in scope. When the institutions had been selected, the heads or directors, or in one or two cases another senior staff member, were recruited to act as leaders at the local level. These project leaders were expected in turn to recruit teams of co-workers in their own institutions.

The institutions selected in this way represented five different countries including Australia, Federal Republic of Germany, Hungary, India and Singapore. Details of the institutions' full postal addresses are to be found in Appendix A. The names of the institutions involved are listed below. For each institution, a shorter name was chosen for the sake of brevity and ease of reference, and these abbreviated titles are shown in brackets after the listing of each full name. The shortened names are used throughout the balance of the report when referring to specific institutions. The list also indicates the names of the local project leaders. These are the people who could be contacted concerning further details of local reports. In this list, and in most other places where the institutions are referred to one after the other, they are presented in alphabetical order by countries.

Australia:

Torrens College of Advanced Education, Adelaide, South Australia
(Abbreviated name: "Torrens")
Project Leaders: Dr. G.A. Ramsey, Mr. G. Dick

Federal Republic of Germany:

Department of Education, University of Trier
(Abbreviated name: "Trier")
Project Leaders: Professor H. Seiler, Dr. U. Holefleisch

Hungary:

Institute of Pedagogy, Attila József University, Szeged
(Abbreviated name: "Szeged")
Project Leader: Professor G. Agoston

India:

Gandhi Shikshan Bhavan, Bombay

(Abbreviated name: "Gandhi Shikshan Bhavan")
Project Leader: Professor V. Patel

Hansraj Jivandas College of Education, Bombay
(Abbreviated name: "H.J. College")
Project Leader: Dr. N.N. Shukla

Singapore:

Institute of Education, Singapore
(Abbreviated name: "Singapore")
Project Leader: Dr. Tan Wee Kiat

It is apparent that there was a degree of variety in the
institutional identities of these colleges. Three (Singapore,
Gandhi Shikshan Bhavan and H.J. College) were teachers colleges,
one (Torrens) was a College of Advanced Education, and two
(Szeged and Trier) were departments within a university. Despite this, each of the participating institutions will be referred to from time to time as a "college" or as a "teachers
college". This is not meant to refer to their organizational
structure, but to their crucial function for the purposes of
the present report (i.e., their function as institutions in
which teachers are trained). Thus, when the terms "college" or
"teachers college" are used, it should be understood that the
usage is somewhat loose, and is adopted only for brevity and
ease of reference. The extent to which the project involved a
broad coverage of courses, programmes and students can be seen
from Table 1 which summarizes some of the main relevant features of the colleges.

After selecting the participating institutions and identifying local project leaders, the UIE staff developed a tentative curriculum plan encompassing an introductory theoretical
course or "core course", a course on the psychological foundations of lifelong education, and a course on general methods of
education, in order to assist the colleges in designing their
own curricular changes. In addition, a basic experimental design was developed at the UIE. Finally, relevant reading material on the concept of lifelong education and its implication
for teachers' roles and for teacher training was collected. The
last step in this phase was the convening of a workshop in Hamburg attended by the local project leaders. This workshop lasted for two weeks and was held in October 1973. The major purposes of the workshop were to clarify understanding of the meaning and implications of lifelong education, to work out a more
detailed curriculum framework for implementation during the lo-

Table 1

Organizational Structures of the Various Colleges

College	Entry Require- ment	Mean Age of Students	Final Qualifi- cation	Length of Programme	Level of Pupils to be Taught
Torrens (a)[1]	Trade of tech- nical qualifi- cations	33	Diploma in Teaching	3 years	Further Education
(b)	Matriculation	22	Diploma in Teaching	3 years	Primary, Secondary and Further Education
Trier	Matriculation	20	Staatsexamen	4 years	Grade 5 to Abitur
Szeged	Matriculation	20	Diploma in Pedagogy	5 years	Upper Secondary
Gandhi Shikshan Bhavan	Bachelor Degree	22	Bachelor of Education Degree	1 year	Upper Pri- mary and Lower Sec- ondary
H. J. College	Bachelor Degree	22	Bachelor of Education Degree	1 year	Upper Pri- mary and Lower Sec- ondary
Singapore	Bachelor Degree	24	Diploma in Education	1 to 1.1/2 years	Upper Sec- ondary

[1]There were two groups of students at Torrens. This is explained more fully on pp. 66-67.

cal, institutional stage, to develop other materials and procedures for the project, and in particular, to work out details
of the experimental design and ways in which it could be adapted to local conditions.

Because of the large differences among the institutions,
the exact form of the project was somewhat different for each
college. In addition, the evaluation procedures were decentral-
ized in that each institution was given the task of developing
its own procedures, evaluative techniques and test instruments.
It was also decided that each college would develop its own
plan for implementing lifelong education, based on the materials supplied by UIE and the procedural decisions taken at the
first workshop. The clarifications achieved, the decisions arrived at, and the plans for future action determined at this
workshop were distributed to the participating project teams in
the form of a set of "Minutes" of the meeting.

Lifelong education as the master concept

The theoretical basis of the changes introduced in the
participating institutions was the concept of lifelong education. The basic notions defining this set of beliefs about education have already been outlined in Chapter 1, while the significance of these ideas for conceptualizing the role of the
teacher and for teacher training have been indicated in Chapters 2 and 3. No recapitulation of these ideas is required at
the present point. However, it is necessary to re-emphasize
that the guiding principle according to which the interventions
carried out were designed and evaluated was that of lifelong
education. This educational principle determined what changes
were made, the purpose for which they were made, and the criteria according to which their effectiveness was subsequently
evaluated. In this sense, lifelong education was the master
concept on which the project was based.

Outline of the project

The focus of interest of the empirical study was to develop practical applications of the concept of lifelong education
to the training of teachers, to implement the changes, and to
evaluate the outcomes of this process. Its basic form may be
summarized in the following steps:

1.   Development of an understanding of the impli-

cations of the concept of lifelong education
among relevant instructional personnel in the
participating teacher training institutions.

2. Collection of appropriate reading and reference
materials.

3. Evolution and try out of a curriculum plan
aimed at developing an insight among student
teachers into the concept of lifelong education and its practical implications.

4. Development within the participating institutions of teaching and learning procedures in
accordance with the instructional implications
of lifelong education.

5. Evaluation of the impact of the programmes implemented.

OBJECTIVES OF THE PROJECT

The overall objective of the study was operationalization
of the concept of lifelong education in teacher education. The
theoretical component of the study (to be found in the first
three chapters of the present text) could therefore be stated
as being to identify the implications of lifelong education for
the teacher, and thus to understand the new knowledge, attitudes and skills that students should acquire during their
teacher training in order to emerge as lifelong education-facilitating teachers. The practical part involved developing
and trying out various changes and innovations in the content,
structure and methods of teacher-training courses in a number
of participating institutions, on the basis of the theoretical
issues previously identified. Stated specifically, the practical objective of the project was to demonstrate that it is
possible to design and implement a number of workable changes
in the functioning of teacher-training institutions in line
with the concept of lifelong education, and through these procedures to achieve desirable effects on student teachers.

Broadly speaking, such effects could be thought of as
having three aspects. The first of these involves possession
of information about lifelong education, the second motivation
to be a lifelong learner and to foster it in others, and the
third mastery of the skills needed to carry out this task. The
first kind of change in curriculum was thus aimed at increasing

students' awareness of the factors in contemporary life creating the need for lifelong education, increasing their familiarity with its basic ideas concerning the organization, timing and content of education, and similar issues. It was concerned with students' *knowledge about lifelong education*.

Lifelong education may also be conceptualized as not only a matter of knowledge, but as a set of principles which require a particular kind of self-image, appropriate values, and positive motivation for continued learning. The second kind of change was thus concerned with fostering the necessary socio-affective qualities in students -- as a matter of *attitudes*, *values* and *motives*. Finally, the third area in which students would be expected to show change would be in development of capacity for self-directed learning, skills in self-evaluation, ability to apply knowledge to life, and similar capacities. Thus, the third area of curricular change was concerned with fostering the *skills that make lifelong learning possible*.

The ultimate aim of orienting teacher training in terms of lifelong education was the development of teachers who not only knew about its "facts", but also endorsed its values and possessed the necessary skills. The hoped-for result of this was development of people who habitually practised the principles of lifelong education, not only as teachers, but also in their day-to-day personal lives.

STRUCTURE OF THE CHANGES

So far the changes introduced in the colleges have been outlined in terms of the effects it was hoped to achieve on student teachers. At this point it is appropriate to describe the changes in terms of the activities made necessary in the participating institutions.

For this purpose, the activities of a teachers college were seen as having three main elements. The first is transmission to students of knowledge about the development of schools, the scholarly basis of education, the theory of teaching, and related topics. It includes study of the history and philosophy of education, of the theoretical foundations of educational psychology or educational sociology, and of teaching techniques, including methods for teaching particular disciplines such as science, mathematics or modern languages. Thus it is concerned with the information taught in teacher-training institutions;

with the *content of courses*.

Quite distinct from the content aspect, it is possible to make changes in the way in which teaching and learning are carried out within a teachers college. This includes the methods through which instruction is carried on (through formal lectures alone, through seminars and tutorials, through discussion groups and so on), the kinds of learning activities students typically engage in during their studies (projects, class presentations, individual study, group projects, etc.), the patterns and forms of evaluation (self-evaluation, co-operative evaluation, formative or summative evaluation, etc.), and similar aspects of curriculum. It involves the *teaching and learning strategies* actually employed in the institution itself.

Finally, teacher training involves provision of practical experiences through which students practise the skills, techniques and roles of the teacher. It is in these activities that the effects of the content of courses and of the teaching and learning methods of the college would be tried out in a practical setting. During the practical experiences, first attempts at putting the principles of lifelong education into effect, both in personal lifestyle and in behaviour as a teacher, would be expected to occur and to be fostered or inhibited, according to the response obtained from pupils, from experienced teachers, and from supervisors. Thus, the area of *practice teaching* was identified as the third element of curriculum in a teachers college in which changes oriented towards lifelong education could be introduced.

The basic questions asked in designing the changes were those of (a) how to change the content of courses in order to make them more consistent with the concept of lifelong education, (b) how to organize the teaching and learning processes within the institutions to make them function as examples of the principles of lifelong education, and (c) how to provide practical experiences likely to foster behaviour oriented towards lifelong education.

It is important to note that this division of the functions of a teacher training institution into three components has been adopted purely to make communication easier. It is not meant to imply that the three functions are independent of each other. In practice it was found that the different kinds of change tended to go together, change in one area necessitating at least some change in others. Nonetheless, although to

some extent artificial, this division simplifies descriptions
of the changes and their outcomes. As a result, Chapter 5
deals separately with changes in the content of courses, Chapter 6 with changes in teaching practice and Chapter 7 with
changes in the colleges' own *modus operandi*.

ACTIVITIES IN THE PARTICIPATING INSTITUTIONS

The project was carried out in a series of steps or stages
of which the first (which has already been described) and the
last (see page 84 - The stage of synthesis) focussed on work at
the Unesco Institute for Education (UIE). The second stage,
however, was mainly conducted within the participating institutions. This "institutional phase" is described in following
sections. After the first international workshop in Hamburg, a
phase of intensive work at the local level commenced in each of
the colleges. For ease of understanding, information about this
work is presented separately for each institution, although a
general pattern is followed in presenting the information. This
consists of a brief description of the role of each institution
in its national system of teacher preparation, a review of the
preparatory activities in the college, and a summary of the actual way in which the project was implemented in that particular institution.

Torrens

Although there are a number of differences among the various states of Australia, it is possible to talk as though the
country possesses a single national system for the education of
teachers. Most universities possess Departments or Faculties
of Education which are involved in teacher training. Generally
such training is of one year's duration following a three-year
Science or Arts degree programme. Although the actual nature
of the one-year course varies from institution to institution,
there is a tendency for the approach to be more scholarly and
theoretical than applied. In addition to the Universities, a
group of institutions called Colleges of Advanced Education
(CAE) are involved in teacher education. The courses in these
institutions tend to be more closely integrated, with study of
the content area, methodology, theory and practice of education,
plus teaching practice, all taking place over a three or four
year period. These colleges are sometimes exclusively involved
in teacher training, but quite often have several faculties or

schools in addition to education, such as Health Sciences, Social Work, Fine Art and Design, or Performing Arts.

The Colleges are generally independent institutions with their own governing bodies, with the right to establish their own programmes and courses and to grant their own degrees and diplomas, subject to the supervision of authorities established to co-ordinate and oversee higher education in Australia. The regulatory and co-ordinating bodies for CAEs are established at both a State and national level, with the State bodies making recommendations to the national body.

As an Australian CAE Torrens is part of the national system of teacher training that has just been outlined. It enjoys a high level of autonomy in internal organization, policies and goals, syllabus and curriculum development, staffing, evaluation, and similar areas. It is answerable to external supervisory agencies for the approval and accreditation of its courses. For example, the co-ordinating body in the State, known as the South Australian Board of Advanced Education, approves all courses the College proposes after it has satisfied itself that a State need exists for the course. Nonetheless, Torrens enjoys great freedom by comparison with some of the other institutions in the study, especially in internal curriculum matters such as teaching and learning processes and evaluation procedures.

The students who participated in the project had entered Torrens on the basis of two different kinds of qualifications. The majority had obtained conventional high school matriculation. These people were preparing for the Diploma in Teaching and would, upon successful completion of their studies, become teachers in primary, secondary, or technical programmes. They ranged in age from about 20 to the early twenties (with rare exceptions), and averaged approximately 22 years of age. The course in which changes were introduced was a one-semester elective. At the time of preparation of the final Torrens report, it had been taught in 1974 and 1975 with 34 and 27 students respectively, making a total of 61 students. These students could be described as following the "standard" route of training within the college.

By contrast with the group just described, a small group of students at Torrens had left secondary school after varying periods, with or without matriculation, and had undergone technical or trade training. This was obtained either through an apprenticeship supplemented by part-time further education and

leading to a tradesman's certificate, or else through part-time
technical courses, again supplemented by work experience, leading to a technician's certificate, to an advanced technician's
certificate, or even to a degree. These kinds of programmes
often occupy up to six or seven years of part-time schooling,
along with on-the-job experience in industry, commerce, agriculture and the like. These people had then decided to become
teachers of their particular trade or technology, and had entered Torrens. They were training to become teachers of pupils
who would themselves be engaged in the further education process through which the teachers had obtained their own trade or
technical qualifications. (This particular group of students
was in fact undergoing teacher training in order to teach people who had left secondary school and become apprentices or
trainee technicians. For this reason, they were ultimately to
become, not school teachers in the conventional sense of the
term, but teachers in the domain of further education.) They
are referred to hereafter as the "further education" students.
The group ranged in age from 28 to 47, with an approximate mean
of 33. They undertook a compulsory one-year course which was
conducted in 1974, 1975 and 1976 with 61, 89 and 100 students
respectively, yielding a total of 250.

Emphasis in the college's orientation had already been on
personal development of students even before the present study
began. As a result, its instructors enjoyed a great deal of
autonomy, and processes like self-learning were part of the
institution's normal mode of functioning. Against this background, the basic ideas of lifelong education were relatively
easy to introduce. There was also a felt need for changes in
the teaching of the further education students. Consequently,
there was a high level of readiness for change of the kind proposed by the UIE.

The first step at Torrens included a report from the project leader to the college's Academic Committee to plan the extent of the college's involvement in the project, and selection
of the key personnel to develop two courses for the purposes of
the project. (The key people who contributed to the project in
all six participating colleges are listed in Appendix B.) The
first of the courses was designed for further-education students, the second for those following the "standard" route.
These steps were taken late in 1973. During January and February 1974 the instructors involved met for one week, during
which they planned the curriculum for the course for further-
education students, in outline for the whole of 1974 and in de-

tail for the first semester. Teaching of this course commenced late in February 1974. A report of this stage of institutional preparation was sent to the UIE at about the end of February. Between March and August 1974 the planning of the course for "standard" students was carried out, and teaching of this course commenced in September. Further planning continued at Torrens during the whole of 1974, although the first phases of the project were already under way, and further changes were introduced during the 1975 academic year. Preliminary reports were prepared and sent to UIE as the project progressed.

In the case of the course for further-education students, the changes involved introduction of a compulsory core course taught for three hours a week, which the students studied on a part-time basis during their second year at Torrens. The course was organized in terms of lifelong education, not only in content, but also in scheduling, teaching and learning methods, and evaluation procedures. The one-semester elective for "standard" students also involved a core of information about lifelong education, and included changes of emphasis in learning and teaching processes similar to those just described for the further-education students.

For ease of understanding and convenience of reference, the steps in the planning and introduction of the revised courses at Torrens are summarized in Tables 2 and 3 which follow. These tables also summarize information about the courses developed at Torrens, including their duration, the kinds of changes made, the basis on which students took them (elective or compulsory), the way in which practice teaching was involved, and so on.

Trier

There are basically two modes of entry to the teaching profession in Germany. There are also variations from *Land* to *Land*, so that although generalizations can be made, various differences will be seen in the differing *Länder*. In general, teachers for elementary schools and for *Hauptschulen* (schools which provide either terminal secondary education or else entry to trades training) undergo, subsequent to matriculation, a three-year programme in *Pädagogische Hochschulen* which, although they are primarily concerned with the training of teachers, have essentially university status. Teachers for academic secondary schools of the grammar school kind *(Gymnasien)*, and for *Realschulen*, which provide either terminal secondary schooling or

Table 2

Outline of Procedures at Torrens
for Further Education Students

Main steps taken and their dates	1. Report of Principal to Academic Committee (late 1973)
	2. Selection of key personnel (late 1973)
	3. Meeting of the instructors involved in the project (January/February 1974)
	4. Planning of the first semester's curriculum (January/February 1974)
	5. Commencement of teaching of the course (late February 1974)
	6. Ongoing planning (throughou, 1974)
	7. Teaching of the further revised course (1975)
	8. Preparation of the final report, which dealt only with 1974 and 1975 although the project continued in 1976 (first half of 1976)
Nature of the changes introduced	1. Introduction of a core course
	2. Re-organization and re-orientation of teaching methods, learning activities, evaluation procedures, etc. in terms of lifelong education
Duration of course	One year
Elective or compulsory	Compulsory
Number of students	1974 - 61 1975 - 89 1976 - 100
Number of instructors	3 in each year
Involvement of practice teaching	Students were assigned to schools during their training and spent only part time at the college. As a result, they were involved in teaching activities during the course. This teaching was closely monitored by the college and an evaluation system worked out. Thus, for this group, the training was essentially inservice training.

Table 3

Outline of Procedures at
Torrens for "Standard" Students

Main steps taken and their dates	1. Report of Principal to Academic Committee (late 1973)
	2. Selection of key personnel (late 1973). These were the same people as for the Further Education students
	3. Meeting of the instructors involved in the project (January/February 1973)
	4. Planning of the course (March to August 1973)
	5. Commencement of teaching of the course (September 1973)
	6. Ongoing planning (throughout 1974)
	7. Teaching of the further revised course (1975)
	8. Preparation of the final report, which dealt only with 1974 and 1975, although the project continued in 1976 (first half of 1976)
Nature of the changes introduced	1. Introduction of a core course
	2. Re-organization and re-orientation of teaching methods, learning activities, evaluation procedures, etc., in terms of lifelong education
Duration of course	One semester
Elective or compulsory	Elective
Number of students	1974 - 34 1975 - 27
Number of instructors	1
Involvement of practice teaching	Not formally involved

else entry to technical training, are usually trained in universities after completing matriculation. They complete a
three-, four-, or five-year programme, the time varying from
state to state. This period is essentially theoretical in nature, and is closely linked with academic training in one or
more scholarly disciplines, although there are courses in the
theory of teaching and the foundations of education. Following
academic training, there is a one-and-a-half year period of
practical teaching experience, which functions both as a period
of practice teaching and as a kind of apprenticeship or proba-
tionary period.

The course which was involved in the present project at
Trier was part of the programme of the Department of Education
of the University of Trier leading to the "Staatsexamen", which
roughly approximates a Bachelor of Education degree. The students were all training to teach in secondary schools (i.e.,
grade 5 to matriculation, since there are normally four years
of primary schooling in Germany). They ranged in age from 18
to 21, with an approximate mean of 20. The course was concerned
with the theory and practice of teaching. It was an elective
of one semester's duration. In 1974 there were 20 students enrolled, in both 1975 and 1976, 120. A total of four instructors
was involved.

In the planning phase at Trier, a project team of five instructors was formed in order to develop curricular modules for
the modification of the single course in the project. This team
constituted a working group which developed the content of the
theoretical analysis of the teaching process forming the basis
of the Trier procedures. No changes could be achieved in the
curriculum for teacher training, nor in the functioning of the
institution as a whole, largely because of the independence
with which German instructors work, and the consequent difficulty of developing a project possessing any degree of breadth
or comprehensiveness. The change introduced involved an existing theoretical course of one semester's duration, modified so
that its first half constituted what may be thought of as a
core course, and the second half what was essentially a general
method of teaching course. In addition to modifying the content of the course, an attempt was made to adopt learning and
teaching processes which were consistent with the theory being
taught.

A number of details of the planning and execution of the
project at Trier are summarized in Table 4 which follows.

Table 4

Outline of Procedures at Trier

Main steps taken and their dates	1. Formation of a project team to plan curricular modules for the course
	2. Teaching of the course in 1974, 1975 and 1976
	3. Preparation of the final report (first half of 1976)
Nature of the changes introduced	1. Introduction of what amounted to a core course
	2. Modification of a simulated teaching practice course
Duration of course	One semester (half devoted to the "core course", half to simulated teaching)
Elective or compulsory	Elective
Number of students	1974 - 20 1975 - 120 1976 - 120
Number of instructors	4
Involvement of practice teaching	No practice teaching in real school settings, but simulation

Szeged

In Hungary, once again, teachers are trained either in universities or teachers colleges. Students who enter teachers college undergo a course of two year's duration for future kindergarten teachers, three years for those who are to teach in the first four grades of general school, and four years for those training to teach in the last four years of general school. By contrast, the university training involves a five year programme leading to a Diploma in Pedagogy. Students in this programme are preparing to work as teachers in academic secondary schools similar to the German *Gymnasium*. The Szeged project was carried out in the Department of Education of the University of Szeged, so that the students were following this latter route.

On entering the university, students declare themselves as trainee teachers. They take academic courses in two disciplines such as mathematics and physics, Hungarian and English, or other similar combinations. However, concurrently with this work they undertake studies in education. The education component of their programme commences in the second semester with studies of general psychology, and continues with developmental psychology in the third semester (i.e., the study of the foundations of education commences at this point). Study of the theory of education commences in the fourth semester, and in the third year (fifth and sixth semesters) more practically oriented studies of the theory of teaching and of the problems of education commence. This period includes two days of observation in co-operating schools in each of the fifth and sixth semesters, and, in either the fifth or the sixth semester, about two hours a week of work within schools but outside the classroom, in youth organizations, hobby groups and similar activities. There is also a compulsory period of two weeks of practical work at the end of the sixth semester, spent in youth camps and other related organizations during the vacation period. The fourth year involves further theory and study of the teaching of the students' specialized subjects in which they have been engaged all along, in parallel with their pedagogical studies. The fifth and final year is spent as an intern in a training school under the university's supervision.

In the case of the present project, it was the second semester of the second year and both semesters of the third year on which attention was focused. The students involved had all completed matriculation-level qualifications, supplemented by some completed university work, as pre-requisites for participation in the project. They were very homogeneous in age, with virtually all aged 19 or 20. The courses involved in the project were compulsory, and were taken by 300 students in the second year of studies and 300 in the third year. Each individual student was involved for three semesters. A total of 12 instructors took part.

Preparation at Szeged went on from March until August 1974. The first step was review and discussion of the project by the local leader with instructors in the institution, directors of the schools in which practice teaching was to occur, and other interested parties. Subsequently the project was reviewed and discussed with the administration of the Faculty of Arts, under whose aegis it was to be carried out. Between April and August 1974, instructors also reviewed the available literature on lifelong education and, after individual study of the literature, three joint meetings were held in which problems in the implementation of the project were discussed. In addition to these planning activities, more practical actions were also taken during the same period, including the building up of a supply of aids to independent learning such as AV/TV devices, and the translation of documents in the area into Hungarian.

At Szeged, changes were much more comprehensive than at the institutions discussed to date. A core course was introduced, while courses in the theory of education, the historical foundations of education, and the theory of teaching were also involved. These courses were compulsory for students in the second half of their second year of teacher training, and for all students in the third year. In all courses, in addition to changes in content, attempts were made to foster the kind of teaching and learning processes indicated by lifelong education.

A further major extension of institutional changes was also seen at Szeged, in that practice teaching was heavily involved in the project. In this area, great emphasis was placed on experiences outside the usual school structure, for example through work with youth groups, participation in extra-curricular activities, leadership of discussion groups, and similar activities. In addition to extending the scope of practice teaching, there was also a change in the roles of instructors and students and in relations between both these groups and teachers in the co-operating schools. For example, students and teachers were incorporated into the planning of practice teaching, so that a degree of self-direction was achieved.

A second major extension of the project methodology at Szeged was a formal evaluation of the effects of the modified curriculum on student teachers. This was done by designing appropriate instruments to measure students' attitudes and opinions in the areas of educational philosophy and classroom practice. These instruments were then administered as a pre-test to 257 students, at the beginning of the third year, and as a post-test to 210 students, at the end of the same year. In addition, they were administered to 280 teachers already practising their profession, in order to ascertain the extent to which ideas and attitudes favourable to lifelong education were already present, and also the extent to which students differed from practising teachers both before and after exposure to a curriculum oriented towards lifelong education. The results of these evaluations will be reported in a later chapter.

The organization of the project in the form it took at Szeged is summarized in Table 5.

Gandhi Shikshan Bhavan

The practical and professional preparation of teachers in India is carried on in three kinds of teachers colleges. The first of these is referred to as a "Junior College of Education". The junior colleges are concerned with training students who will become teachers in the first four grades of primary education, and offer a two year programme for students with secondary school educational background. The second kind of teachers college in India is referred to as a "College of Education". Students in these colleges already have a university degree on entry, such as a Bachelor of Arts or a Bachelor of Science. They undergo a one-year programme of training in the theory and practice of teaching which leads to a BEd degree, in preparation for teaching in grades 5 to 10. This approach separates academic training in special disciplines (carried on at university in the course of the bachelor degree programme) and pedagogical training (carried on in the College of Education). However, the basic curriculum for pedagogical training is laid down by the university with which each college is affiliated. Finally, there are a small number of Regional Colleges of Education. These colleges admit high school matriculants directly into a four-year programme of training to teach from grades 5 to 12.

Gandhi Shikshan Bhavan is a College of Education. It admits people who already have a BA, BSc or BCom degree, with an age range from 21 to 50, although virtually all students lie between 21 and 30, and the approximate mean age of the students in the present project was 22. The students were preparing for the Bachelor of Education degree, and were eventually to teach pupils at upper primary and lower secondary levels.

Table 5

Outline of Procedures at Szeged

Main steps taken and their dates	1. Review and discussion of the project with college instructors and principals of co-operating schools (March 1974)
	2. Review and discussion of the project with the administration of the Faculty of Arts (March 1974)
	3. Review of the literature on lifelong education and conduct of three planning meetings by instructors (April to August 1974)
	4. Development of learning aids and materials (April to August 1974)
	5. Introduction of the modified curriculum in 2nd and 3rd year courses (September 1974 to the end of 1975)
	6. Administration of pre-tests at the beginning of 3rd year and of post-tests to the same general group of students at the end of the 3rd year
	7. Preparation of the final report (first half of 1976)
Nature of the changes introduced	1. Introduction of a core course
	2. Modification of the Historical Foundations course
	3. Modification of the Theory of Education course
	4. Modification of the Theory of Teaching course
	5. Modification of practice teaching methods
Duration of course	One and a half years
Elective or compulsory	Compulsory
Number of students	600
Number of instructors	12
Involvement of practice teaching	Yes. Practice teaching was also extended to include activities outside classrooms

At this college the period of preparation lasted from November 1973 to May 1974. This activity included meetings among the college's instructors in order to specify the implications of lifelong education for teaching practice within the college, and to work out details of the experimental design. A special issue at Gandhi Shikshan Bhavan was the need to reconcile the concept of lifelong education with the educational philosophy of the Indian Council of Basic Education, the body which established the college and which is its major funding agency. Consequently, meetings were held with the national executive of the organization for this purpose. Meetings were also held in March 1974 with the headmasters of the 20 co-operating schools in which practice teaching would be done, in order to prepare a plan of pupil involvement in the study of the curriculum. Subsequently, the instructors in the college prepared a final project design, including a curriculum framework.

An important step at Gandhi Shikshan Bhavan was the development of the necessary instruments for measuring the effects of the programme. These tests included both pre- and post-tests and necessitated administration of the pre-test instruments to certain students as early as February, 1974, in order to ascertain how the students scored before the commencement of the project. The project proper commenced in June. Some of the test instruments were also administered to the students in the 1973-74 academic year so that their data could provide baseline or control information for students who did not experience the lifelong education-oriented curriculum. This group thus constituted a control group.

The curricular changes at Gandhi Shikshan Bhavan involved a compulsory course of one year's duration. All 83 students enrolled in the 1974-1975 academic year participated, while all 13 instructors in the college were also involved. Not only was a core course in lifelong education introduced, but all foundations courses were modified, as well as courses in special and general methods of education. Teaching and learning methods were adapted in accordance with the principles of lifelong education, and evaluation too was changed in order to introduce more self-evaluation as well as group-evaluation. Finally, the principles of lifelong education were extended to practice teaching, where students were encouraged to use methods and processes in line with lifelong education, to draw examples and materials from real life, to manufacture learning materials from everyday resources, to foster a co-operative spirit among their pupils, and many more procedures derived from the concept of lifelong education, as will be seen from later chapters.

It is thus apparent that the tactic of change adopted at Gandhi Shikshan Bhavan (and at H.J. College too, as will become apparent from the next section) involved not only modification of the content and methods of all courses in the college, but also a major re-organization of the whole teaching and learning atmosphere of the college, a change in the relationship between instructors and students, a change in the relationship of the college to the community, and changes in the methods and forms of practice teaching. The changes introduced in the course of the project are summarized in Table 6.

H.J. College

Details of the organization of teacher training in India are, of course, the same for H.J. College as for Gandhi Shikshan Bahvan, and they will not be repeated here. In the case of H.J. College, the students involved in the project were in a one-year programme leading to the BEd degree, with the intention of teaching at upper primary and lower secondary levels. These students all had bachelor degrees and were about 22 years old, on average. One feature of the H.J. College which differed from that at Gandhi Shikshan Bhavan was that 78 students did their practice teaching in the form of a six-week internship, whereas 76 did it in the form of one hour a week of practice teaching in co-operating schools. Some of the findings of the H.J. College project presented in Chapter 8, for example, are based on this division of students into those who had an internship and those who had not.

The preparatory stage at H.J. College lasted from December 1973 until June 1974. An initial meeting of the staff of the college was held, and a series of weekly "Think Tank" meetings then ensued. These meetings, at which things like the meaning of lifelong education and its implications for teaching methods and materials were clarified by discussion among the instructors, continued throughout the project. A series of sub-committees was formed to revise existing syllabuses for the various disciplines in the light of lifelong education, and to consider the implications of the concept for such areas of college life as the library. A number of workshops were held, in which instructors analyzed the content of the existing syllabus, which was laid down by the University of Bombay and could not be substantially altered, and considered the possibility of

Table 6

Outline of Procedures
at Gandhi Shikshan Bhavan

Main steps taken and their dates	1. Meetings among the college's instructors to specify the implications of lifelong education and to work out the experimental design (November 1973 to May 1974)
	2. Meetings with the national executive of the Indian Council of Basic Education (early 1974)
	3. Preparation of the final project design and development of test instruments (November 1973 to June 1974)
	4. Administration of tests to control group (February 1974)
	5. Meetings with the headmasters of the co-operating schools (March 1974)
	6. Administration of pre-tests to experimental group (June 1974)
	7. Commencement of teaching according to the modified curriculum (June 1974)
	8. Administration of post-tests to experimental group (February 1975)
	9. Preparation of the final report (February to October 1975)
Nature of the changes introduced	1. Introduction of a core course
	2. Modification of Foundations courses
	3. Modification of courses in General and Special Methods of Education
	4. Modification of teaching and learning processes within the college
	5. Modification of teaching practice
Duration of course	One year
Elective or compulsory	Compulsory
Number of students	83 (total college enrollment)
Number of instructors	13 (all college staff)
Involvement of practice teaching	Yes

introducing lifelong education concepts into these courses. These committees also developed lists of appropriate reference materials, and of teaching aids and suitable practical projects. Thus, they worked on developing what could be called a lifelong education *supplemented* curriculum, since although its basic form was specified by an external agency and could not be drastically altered, it could be added to, deepened, and broadened.

A series of meetings was also held with the principals of co-operating schools in which students were to do their practice teaching. At these meetings there were discussions concerning what was expected from the schools and their teachers, what time demands this would make on the schools, and what benefits might accrue to the schools as a result of their participation in the project. Finally, details of the implementation of the project were worked out, and committees assigned to the development of research instruments for the assessment of the effects of the modified curriculum, and for similar purposes.

The entire student body of 154 participated in the project, along with all 19 instructors. A core course was introduced, and in addition all foundations courses, as well as the courses in special and general methods of education, were modified in keeping with the principles of lifelong education. Teaching methods, learning activities and evaluation procedures were also modified in the light of lifelong education. As at Gandhi Shikshan Bhavan, activities were introduced which emphasized the links between the college and the community, and emphasis in practice teaching was given to the adoption by students of methods and techniques of a kind consistent with lifelong education. Thus, there was an extensive modification of the content and methods of all courses in the college, along with a major change in the whole teaching and learning atmosphere of the institution.

An important methodological step at H.J. College, as at Gandhi Shikshan Bhavan, was the adoption of a research design involving not only pre- and post-test measurements, but also the use of an experimental group/control group design. This was achieved by comparison of the scores of H.J. College students on some of the test instruments with scores obtained by students in another college not in any other way involved in the project. A summary of the procedures at H.J. College is to be found in Table 7.

Table 7

Outline of Procedures at H. J. College

Main steps taken and their dates	1. Initial meeting of the college's staff followed by a series of "think tank" meetings. Formation of subcommittees to revise syllabi and workshops for instructors (December 1973 to June 1974)
	2. Development of lists of reference materials and collection of teaching aids (first half of 1974)
	3. Meetings with principals of co-operating schools (early 1974)
	4. Development of research instruments (first half of 1974)
	5. Administration of pre-tests (commencement of 1974-1975 academic year)
	6. Implementation of modified curriculum (June 1974 to early 1975)
	7. Administration of post-tests (end of 1974-1975 academic year)
	8. Preparation of final report (completed by February 1976)
Nature of the changes introduced	1. Introduction of a core course
	2. Modification of foundations courses
	3. Modification of courses in General and Special Methods of Education
	4. Modification of teaching and learning processes within the college
	5. Modification of teaching practice
Duration of course	One year
Elective or compulsory	Compulsory
Number of students	154 (all students enrolled)
Number of instructors	19 (all staff members)
Involvement of teaching practice	Yes

Singapore

The Singapore Institute of Education is responsible for all pre-service teacher training in Singapore, and also for a major portion of in-service training. Three diplomas are offered. The first of these involves students with matriculation standing who enter the Institute directly from secondary school at the age of about 18 or 19, and work towards a Certificate in Education. Secondly, persons already possessing the Certificate in Education who have subsequently completed five years of teaching experience may study at the Institute for two years for the Advanced Certificate in Education. Finally, students who already possess a bachelor degree may enter a course of studies leading to the Diploma in Education, which requires from one to one-and-a-half years. The Institute also has students preparing for MEd and PhD degrees.

The first step at Singapore was the formation of a five-member "nucleus committee" which met every two weeks during the project. The various background papers supplied by the UIE were circulated within the college, with a view to incorporating some of their contents into the college's own core education programmes. However, as the existing programmes had only recently been adopted, no substantial curricular changes were made. In a similar way, materials from the other participating institutions were received and distributed among the staff and students involved in the project. Bibliographic material was also studied, and selected background materials were recommended to the library for purchase.

A second step undertaken in the early stages of the project at Singapore involved the dissemination of lifelong education concepts among other organizations and institutions engaged in education. In pursuing this purpose two major reports were translated into both Malay and Chinese and published in a professional journal produced and distributed by the college itself. In addition, a brief note about the project was published in the journal of the Singapore Teachers' Union. It can thus be seen that a major aspect of the preparatory work at Singapore involved dissemination of the concept of lifelong education to a wide audience.

The students involved in the present project were studying for the Diploma in Education, and preparing to teach at grades between grade 7 and grade 12, with most of them concentrating on the senior secondary level (grades 9 to 12). They were mostly about 22 or 23 years in age. The changes made in instruction in

the college at Singapore centered on introduction of a one-semester elective, "special education" course as part of the Diploma
programme. This course was taught for three semesters and had 4,
7 and 13 students respectively. The total number of instructors
involved in the project was four. In addition to changes in the
content of the class, changes were made in the teaching and
learning strategies, and links with community learning agencies
were emphasized. The changes are summarized in Table 8.

Table 8

Outline of Procedures at Singapore

Main steps taken and their dates	1. Formation of a "nucleus committee" which met every two weeks during the project (January 1974 - May 1974)
	2. Circulation of background papers on life-long education and consideration of possible programme changes (January 1974 - December 1975)
	3. Wider dissemination of lifelong education concepts (July 1974 - July 1975)
	4. Commencement of teaching according to the modified curriculum (July 1974)
	5. Preparation of the final report (June 1975 - September 1975)
Nature of the changes introduced	1. Introduction of a one-semester core course
	2. Modification of teaching and learning strategies in the course
Duration of course	One semester
Elective or compulsory	Elective
Number of students	First semester taught (July 1974) - 4 Second semster taught (Jan. 1975) - 7 Third semester taught (July 1975) - 13
Number of instructors	4
Involvement of teaching practice	No

THE STAGE OF SYNTHESIS

The final step in the project was the stage in which the
data collected in the various institutions were synthesized into a single, coherent statement. This stage may be thought of
as having two phases, a local or institutional phase and an international phase. For convenience, these two phases are brief-
ly described in separate sections.

The institutional syntheses

Each college prepared a local report giving details of the
rationale and aims of the project as it had been conceived at
the local level, the actual changes introduced in the college,
and evaluative remarks of one kind or another. This latter material was based in some cases (e.g., Szeged, Gandhi Shikshan
Bhavan, H.J. College) on the analysis of a variety of formal
test instruments and protocols of various kinds. In others, it
involved observations, opinions, subjective impressions, and
similar data. These local reports were distributed among the
participating colleges, and were also sent to the UIE. A copy
of the tables of contents of the various final institutional
reports is to be found in Appendix C. In most cases the reports are available from the project leaders in the various institutions.

The international synthesis

When the local reports had all been circulated among the
participating institutions and had also been received at the
UIE, a final project workshop was organized. This meeting took
place in June 1976. At the workshop, each local project leader
presented the report from his institution, amplifying and clar-
ifying the points raised and emphasizing the central features
of the project as it had been implemented locally. Subsequently, key issues such as that of identifying the major findings
arising from the reports were hammered out. At this stage, the
emphasis was on achieving broad understanding of the implications of the project as a totality, and on identifying findings
that transcended the boundaries of a single local variant. In
other words, the six national reports were treated as data, on
the basis of which a broader fusion and an overall view was to
be developed.

Subsequently, after the conclusion of the final workshop,

a plan for the structure of an international report was prepared
at the UIE. This report was to synthesize the findings of the
institutional reports, incorporating the insights gained at the
workshop. (The present report is, in fact, the resulting document.) This outline was circulated to the project leaders with
a request for their comments and suggestions, and then the preparation of the final international report began, eventually occupying the second half of 1976. By early 1977 the project
leaders had been given an opportunity to read and criticize the
first draft of the international report, and the present revised
version was prepared.

Although the present document claims to be a synthesis of
the six institutional reports, it is not a summary of them in
the sense that each has simply been reproduced, possibly in
shortened form. As has been stated already, the institutional
reports were treated as data, and conclusions drawn on the basis of those data. Some of the findings are reported in the
first three chapters, but most are given in Chapters 5, 6, 7,
8 and 9. As a result of this approach to the preparation of
the international report, a structure has been imposed on the
materials presented in the institutional reports which does not
necessarily correspond to the original structure. The data
have, in fact, been re-organized for the purpose of the present
report. Among other things this means that there has been selection of materials from the institutional reports, and that
the emphasis given to various aspects of these reports has sometimes been altered for the purpose of the international report.
Some material contained in the institutional reports may even
have been omitted or scarcely mentioned. For this reason, people interested in the project may wish to obtain copies of the
institutional reports from the local project leaders. Nonetheless, it is probable that the key procedures, methods and findings are all to be found in the present document.

VARIABILITY IN THE FORM OF THE PROJECT

One of the intentions of the present project which became
explicit in the international planning stage was that it should
cover a variety of institutions in differing socio-political
systems, a variety of forms and methods of teacher training, a
variety of different kinds of students, and a wide variety of
pupils for whom the students were preparing. The extent to
which a broad coverage was achieved can be seen from Table 9.
Student numbers ranged from several hundred to four, at any giv-

Table 9

Summary of Change Structures in the Various Colleges

College	Compulsory or Elective	No of Students	No of Instructors	Courses Involved	Duration	Involvement of Practice Teaching
Torrens (a)[1]	C	250	1	Core Course	1 year	Yes
(b)	E	61	4	Core Course	1 semester	No
Trier	E	260	4	Core Course; Simulated teaching practice	1 semester	No
Szeged	C	600	12	Core Course; Historical and Theoretical Foundations; Theory of Education; Theory of Teaching	1.1/2 years	Yes
Gandhi Shikshan Bhavan	C	83	13	Core Course; Foundations Courses; Special and General Methods of Education	1 year	Yes
H. J. College	C	155	19	Core Course; Foundations Courses; Special and General Methods of Education	1 year	Yes
Singapore	E	24	4	Core Course	1 semester	No

[1]These data refer to the further education students

en time, programmes ranged from one semester in length to one-
and-a-half years, some programmes included marked re-organization of the institutions involved, others merely slight addi-
tions to the available options, and so on. Some of these dimensions along which the project varied are discussed more fully in the following sections.

Differences in experimental design

In the planning phase of the project an attempt was made
to develop a broad and general plan of action which would provide guidelines for the various colleges. However, the institutions were situated in national education systems with different
socio-political ideologies and structures and, as a result,
there were substantial differences between colleges in their
rights and responsibilities, in the degree to which changes
could be freely made without reference to outside bodies, and
in similar factors. There was also great variability in the
internal structure of the colleges and in factors like their
degree of commitment to existing curricula. This meant that it
was impossible to lay down precise details of the way in which
the project was to be implemented in each college, and to expect these details to be strictly observed. Consequently, the
experimental design was expressed in broad terms, in order to
permit each institution to develop its own variant, consistent
with the way in which the principles of lifelong education
could be realized within a particular national context, and
consistent with what was feasible within the college itself.

This does not mean that no agreement was reached concerning the meaning of lifelong education, or concerning the general form of the project. However, it is true that there was
a deliberate and indeed essential, flexibility in specifying
the form of the project, and that precise details of what
changes were made differed from institution to institution. An
important advantage which flowed from this variability in the
details of experimental design was that, over and above the
broad areas of overlap between projects, there was an opportunity for each college to make a unique contribution arising out
of the idiosyncracies of its local variant of the project. It
is true that strict comparisons could not be made between institutions; it was impossible to ask, for example, whether
greater changes in the attitudes of students had been achieved
at Szeged or Gandhi Shikshan Bhavan. However, such comparisons
were never intended to be a part of the project. On the other

hand, permitting each college to develop the details of the project according to the ingenuity of its participating instructors led to the testing of many procedures which would not have been permitted by imposition of a single, detailed experimental design on all of the colleges. Thus, the variability in details of the ways in which it was implemented in the various institutions added greatly to the project's richness.

Differences in level

The teacher training institutions involved in the study were preparing teachers for work at a wide variety of levels of school instruction. For example, H.J. College and Gandhi Shikshan Bhavan were involved with students who would become teachers at upper-primary and lower-secondary level, students at Trier were preparing to teach at grades 5 to 10, students in Singapore at lower- and upper-secondary, students at Szeged at upper-secondary level, and students at Torrens at both school level and also post-secondary ("further education") level. Thus, it is clear that a wide range existed in the levels of the pupils ultimately to be taught by the student teachers involved in the study. In this respect, the project could be said to be comprehensive in scope.

Differences in types of course

A wide range also existed in the kinds of courses introduced in the various institutions in their implementation of the project. In Singapore, the curricular change consisted of the introduction of a single elective course, concerned with explication of basic information about lifelong education and occupying two hours a week for one semester. In Trier it involved a course on the theory of teaching occupying four hours a week for half a semester, plus a course in teaching method which occupied the other half. At Torrens there were two relatively unrelated changes involving introduction of a one-semester course on lifelong education as an elective available to all third year students, and introduction of a compulsory introductory core course occupying three hours per week for further education students. The curricular changes were considerably more extensive at Szeged where they involved not only introduction of a compulsory core course taught for one semester for two hours a week, but also modification of a course in Historical Foundations of Education to give emphasis to lifelong education concepts, along with similar changes in a course in the theory of education and in instruction in the theory of teaching. Finally, at both Gandhi Shikshan Bhavan and H.J. College, the curricular changes involved not only the introduction of core courses, although on a somewhat different organizational basis for the two colleges, but also re-orientation of the entire curriculum of Philosophical, Sociological and Psychological Foundations of Education, of study of evaluation, of general methods of education, and of special methods of education. These changes were compulsory for all students in the two colleges.

Differences in extent of change

It is apparent from the preceding paragraph that there was considerable diversity in the kinds of changes attempted at the various colleges. These ranged from the relatively restricted introduction of an elective course at Singapore to wholesale re-organization of teaching, and indeed of college life, in the two Indian colleges. In some institutions changes were compulsory for all students, in some elective. As a result, in one institution (Szeged) as many as 300 students were involved in each of two semesters, making 600 individual students in all, whereas in another (Singapore) as few as four students in a single semester or 24 students in all took part. Similarly, staff involvement ranged from all the staff of a college (Gandhi Shikshan Bhavan and H.J. College) to a small subgroup of four (Trier, Torrens, Singapore). In much the same way, the proportion of the institution's programme given over to the lifelong education project ranged from a complete re-orientation (as in the Indian colleges), to a relatively small addition to the normal workload (as in Singapore), with various intermediate stages. This was also seen in the number of courses in a college affected by the lifelong education project, again ranging from all of them involving all students for all their time, to a single elective involving each student for two hours a week for a single semester. Finally, the extensiveness of changes could be seen in whether or not students were *required* to participate in the lifelong education-oriented curriculum, as they were at H.J. College, Gandhi Shikshan Bhavan, Szeged and Torrens (further education students only), or whether participation was *elective* (Trier, Singapore and part of the Torrens project). One major dimension along which the various projects differed was thus the extensiveness of the changes introduced.

LIMITATIONS OF THE PROJECT

The project described in this report had two important lim-
iting conditions. The first of these was the high level of
variability from institution to institution in the precise details of its implementation. These variations were imposed by
differences in the colleges' abilities to carry out sweeping
changes in curriculum, and also by the great variety from college to college in students, kinds of course being followed,
and similar aspects. Although it has been argued in the preceding section that this heterogeneity of the participating institutions had advantages, for example because it resulted in
development of a rich variety of methods and materials, it was
a limitation as far as the carrying out of strict evaluations
of the changes implemented in the colleges was concerned. The
second problem was one of time and cost. Practical considerations required that the project be of short-term nature only
(concerned with no more than one-and-a-half or two years of
each college's life), while cost considerations precluded hir-
ing of personnel, development of materials, and similar actions,
except to the extent that these could be provided from the normal resources of the participating institutions. As a result,
a strict, formal study following the lines of a rigorous experiment could not be carried out. Nonetheless, although no claim
is made that a controlled experiment has been completed, the
implementation of the project in the colleges did permit the
drawing of some conclusions, while all of the colleges provided
a number of hints and observations which consist, at the very
least, of the impressions gained by careful observers. However, these generalizations must be regarded as tentative, and
should be treated with caution.

In addition to obtaining such "quasi-experimental" findings, the project had a second function, linked with the one
just described but distinguishable from it. This was the developmental function. A major purpose was to develop better
understanding of the practical implications of lifelong education, and to foster attempts to turn these understandings into
real-life activities that could be carried on in teachers colleges. Thus, the varied procedures adopted in the participating institutions provide many example of novel forms of classroom organization, of techniques of evaluation, of course content, of instructor-student relations, of integration of colleges with community organizations, of forms of practice teaching, and similar innovations. In this sense, the project can
be regarded as a source of ideas and a demonstration of the

practicability of a variety of methods and procedures, some of
which other colleges may wish to adopt.

In effect, then, the project tried to combine practical
usefulness and informal methods of formulating and testing
ideas, with some degree of rigour, where this could be achieved.
It has many methodological flaws when viewed from a strictly
experimental position. However, the intention was to generate
and stimulate ideas, above all, and to provide some guidelines
concerning various ways in which the concept of lifelong education could be introduced into teachers colleges. It is hoped
that the findings reported in coming chapters will be viewed
in this light. The study is broad and comprehensive, and is
meant to be seminal rather than definitive. Hopefully it will
be read from this point of view.

SUMMARY

On the basis of lifelong education as the guiding principle, various changes in curriculum, instructional procedures,
institutional organization and practice teaching were introduced in six teacher-training institutions. The intention of
the changes was to increase student teachers' knowledge about
lifelong education, to modify their attitudes and motives in
the area, and to encourage practical teaching behaviours of a
kind thought likely to foster lifelong learning in pupils. It
was hoped, in this way, to develop students who not only adopted different teaching behaviours, but who also adopted the habits of lifelong learning in their own lives.

The changes were concerned with basic courses containing
information about lifelong education, with teaching and learning methods employed in the colleges, with internal functioning
within the college, and with practice teaching activities. However, not all institutions made changes in all areas. As a result, the nature of the changes differed widely from institution to institution, ranging from introduction of a one-semester elective taken by a handful of students to total re-organization of all activities within the college including participation of all staff and all students. Data concerning the effectiveness of the procedures adopted were also collected,
again in a variety of ways encompassing both subjective, qualitative data and also more objective, quantitative kinds.

This lack of uniformity was made necessary by the widely

differing settings within which the colleges functioned. For example, some were located in universities, some were independent, and some were partly independent and partly under the supervision of other agencies. Some were in less-developed countries, some in more-developed ones, some in capitalist, some in socialist societies. In some there was a strongly felt need for curricular change, in others no such need at all. One result was that the project took a differing form in each college. On the other hand, the variety of settings in which the project was implemented meant that the concept of lifelong education was developed and applied in a variety of ways, although all showed agreement on certain common principles. Many different techniques and procedures were thus employed and, in this sense, lack of uniformity led to richness and variety.

CHAPTER 5

CHANGES IN THEORY COURSES

Chapter 2 has indicated that teachers need many special properties to foster lifelong learning in pupils. The objectives of teacher training in the context of lifelong education will be the development of these properties in student teachers. The present chapter describes the changes which were implemented in the various colleges with this purpose in mind, concentrating on changes in theory courses.

CONTENT OF THE CHANGES

For the present purposes the theoretical portions of teachers college curricula may be thought of as having three components - a course on the origins, meaning and implications of lifelong education (a "core" course), a course or courses concerned with the theoretical foundations of education, and a course or courses in the theory of teaching. The changes implemented in the various colleges are described here from this point of view.

Core courses

The first step in the introduction of the principles of lifelong education in a teachers college may be seen as development of a core course concerned with the history, rationale, main characteristics and use of the concept. All of the participating institutions developed such a course in one form or another.

In the case of Gandhi Shikshan Bhavan, a core course taught for two hours a week for one whole year was introduced. At H.

J. College a somewhat similar course was developed. However, it
was taught for one hour a day for the first four weeks of the
year, and the content of the course was also somewhat different.
The main themes of this course at H. J. College are listed below
in Table 10 which is taken from pp. 10-11 of the original report.
Thereafter the principles which had been outlined were applied
to all other teaching, as was the case at Gandhi Shikshan Bhavan
too.

Table 10

Themes in the Core Course at H. J. College

1.	The student teacher (ST) recalls/recognizes the need of life-long education.
2.	The ST recalls/recognizes nature, scope and function of the concept of lifelong education.
3.	The ST recalls/recognizes features of the concept of lifelong education.
4.	The ST discusses impact of the concept of lifelong education on various aspects of education.
5.	The ST identifies role of teacher in promoting lifelong education.
6.	The ST identifies potentialities of formal and informal education in the process of lifelong education.
7.	The ST formulates procedures of measurement and evaluation.
8.	The ST discusses implication of explosion of knowledge for the concept of lifelong education.
9.	The ST identifies changes in all spheres of life.
10.	The ST discusses implications regarding education of/for tomorrow.

At Torrens College, two courses concerned with information
about lifelong education were involved. The first of these was
a compulsory course for further education students. This course
was organized around four themes consisting of (1) Education and
society, (2) The teacher in further education, (3) The student

in further education, (4) The school and further education.
Each of these themes was studied from the point of view of lifelong education. The second course at Torrens was a one-semester
option for final year students. In this course, the first half
(eight weeks) was spent focusing on several themes which can be
seen as comprising a course in the basic principles of lifelong
education. These themes were (1) Some basic concepts of lifelong education - their history and development, (2) some psychological foundations of lifelong education, (3) some sociological
foundations of lifelong education, (4) the economic implications
of lifelong education, (5) some insights which anthropology and
ecology may have for lifelong education, (6) some implications
of lifelong education for curriculum, (7) the community as a
learning resource, (8) living-working-learning; the integration
of man's activities.

At Szeged, the introduction of core material involving information about lifelong education was achieved by inserting the
material into an existing course of two semesters' duration.
This was done in the first instance by the use of six hours of
class time at the beginning of the first semester for an introduction to lifelong education (four hours of lectures and two
hours of group discussion). This introduction was organized
around three themes (1) The mass need for lifelong education
produced by the scientific-technological revolution and socialist democratism, (2) The concept and characteristics of
lifelong education, (3) The influence of lifelong education on
the instructional-educative process. The ideas communicated
during this six-hour introduction served as the basis for all
subsequent themes elaborated during courses on educational
theory.

Building up of a basic stock of information about lifelong
education was achieved in Singapore by the introduction of what
amounted to a core course as a one-semester elective occupying
two hours a week of teaching time. The course concentrated on
the following ten topics: (1) Aspects of life leading to educational change, (2) The concept of lifelong education, (3)
The new role of education in the light of lifelong education,
(4) Implications of lifelong education for curricula, (5) Implications for educational management, (6) Implications for
evaluation, (7) Implications for guidance, (8) Implications for
educational technology, (9) Implications for the teacher's
roles, (10) How can we personally contribute to lifelong education?

The change in curricular content at Trier involved a one-semester course with four hours of activities per week. In actual practice, however, it was run as a "block" course consisting of ten days of more or less full time work, held in the normal vacation period. Relevant texts were distributed for reading about four weeks in advance. The first half of this programme contained the theoretical material related to the concept of lifelong education. However, there was a pronounced difference between the content of this course and that of core courses in the other participating colleges. At Trier, no mention was specifically made of the idea of lifelong education. Rather, an attempt was made to develop understanding of the concept of *interaction* as the key theme. The emphasis was mainly on developing attitudes and values thought likely to lead to teaching behaviours facilitative of lifelong education, through fostering student teachers' awareness of themselves as interactors and helping them learn to modify their interactions with other people.

For the present purposes the key ideas of this course may be summarized as follows (see pp. 16-19 of the Trier report):

- The task of socializing institutions such as schools is to prepare the young for the requirements of society.

- As it is impossible to foresee these requirements, this preparation consists mainly in the fostering of *dispositions* (especially attitudes) which will ultimately enable pupils to cope with the changes of society.

- Pupils' personalities and identities develop in interaction situations. In our society children's interactions with teachers are a decisive influence. For this reason, special emphasis must be placed on teachers relationships with their pupils.

- Consequently, it is crucial that teachers can preserve their own identities under conditions suitable to develop their pupils' identities.

- This means that one of the most important things teachers must learn is to regard their knowledge of people, society and themselves

as changeable and in need of change, and
to contribute to such change by their own
efforts. This applies in particular to
their knowledge of school and teaching as
well as to the knowledge they should transmit.

On the basis of this rationale, the purpose of the course was
to make students aware of the principles of lifelong education
as they apply to their everyday social interactions, to connect
this knowledge with action, for example in the classroom, and
to encourage the use of theory as a tool for reflecting upon
practice.

Theoretical foundations of education

The second aspect of the lifelong education curriculum involved courses in the theoretical foundations of lifelong education as seen in such disciplines as psychology, sociology, philosophy, economics, and so on. The aim of this aspect of the
curriculum was not to provide information about the origins,
nature and implications of lifelong education, but to examine
whether or not it has a sound basis in the disciplines, such as
those just mentioned, out of which educational theory largely
arises.

A change in curriculum content of this extent, one step
further than simply introduction of a core course, was not attempted at all of the participating colleges. At Torrens,
Singapore and Trier, for example, no direct and conscious
changes were made in foundations courses. It is true that the
core courses included discussions to a greater or lesser extent
of the foundations of lifelong education (see the outline of
the core course for Torrens College on page 95 for an example).
However, special courses were not introduced, nor were existing
foundations courses systematically modified with the deliberate
intent of bringing out their implications for lifelong education.

By contrast, at Szeged, Gandhi Shikshan Bhavan and H. J.
College systematic attempts were made to teach foundations of
education from the standpoint of lifelong education. In all
three cases, this did not involve the introduction of new
courses, but re-orientation of existing ones so that they became infused with ideas arising from the concept of lifelong
education. A major reason why modification of the teaching of
foundations of education had to be done in this way, regardless

of whether it is or is not the best, was the existence of external requirements, such as a programme structure imposed by an external body or a body not entirely within the decision-making framework of the co-operating institutions. For example, both H.J. College and Gandhi Shikshan Bhavan were required to prepare their students for the final examinations of the Bombay University. This meant that the content of courses in Educational Psychology, Educational Sociology, Educational Philosophy, and so on was largely determined by forces outside the colleges. What happened at these two colleges was that the existing content was taught from a new viewpoint, that of lifelong education.

At Szeged, core information about lifelong education presented in six hours of class contact between students and instructors served as the jumping off point for infusing teaching of the historical and theoretical foundations of education with the principles of lifelong education. In particular, study of the foundations of education involved treatment of the topics listed in Table 11.

General and special methods of education

The third kind of course identified for the purpose of analyzing changes in the content of curriculum involved both general and special methods of education. Changes in these areas were most specifically and systematically carried out at the two Indian Colleges and in Szeged. Once again, both H.J. College and Gandhi Shikshan Bhavan were restricted by the necessity to follow the curriculum requirements of Bombay University, and again the approach adopted involved infusing the contents of the university-specified curriculum with ideas emanating from the concept of lifelong education. The way in which this was achieved is demonstrated by the example from the H.J. College report given in Table 12 (see pp. 88 and 90 of the original report). As this table is intended merely to give some illustrative examples, it contains only a portion of the material to be found in the original report.

A similar attempt was made to infuse instruction in the methods of teaching with the principles of lifelong education. This was attempted in all methods teaching, of course, but it may be illustrated here using the example of the special methods curriculum for the teaching of mathematics. Material from

Table 11

Topics Discussed at Szeged in the
Foundations of Education

1. Historical background leading to a wide, overall social process of education.

2. The role of the family in the system of educational constituents.

3. The educational role of youth organizations, cooperation of school with youth organizations.

4. The educational role of factories and other productive plants, the connections between school and the process of industrial as well as agricultural production.

5. The educational role of political, social and state institutions, links between school and the above establishments and organizations.

6. The educational role and responsibility of means of communication, how school relates to mass communication.

7. The place of public educational institutions and research institutes in the system of education, the relationship between school and these establishments.

8. The role of sport and tourist clubs in education of young people.

9. The rights and duties of creative youth; the Hungarian Youth Law.

10. Students' self-government in school, the meaning of self-governing activity, its organizational forms, methods of influencing the students' self-governing institutions by adults, the development of qualities which improve the students' participation in the self-governing process.

11. Training students for becoming involved in public life and in the political, economic and cultural life of their village or city, the possibilities for accomplishment of pursuits of public interest.

Table 12

Contents of the General Methods
Curriculum at H. J. College

List of Topics (Bombay University Curriculum)	Changes Made for the Diffusion of the Concept of Lifelong Ed- ucation

Section I: Methods of Instruction

1. Organization of curriculum	1. Need of a curriculum to prepare the child for lifelong learning
(a) Meaning of curriculum. (b) Objectives of the school curriculum.	(a) Learning through life. (b) Objectives of school cur- riculum to make them learn- ers throughout life.
(c) Planning of units. Objectives of various courses and their specifications.	(c) Developing a desirable at- titude towards lifelong learning.
2. Fundamental basis of teaching and learning.	2. Education is a continuous process. True learning is interactive and co-operative. Teaching-learning
(a) General principles of in- struction and their ap- plication to the teach- ing and learning process.	is formal and informal. Under- standing of the psychological principles of maxims enables the teacher to adopt dynamic strate- gies of learning.
(b) Maxims and principles of teaching.	
3. Types of lesson.	3. Emphasis on the development of the skills of:
(a) Types of lessons aimed at acquisition of knowledge and skills - development of critical thinking - problem solving - ap- preciation - review - drill - radio lesson.	(a) conducting a knowledge lesson. (b) conducting a skill lesson. (c) helping students to think critically. (d) practising effectively. (e) getting the most out of a radio or TV lesson.

Section II: Evaluation

1. Theory of evaluation

(a) Basic concept of evaluation.	(a) concept of self-evaluation; group evaluation and project evaluation - need and importance from lifelong education point of view.
(b) Source and criteria of instructional objectives.	(b) skills of self and group evaluation.
(c) Relation between instructional objectives, teaching-learning procedures and evaluation.	(c) relation of instructional objectives to life.
(d) Objectives and their specifications.	(d) relation between lifelong learning and evaluation throughout life.
(e) Learning experiences in various school subjects.	(e) importance of life-like situations and learning through life situations.

the mathematics curriculum is shown in Table 13 which follows.

At Szeged, the methods class lasted for one whole semester, occupying two hours of lectures per week. Emphasis was placed upon individual study with the help of a set text. All of the themes in the class were taught from the point of view of lifelong education, to the extent that this was possible. As the Szeged report put it (Part C, p. 7):

> The modernization of the content of didactics training according to the principles of lifelong education is a continuous process determined by objective and subjective conditions. In numerous areas the conditions have already been complied with, so that it is possible to effect modifications in the didactics curriculum in order to contribute to the realization of lifelong education.

At Trier, the second half of the course involved in the present project can be conceptualized as a course in general methods of education. The aim of this course was to foster in student teachers awareness of themselves as being engaged in a continuous process of interaction, and to help them to learn to do something about it. The teacher is a permanently developing system of feelings, attitudes, opinions and so on engaged in a process of interaction with pupils who are themselves similar

Table 13

Contents of the Special Methods
Curriculum at H. J. College

MATHEMATICS

List of Topics (Bombay University Curriculum)	Changes Made for the Diffusion of the Concept of Lifelong Education

---

1. Value of teaching mathematics. Utilitarian, disciplinarian, cultural and vocational.	1. Emphasis on cultural value with respect to development schemes, industrial work, etc. Adaptation to the changing situation in life.
2. Nature, Scope and History of Mathematics.	2. Emphasis on changing concepts of Mathematics and its utility in daily life and development of scientific knowledge.
i) Meaning of Mathematics according to the various schools of thought.	
ii) Structure of Mathematics.	
iii) Contribution of the following Mathematicians to the Sciences of Mathematics:-	
A. i) Arya Bhatt	Great Mathematicians as lifelong learners.
ii) Bhaskaracharya	
iii) Ramanujam	
B. i) Euclid	
ii) Pythagoras	
iii) Gauss	
3. Objectives of teaching Mathematics	3. (a) Emphasis on the development of personality traits - precision, etc., and attitude.
i) General objectives	
ii) Classroom objectives	(b) Development of skills, reasoning and application for life.

systems. Awareness of this is a key factor encouraging teaching practices facilitative of the goals of lifelong education, such as joint planning with pupils, or self evaluation. Particular application of the interaction model to teaching was fostered through the use of simulated classroom situations, and especially through microteaching.

TEACHING AND LEARNING PROCESSES

Curricular changes in keeping with the concept of lifelong education do not involve merely changes in the content of theory courses. Realization of the goals of lifelong education in teachers college curricula also involves values, attitudes, habits and skills of a lifelong learning-facilitating kind. As a result, modification of curriculum in the light of lifelong education requires, in addition to changes in the content of theory courses, changes in the teaching and learning processes through which that content is mastered. The present section is concerned with enunciating some of the major changes in this area which were introduced in the various institutions participating in the project.

Activity

The general goal of lifelong education-oriented teaching and learning processes was summarized by the Szeged report as being that of "activity" (Part D, p. 1). The effect of activity is "extending the sphere of independent work" (Part D, p. 3), with the ultimate goal of:

> improving and developing skills and abilities
> to follow accelerating progress, as well as
> to absorb ever renewing knowledge and to
> realize the increasing demands of independent
> teaching work (Part D, p. 1)

This student activity took a variety of forms in the various colleges, some of them common to several colleges, some limited to one or two of them. However, all of the activities discussed in following sections were regarded by participants in the project as having been effective and successful.

Self-learning

Great emphasis was placed in all of the colleges on increasing the ability of students to learn by themselves. Many kinds of activities such as research projects, term papers, seminar reports and similar measures were adopted as learning tools. In particular, efforts were made to equip students with the skills needed to work effectively on their own, not only by using libraries and similar conventional resources, but also by observing the society in which they lived, asking questions of persons possessing special skills and knowledge, and so on. At Torrens, this kind of learning was referred to as "investigation based learning".

Self-directed learning

Even where learning required some degree of input and organization by other people, teaching and learning processes in the participating colleges continually emphasized giving control of the learning process to students themselves, so that it was self-directed. Other-directed learning such as the guided learning that results from a lecture programme selected and planned by a college instructor was not ignored, of course. However, even where some learning experiences were substantially controlled by instructors, efforts were made to interpose episodes of self-directed learning among the other-directed experiences. Devices that were frequently employed included student-selected research projects, papers on topics of interest to students, seminars, joint planning of course content with instructors, and similar activities.

Inter-learning

One major feature of teaching and learning processes was the emphasis placed upon learning from each other, referred to here as "inter-learning". At Szeged, for example, great emphasis was placed on group learning projects, as was the case at Torrens and to some extent at all the colleges. They all conducted workshops in which students reported to each other and discussed their work, a practice which was supplemented, for instance at both the Indian colleges and Torrens College, by peer evaluation, or in other words participatory evaluation. At H. J. College, this was particularly emphasized in practice teaching. Commonly, oral reports were given to peer groups, in which students reported on the results of their self-learning and self-directed learning tasks. At Gandhi Shikshan Bhavan, for example, there was an assembly of the whole college every day, at which a student gave an oral report about some topic that had been studied individually.

Learning to improve

It is clear that a number of different forms of learning and evaluation were fostered in the colleges participating in the project. These included both self-directed and other-directed learning, as well as self-learning and peer-learning. Similarly, evaluation involved not only traditional forms in which instructors assigned grades, but self-evaluation and peer-evaluation, as well as evaluation as a continuous process fostering improvement, rather than as a judgement of final success or failure. In a sense, then, a further form of learning was made use of: a form that may be called "learning to improve".

Non-classroom-oriented learning

Although they deviated from traditional classroom instruction in, for example, their emphasis on self-directed learning, the teaching and learning processes outlined to this point have still been classroom-centered. However, a wide range of activities was introduced in the various colleges that involved the community itself as the place of learning. Among these activities were visits to community sites in which non-school learning would be expected to occur, such as an adult education centre, the headquarters of a union, and a radio station where educational programmes were made. In the case of Torrens College, the visits were incorporated into the formal teaching structure. In Singapore a system of visits was also part of the learning and teaching processes. Visits here included a school for spastic children, a kindergarten, a home for the aged and a community centre.

An additional use of non-school sources was made at Torrens in the form of an "important growth events" period at the commencement of lectures in the elective course. Here students were encouraged to talk about the learning experiences that could be gleaned from everyday life such as through reading a book containing important growth facilitating ideas, seeing a film or TV programme, or hearing a programme on the radio, or even important lifelong learning-facilitating personal encounters with other people. This procedure stressed that learning is a process that goes on in the course of everyday life itself, and helped to make it possible for students consciously to recognize major learning experiences in their lives as well as to identify some of the sources of such experiences. This learning from life itself was also stressed at both Gandhi Shikshan Bhavan and H. J. College. In these institutions, students participated regularly and systematically in "work experience" such as gardening, bookbinding, needlework, and so on. The aim here was that they should not only learn by doing, but that they should participate in the everyday manual work that is the lot of most people in India.

Learning from life itself also involves participating in life. This was heavily stressed in the teaching and learning processes at Gandhi Shikshan Bhavan. For example, the college had an assembly every day. At these assemblies, not only did students deliver papers to their peers, thus facilitating learning from each other, but many members of the outside community gave talks to the assembled college. These included talks on professional topics such as "Learning theories", as well as personal discussions emphasizing key experiences in the lives of students and staff ("My memorable experiences "). Learning about the social life of India was also seen as an important non-classroom learning process, and many of the addresses were on topics in this area such as "Present malaise in India", or "What is happening in Bihar?". In addition, the culture of the country was regarded as an important source of learning experiences, and many of the addresses were in this area (e.g., "India's literary personalities", or "Tagore as a poet"). Finally, feast days and historically important days from the traditions of many of the racial groups comprising the Indian population were celebrated such as Ramzan Idd, Christmas, or Sankrant, while important national events such as Independence Day were commemorated.

The theme of learning by participating in community life was continued in both Indian colleges in a number of other ways. One of these involved "social work" with disadvantaged members of the society. Both H. J. College and Gandhi Shikshan Bhavan formed close associations with a slum area, and all students spent a certain amount of time in formally recognized, organized contact with the slum dwellers. Not only did they learn about life for people in these circumstances, but they acted as out-of-school teachers too, fostering non-school learning in areas like personal health care, nutrition, basic

life skills and so on. They also undertook tutoring with
backward children, again becoming part of the network of non-
school educative experiences of which life is composed. This
theme of non-school teaching and learning was also seen in
other colleges in various ways. At Szeged, for instance, great
emphasis was placed on working with young people in informal
teaching and learning relationships. This was achieved through
participation in youth groups during term time, and through involvement in youth camps during the summer.

Evaluation

A major theme in the evaluation processes introduced in the
participating institutions was, on the one hand, that of shifting the locus of evaluation away from authority figures onto
students themselves and their peers, and, on the other, shifting
the purpose of evaluation from judgments of adequacy or in-
adequacy to a planning function. In this latter function, attempts were also made to introduce continuous evaluation. At
Torrens, for example, students' project reports were graded on
the basis of evaluation by the presenting groups themselves
(self-evaluation), by the peer group to whom the reports were
presented (peer-evaluation), and also by the instructors. According to the report, this did not produce any marked distor-
tion of final assessments, as grades from all three sources
tended to be similar. However, the experience of self-evaluation would be expected to provide a valuable learning experience for the student teachers.

A major example of self-evaluation practised for the purpose of taking stock and subsequently making plans for the
future took the form at Torrens College of a "personal growth
plan" developed by each student. In these plans they reviewed
the course of their lives to date and tried to develop growth
plans for the future, thus including life itself in the formative self-evaluation. The personal growth plan prepared by
one student is shown in Figure 1.

Use of media

A number of the colleges made substantial use of various
educational media, and especially videotape. In Singapore for
example, the core course was followed by a videotaped discussion of lifelong education in which the participating students were encouraged to express their opinions and criticisms

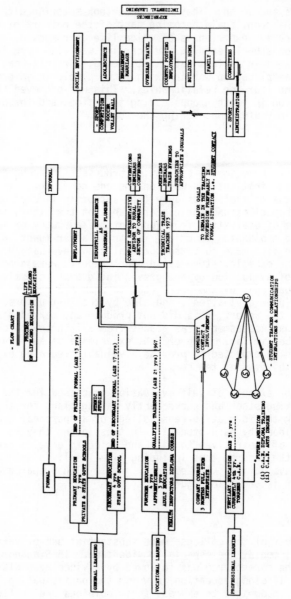

FIGURE 1: AN EXAMPLE OF A STUDENT'S PERSONAL GROWTH PLAN

both of the concept and of the course. At Trier, videotape was used in the second half of the course when attention turned to the basic elements of classroom teaching. An interesting use of videotape was achieved at Torrens College where students interviewed both formal and informal educators such as teachers and parents, and also children. Here, use of media made it possible for many people to share a learning experience. Educational media were also used at Torrens for the presentation of class reports. Students were encouraged to use other forms of communication than formal language, and several variants did in fact emerge. Not only did students use videotape, sound tape and transparencies, but in one case even cartoons were employed in order to achieve communication by an alternative means to the spoken and written word.

SUMMARY

One of the areas in which changes were introduced in the colleges participating in the project was in the curriculum of theoretical courses. In all of the institutions what may be called a "core" course was introduced. This involved, in most cases, an introduction to the ideas of lifelong education and its implications for teaching. Some of the colleges made more extensive changes including adaptation of existing courses on the theoretical foundations of education and, in some cases, modification of courses on the general and special methods of education.

In addition to changes in the content of courses, curricular changes affected the ways in which teaching within the colleges was done; there were in fact changes in teaching and learning processes. Not all changes were made in all colleges, of course. Similarly, the specific forms taken by various changes differed from college to college. However, a general set of changes could be discerned involving a number of different kinds of activity and of different areas of the teaching and learning process. In particular, there were changes in learning processes involving emphasis on self-learning, self-directed learning and inter-learning, and an attempt to link classroom learning with events and processes outside the classroom or even outside the college. There were also changes in the forms and uses made of evaluation, with a movement towards adoption of continuous, formative evaluation, self-evaluation and group-evaluation. Finally, there was emphasis on use of media, library resources, teaching and learning aids, and similar resources.

This resulted from recognition of the importance of familiarity with sources of information outside the traditional classroom and of the need for teachers to have well-developed communication skills.

CHAPTER 6

CHANGES IN PRACTICE TEACHING

BROADENED CONCEPT OF PRACTICE TEACHING

New settings

One important aspect of lifelong education is the close relationship it implies between activities taking place in schools and the events of everyday life. As a result, teachers would need, among other things, skill in linking schooling and life. This implies that practical activities in teacher training institutions aimed at providing experience of teaching ought to be more closely linked with day-to-day life. Practice teaching should thus involve opportunities for student teachers to participate in not only the formal, school-based learning of pupils, but also in their learning activities in non-formal and even informal settings. As a result, there would be a broadening of the kinds of activity constituting practice teaching, so that they would come to include contact with pupils both in and out of schools, for example through tutoring exceptional children, leading youth groups, working in clubs and societies, and similar activities.

Different age groups

Lifelong education also stresses that educative learning goes on at all ages, so that practice teaching could be further broadened to include experiences with learners beyond conventional school age, for example through contacts with parents, working with underprivileged social groups, participation in the activities of community centres, involvement in cultural, social or political activities and so on. Thus it is possible to conceive of practice teaching as going on not only in schools, but in other places as well, and as concerned not only with school age learners, but with other ones too. Such a broadened concept of practice teaching was, in fact, adopted in several of the colleges participating in the present project, as will be seen from the material which follows.

Special methods and procedures

The broadening of practice teaching discussed in the previous two paragraphs could be called "structural". However, lifelong education implies broadening of a second kind, in the sense that there would also be an extension and modification of methods, techniques, practices and procedures of instruction. Thus, the extended concept of practice teaching is also concerned with the processes which would receive special emphasis in teaching with a lifelong education orientation. The discussion of practice teaching from the point of view of lifelong education in the balance of the present chapter centres on three themes; the locations and settings in which it occurs, the age groups involved, and the special methods, approaches and techniques employed.

TYPES OF CHANGE

As a result of the broadening of the idea of what constitutes practice teaching, the kinds of activity students in the various colleges engaged in during their practice teaching experiences varied considerably. They included conventional contacts with pupils in a classroom setting, of course, since the classroom role of the teacher will continue to be important. However, they also included activities going on inside schools but outside classrooms, activities taking place outside schools altogether, and even activities which did not involve school-age children. This wide variety of practice teaching experiences is described in following sections. The main emphasis is given to procedures in which the broader conception of practice teaching is apparent, although this is not meant to imply that more conventional experiences in the classroom are unimportant, and they will not be ignored.

Teaching practice with school age learners

The traditional age group to be involved in practice teaching is that of pupils of school age, and much of the practice teaching in the project was done with this group. Even in this case, however, emphasis was on not only formal learning process- es of the more traditional kind, but informal learning too. For this reason, a wide variety of activities, both in and out of the classroom, were regarded as providing legitimate oppor- tunities for practice teaching experiences. Even where within- the-classroom activities were involved, an attempt was made to develop skill in practices regarded as of particular importance in a lifelong education orientation. Furthermore, since the concept of lifelong education stresses that teachers themselves are part of a dynamic learning process, teaching practice stres- sed not merely things like exercise of control, or specification of learning outcomes, but also the ability of teachers to share planning, learn themselves, energize self-directed learning in students, and on on.

This broad concept of teaching practice with school-age learners was emphasized in the curriculum plan for teaching practice developed at H. J. College. A section of the college's plan is contained in Table 14 which follows.

In teaching practice with school age learners, a number of special aspects of teaching activities oriented towards lifelong education were seen in the various colleges. Some of these cen- tered on schools, some did not. Practices and emphases of rele- vance to the present report are discussed below.

Individualized teaching and learning. Broadly speaking, teaching practice has two components: observing other people (often experienced teachers) in the act of teaching on the one hand, and carrying out actual teaching behaviours, on the other. In both of these activities, participating colleges placed great emphasis upon the fostering by teachers of independent pupil work or, as it was called in the Szeged report "individual ac- tivity". For example, students at Szeged were given sets of teacher behaviours to watch for when observing lessons, which included items like:

1. Was the need for independent and differ- entiated student work reflected in the or- ganization, set up and conduct of the lesson?

2. Which forms of activity and what combination of them were applied in the course of the lesson (e.g., individual ...)?

Table 14

Goals of Teaching Practice

Specifications

---

1. The student teacher acquires skills of communication

    i) Listening
    ii) Speaking
    iii) Reading
    iv) Writing

2. The student teacher acquires skill in self-learning

3. The student teacher acquires skills of:

    (a) Co-Learner
    (b) Co-ordinator
    (c) Animator and guide in his classroom and in the school.

4. The student teacher acquires skill in the practical art of teaching and evaluating.

5. The student teacher acquires skills related to the planning of teaching-learning and testing processes.

6. The student teacher acquires skills in promoting participatory learning.

7. The student teacher develops co-operative studies.

Recognition of the importance of individualized teaching and learning is also evident in the teaching practice goals listed in Table 15 (see p. 188 of the Gandhi Shikshan Bhavan report).

In evaluation of student teachers at H. J. College, (this was both evaluation by instructors and also by students themselves), behaviours observed and evaluated when the students took the role of teachers included the extent to which they undertook individual diagnostic measures and followed them up with remedial measures, the question of whether or not they encouraged development of self-study methods in their pupils, and similar issues. At Trier too, where practice teaching was confined to simulation, the theory of teaching developed as the

Table 15

Goals of Practice Teaching

Objective: Promotion of self-directed learning

Employing learning strategies that will encourage the following
abilities among pupils:

(a) raise questions and answer questions raised by other pupils
    in cogent language.

(b) express thoughts in precise writing.

(c) analyze situations and tasks.

(d) synthesize different points.

(e) use reading material for their own benefit.

(f) preparing their own notes on the bases of their study of an area.

(g) constructing or drawing up a plan or sketch of a project or theme.

---

theoretical basis for practical teaching emphasized joint planning with pupils, awareness among pupils of their role in the
interactions with the teacher, mutually intelligible activities
in the classroom, and so on.

Classroom methods. At the level of classroom management,
alternatives were sought to traditional "frontal teaching" which
is teacher-centered, involves almost exclusively other-directed
learning processes, and gives few opportunities for, for example, the kind of learning in which one student teaches another.
In instruction at Szeged this was attempted through the use of
various combinations of other-directed and self-directed learning, along with opportunities to learn from teachers, to learn
on one's own and to learn from peers. Various kinds of activities were alternated with each other, in order to attain a combination of different kinds of classroom learning processes.
For example, three basic patterns of instruction were used consisting of lectures based on independent work, lectures with in-
serted individual assignments and finally, lectures having independent activities in their final sections.

At H. J. College, not only were student teachers asked to

judge themselves on the extent to which they had achieved classroom roles such as guide, friend, co-learner and animator, but
they were encouraged consciously to seek to introduce into their
classroom methods combinations of lectures, discussions, problem-solving alone and in groups, and project work. Similarly,
classroom methods emphasized at Gandhi Shikshan Bhavan included
self-study and group-study methods. Trainees were expected to
try inspiring school pupils to use different learning sources
such as the library or a knowledgeable person, and, at the same
time, to help them participate in group presentations, ask questions of others, assist pupils who were backward in their work,
and engage in similar group learning activities. Thus teaching
and learning processes at the classroom level emphasized combinations of guided learning, in which teachers have a more central role, group learning, in which the teacher is of less prominence, small group learning and collaboration with other students, and finally self-directed learning.

   Out-of-the-classroom activities. A major departure from
traditional teaching practice was the emphasis several of the
colleges placed on activities which, while still going on in
schools and involving school-age learners, lay outside the con-
fines of the classroom. One way in which this was achieved was
by having student teachers work as tutors for backward pupils or
for especially gifted pupils, a practice which was seen in
various forms at Szeged, H. J. College and Gandhi Shikshan
Bhavan. Student teachers in these colleges also participated
as part of their practice teaching activities in a number of
school-centered but out-of-the-classroom activities (co-curricular activities) such as leading study circles, going on excursions and field trips, or helping to organize cultural activities such as drama or folk dancing groups. At Singapore,
students participated in a number of co-curricular activities
which can be discussed within the context of practice teaching.
The purpose of this co-curricular training was to enhance the
students' ability to participate in the extra-curricular activities of the schools in which they would eventually teach.
These included art, music, librarianship, dietetics, guidance
and counselling, and textbook writing. Closely related to them
were so-called "personal growth" activities which were considered to foster the development of "fulfilled" individuals.
These included sports, folk dancing, handicrafts and music.

Out-of-school activities. Not only was the concept of teaching practice extended in the ways just described, but it also included activities outside schools altogether, although still involving educative agencies of society. For example, at Szeged students carried out some of their practice teaching in vocational training centres and halls of residence in which children lived while attending school. The students were also able to work with groups of young people through a national youth organization known as the Pioneers, and through Communist Youth Groups. In addition to these activities, they had the opportunity of assisting in the supervision of summer camps for school-age children, thus experiencing a further kind of contact with pupils in out-of-school settings. At H. J. College and Gandhi Shikshan Bhavan students also participated in out-of-school work with children. This involved working in slum areas "adopted" by the colleges, tutoring backward children, giving basic hygiene instruction, and carrying out similar activities. Many students reported that they found a period of teaching practice spent in such settings extremely rewarding, and that it gave them a more comprehensive understanding of the process of education and of children's participation in it.

Practical experience with learners beyond school age

Practical teaching usually involves contact with children of school age. As has been shown, a wider range of such activities was included in the present project. Teaching practice was also broadened in a second way. A number of activities not directly involving children of school age were recognized as valuable experiences for student teachers in the context of lifelong education. Some of these are discussed below.

Co-operation with parents. One such group of people beyond conventional school age was parents. As part of the elective class at Torrens, for example, students interviewed parents. These interviews were recorded on videotape and played back to the rest of the class. Interviews were also conducted with pupils and teachers and shared in a similar manner. At Gandhi Shikshan Bhavan and H. J. College the students "adopted" slum areas and worked with parents (as well as children). They gave advice, information and practical help on matters such as health care, nutrition and similar factors.

Co-operation with other educational agencies. Another way in which experience with non-school agencies was obtained was through cooperation with other community institutions of an educative kind. For example, a wide-ranging cooperation was established at Singapore between the Institute of Education and a large number of other community educational agencies, although the activities were not integrated into the practice teaching programme. These activities were authorized by the Institute's formal statement of purpose which requires it to serve as a centre for the dissemination of new ideas. In practice, this has resulted in courses in teaching methods for instructors in a dental nurse training school, the Ministry of Defence, the Industrial Training Board, the Adult Education Board, and a number of others.

Participating in community learning. As has already been mentioned, students in the lifelong education-oriented programmes at Torrens and Singapore were involved to varying degrees with learning agencies in the community, such as schools for spastic and blind children, a home for the aged, a creche, and a community centre, among others. Students at Singapore prepared project reports on the Outward Bound School, community centres, and the Adult Education Board, among others. Projects were also planned on the aquarium, the zoo, the museum, the botanical gardens and similar agencies. At Torrens, emphasis on foci of learning in the community included a programme of visits to an educational radio station, a union headquarters, and so on.

Participation in the everyday learning of the community was also strongly developed at H. J. College and Gandhi Shikshan Bhavan, where students were required to spend some time each week working in manual occupations, which are the lot of a high proportion of the people of India. Work experiences included needlework, bookbinding, gardening, and similar activities. In this way, the students gained actual practical experience of the kinds of tasks involved in the life of their society.

FOSTERING EDUCABILITY

Learning is a natural and normal process that occurs with or without schooling, and both in and out of school. Within the context of lifelong education, a major task for teachers is to cultivate skills and attitudes in pupils so that they can carry on worthwhile, socially valid learning experiences through-

out life, and especially so that they can both learn from and
also apply learning to experiences that occur out of school.
In other words, the function of school is to foster what may be
called *educability*. Highly educable people have well-developed
learning skills such as reading, observing, listening, and so
on, and have well-developed intellectual skills such as reasoning, critical thinking and interpreting. They are skilled in
different learning modes such as learning under the guidance of
a teacher, learning without a teacher, and learning in small
groups, and are able to use a wide variety of learning media
and aids. They can learn in many different settings and are
skilled at learning with and through other people, being able
for example, to take the role of learner or teacher, according
to the demands of a particular situation. Finally, they are
skilled in identifying their own learning needs and in planning,
conducting and evaluating their own study.

The highly educable are able to assess their own needs for
change, can work out for themselves how to make the necessary
changes, and possess the skills to carry out the change plans
they have formulated. Thus, the growth of educability involves
learning to learn in a variety of ways and forms, learning to
learn by sharing with others, learning to evaluate, and learning
to improve. As far as practice teaching is concerned, this implies that student teachers will need practical experience in
identifying learning resources and developing learning materials
from resources outside the formal school system, in fostering
self-learning and a wide variety of learning modes both in their
pupils and in themselves, and in building not only their own
skills of self-assessment, but also those of the pupils they
teach.

Educability is not, however, merely a matter of cognitive
skills of the kind just discussed. It also involves emotional,
motivational and attitudinal aspects. For example, people will
be highly educable only when, in addition to capacity for learning in many settings, mastery of many different learning modes,
and all the cognitive skills which have just been discussed,
they see themselves as the kind of persons for whom it is natural
and normal to learn, when they are excited and stimulated by the
opportunity to learn or even by the existence of pressure to
learn, and when they feel a personal commitment to learn, including a willingness to expend the necessary effort. These
non-cognitive aspects of educability, which have previously
been referred to as the personal "pre-requisites" for learning
(p. 11), should not be overlooked when considering the role of

teachers in fostering educability and hence the kind of things student teachers should emphasize in their practice teaching.

Self-directed learning

For each individual person, learning is a personal and idiosyncratic process, despite the fact that common basic principles may exist. For example, individual people have differing opportunities for learning and are exposed to different patterns of learning experiences. Different people have different needs for learning and different motivation to learn. When individual people recognize that they themselves need to take responsibility for the management of their own learning in order to accomplish their own patterns of social and vocational development, they are recognizing the importance of self-directed learning. Self-directed learning requires that learners be capable of recognizing their own learning needs, identifying the resources available for carrying out learning tasks, and skilled in the techniques for carrying out the learning that has been found to be needed. A lifelong education-oriented system of teaching practice would be expected to give student teachers opportunities to develop skill in fostering such abilities in pupils.

Use of learning resources

One necessary skill for teachers within the context of lifelong education is the capacity to make use of a broad range of learning resources in order to foster both in themselves and in their pupils, the ability to learn without the supervision of teachers or the structures of formal schooling. In the present project many practical activities involving the use of non-teachers and non-school resources were engaged in by students at the participating institutions.

Media and teaching aids. All of the colleges placed heavy emphasis on the use of educational media to supplement conventional teaching, including filmstrips, transparencies, slides, audio and videotape and similar devices. Similarly, there was unanimous emphasis on the use of teaching aids. At Singapore, for example, students were encouraged to make use of (a) display boards (e.g., chalk, felt, flannel, magnetic), (b) non-projected materials (e.g., pictures, charts, photos, etc.), (c) projected materials (e.g., slides, filmstrips, etc.), (d) overhead pro-

jector and transparencies, (e) television, and (f) audio aids
such as audiotape. However, rather than relying exclusively on
expensive and scarce technologies, emphasis was also placed on
the construction of teaching aids from everyday materials available in ordinary life. Such utilization of commonplace materials
found in the day-to-day environments of ordinary people for the
construction of learning materials was particularly emphasized
in H.J. College and Gandhi Shikshan Bhavan. At Singapore,
students had access to art media and wood, metal, electrical
and electronic equipment to assist them in the development of
teaching materials.

Individualized learning resources. A second point of emphasis was the importance of highly individualized learning resources. For example, at Szeged emphasis was placed on the use
of programmed instructional materials and teaching machines.
In other institutions, students were expected to help their
pupils to acquire familiarity with resources such as text books
and other library materials, so that they could carry out independent research on a particular topic, pursue a theme of personal interest, or seek to remedy a defect in their knowledge or
understanding.

Resources in the community. Learning resources to be found
in the community or in life itself were also emphasized. At
Torrens interviews were conducted with parents and community
centres of learning were visited, as was also done at Singapore.
At Gandhi Shikshan Bhavan persons from the community with special knowledge or skills became resource persons and delivered
addresses to the students. Newspapers and magazines were utilized as sources of learning materials at Singapore, where clippings concerned with real-life lifelong learning experiences
were collected and distributed. That life itself is a rich
source of learning was emphasized at Torrens where students
were asked to note each week significant growth experiences
they had experienced during the week, including things like
seeing a film, or meeting someone, or reading a newspaper ar-
ticle. In a similar vein, at Gandhi Shikshan Bhavan students
wrote reports on "My memorable experiences" in which they outlined significant learning experiences that had occurred in
their own lives. Again at Gandhi Shikshan Bhavan, the everyday
life of India was used as a source of learning resources through
the celebration of important feast days for the various religious groups that make up Indian society, through discussions of

significant social problems in Indian society, and through
learning about important people and events in the history of
the nation.

Varied learning modes

Learning can be conceptualized as involving two forms, the
one occurring when people learn on their own (individual learning), the other when they learn with and through other people
(group learning). Within these two forms, two further kinds of
learning can be observed, self-directed learning and other-directed learning. Thus, people may learn on their own, and without direction or guidance from other people (self-learning).
This kind of learning occurs, for example, when a person identifies the need to learn something and then carries out the
necessary learning, for example through the use of text books
or programmed instruction. On the other hand, if the learning
need and the methods for satisfying it were identified by someone else, such as a teacher, this would be guided individual
learning. These two kinds of individual learning can be contrasted with the corresponding modes when learning goes on in groups
(group learning). For example, guided group learning occurs
when a teacher leads a discussion group or seminar. A form of
group learning which may be called inter-learning takes place
when learners learn from each other, rather than from a teacher
or from text books, programmed material or other devices.

In the case of classroom practices oriented in terms of
lifelong education, all of these learning modes are important.
Learners need to be able to work alone or in groups. They need
to be able to learn with and without guidance, and to be able
to identify their own learning needs as well as to profit from
the guidance of other people. Thus, teaching practice from the
viewpoint of lifelong education should involve experience in
fostering many learning modes.

Individual learning. All of the basic learning modes including learning alone and in groups, as well as learning without guidance, were emphasized in the colleges involved in the
study. Use of the library as a major vehicle for self-learning
was universally emphasized, with recognition of the importance
for pupils, if they are to engage in self-learning, of resources
like dictionaries, atlases, and encyclopaedias. Textbooks too
are a major source for guided individual learning. The use of

projects, the conduct of research on selected topics and similar activities were common in the colleges. If self-directed
learning using these kinds of tools is to occur, it is important
that goals be apparent to learners. This was emphasized at
Trier where great emphasis was placed on the importance of
having classroom goals that are apparent not only to the teacher
but to pupils as well. For self-directed learning to occur,
what is needed is that the goals of a lesson be transparent for
pupil as well as teacher.

Group learning. Group learning was also strongly emphasized in the participating colleges. At H.J. College, for example, much use was made of tutorials, seminars and group discussions. This was also true of the other colleges. At Gandhi
Shikshan Bhavan students evaluated themselves on the extent to
which they had successfully introduced into their practice
teaching discussions, activity lessons, dramatizations and similar activities, as well as pupil participation in lesson planning at the group discussion level. Another form of group learning during practice teaching consisted of "post mortems" of
lessons taught by experienced teachers. The practice of
conducting such group reviews was systematically developed at
Szeged and Singapore.

Inter-learning. Inter-learning involves sharing of knowledge among learners - learning from other learners. Sharing
knowledge was emphasized at Gandhi Shikshan Bhavan and H.J.
College with, for example, older pupils acting as teachers for
younger, or more advanced pupils sharing their skill with those
who had made less headway. At Singapore one form of inter-
learning occurred when videotapes were made of micro-teaching
lessons, then played back for discussion and analysis by other
students. At H.J. College and Gandhi Shikshan Bhavan students
presented papers and addresses to other students. At Torrens,
not only were project reports prepared and presented to other
students, but these reports were prepared by *groups* of students,
with emphasis placed upon teamwork and cooperation.

Developing evaluation skills

A fundamental notion in educability is that of evaluation.
Pupils would be expected to be able to assess their own learning needs in order to plan their learning activities. They

would also need to be skilled in sharing evaluative information with others in a process of mutual evaluation. The aim of evaluation from the lifelong education perspective is to foster skill among people in identifying their own and other people's learning needs so that they may become competent in planning and carrying out their own programmes of learning and personal development, and in helping others. This means that evaluation, in a lifelong learning-oriented system, would cease to be a matter of judgment of learners by external authorities with the goal of determining whether some prestated criteria of excellence have been reached, and would become instead a co-operative activity in which individual learners diagnosed and evaluated their own learning needs in pursuing self-improvement and personal development. This orientation suggests a number of special kinds of evaluation that were seen in the various colleges involved in the project.

Self-evaluation. One major concept in evaluation from the lifelong education perspective is that of self-evaluation. At Torrens, for example, students evaluated their own assignments as part of the process of assigning grades. They also participated in a form of self-evaluation with the construction of self-growth plans, in which they were required to assess the growth of their lives to date and to plan for the future. At both H. J. College and Gandhi Shikshan Bhavan great emphasis was placed on self-evaluation by students. During practice teaching the need for students to foster self-evaluation by pupils was also emphasized in these two colleges.

Cooperative evaluation. Frequently, evaluation was a joint venture in which several agencies worked together. For example, at Torrens students worked with other students and their instructors to arrive at a final consensus in the assigning of grades. At Singapore, peer evaluation was employed in evaluating microteaching. At Szeged part of the evaluative process was group interviews between instructors and students in order to discuss experiences during practice teaching. At Trier emphasis was placed upon the need for evaluative activities to be joint actions of teachers and pupils. Students evaluated each other at Gandhi Shikshan Bhavan and H. J. College. In all of these cases, evaluation was seen as a joint activity engaged in by students, by their peers and by instructors, acting in co-operation and pooling their particular competencies and knowledge in each situation.

Self- vs. external evaluation. An important idea underlying both self-evaluation and cooperative or group evaluation,
as contrasted with the older model of evaluation as something
done to a learner by an external authority, is that of self-
evaluation versus external evaluation. Both evaluation by
learners themselves and also cooperative evaluation imply an
active role for learners in the evaluation process. The locus
of evaluation moves from external authorities to learners themselves. This does not imply that there is no place for other
people in the evaluative process, as the emphasis on cooperative
and group evaluation makes clear. However, it does imply, on the
one hand, that the purpose of evaluation will be to serve the
needs of the person being evaluated, not those of the evaluator,
and on the other that learners themselves will take responsibility for evaluating themselves.

Diagnostic evaluation. A major purpose of evaluation from
the lifelong education viewpoint is its role in providing information about the present status and needs for future development of each learner. Evaluation is thus seen as a diagnostic
process which analyzes special needs and helps in the formulation of plans for the future. To this end, students at Singapore had access to teaching aids which included standardized
test materials to be used for diagnostic and counselling of
pupils. At Torrens, the joint evaluation of projects by students, their peers and instructors was carried out with a
strongly diagnostic purpose. This included assessing the adequacy of use of resources such as library and media, the degree of teamwork developed, and the potential of the work to
energize future inquiry in others. At Gandhi Shikshan Bhavan
evaluation was a continuous process, with staff making structured observations throughout the semester and providing feedback through faculty advisers. At H. J. College every activity of the students was monitored and, in some cases, they were
provided with feedback. In each case evaluation functioned as
a diagnostic tool in an ongoing process.

Formative vs. summative evaluation. A major thrust of
the emphases indicated in preceeding sections is that evaluation
ceases to be a terminal activity occurring at the end of some
learning process and useful primarily for indicating the extent to which pre-stated goals of some kind have been reached,
such as whether or not a certain proportion of the pupils in a

class can carry out a particular arithmetic operation correctly. This kind of evaluation (summative evaluation) is replaced by evaluation for the purpose of guiding the continuous development of ongoing learning processes (formative evaluation). Evaluation becomes a feedback in a dynamic, self-regulatory process, in which learners check their present status against information provided by their own analysis of the situation, that of their peers, and that of authority figures, in order to form plans for future learning. It was the formative aspects of evaluation which were given emphasis in all of the colleges participating in the present project.

Evaluation of the learning environment. Evaluation is typically thought of as concentrating on the learner, even if it be of the formative rather than the summative kind. However, it is also possible to evaluate the environment within which learning has occurred, and to make statements about how that environment could be designed to facilitate future learning. This kind of evaluation can be referred to as "conditions evaluation" or "C-Evaluation" as against "learner evaluation" or "L-Evaluation" (see Skager, 1978). A form of C-Evaluation was given prominence in several of the colleges. At Singapore, for example, the lifelong education core class was evaluated by the students participating in it (the structure, content and other details of a class constitute part of the learning environment). Similarly, at Szeged, students evaluated their own practice teaching experiences, both through group interviews and also through formal questionnaires. At both H. J. College and Gandhi Shikshan Bhavan, pupils also evaluated the students who had been their teachers. Thus, learners themselves evaluated the learning environments to which they had been exposed.

SUMMARY

Emphasis in lifelong education is on linking school learning with life, encouraging systematic learning at all ages, and developing the prerequisites for learning, both in the cognitive and non-cognitive senses. This orientation means that the purposes and forms of practice teaching can be conceived more broadly than has traditionally been the case.

In the present project practice teaching included not only conventional classroom activities, but also activities taking

place in schools but outside the classroom, activities with
school-age learners but outside schools altogether, and activities not only outside schools but with learners beyond traditional school age. Examples of such extension within a school
setting were tutoring backward or gifted pupils, or leading
study or cultural groups. Activities outside schools altogether included working in youth organizations, social groups,
political or recreational clubs, and so on. Finally, practice
teaching encompassed work with parents, citizen groups, and
disadvantaged social groups.

Lifelong education also requires the fostering of special
skills, values and attitudes in pupils. Consequently, emphasis
was placed in all of the colleges on giving student teachers
practical opportunities to practice teaching methods, techniques
and procedures which would encourage pupils to learn through
many modes, employ many different study techniques, direct and
evaluate their own learning, and acquire confidence and motivation for further learning.

CHAPTER 7

CHANGES IN THE INSTITUTIONS THEMSELVES

NEED FOR INSTITUTIONAL CHANGES

Teacher training institutions which genuinely accepted the principles of lifelong education would not only teach about it, but would themselves become models of teaching and learning in a lifelong education setting. Students would then learn not only from the content of formal instruction, but from the colleges' "way of life" as well. For this reason, instructional and organizational changes in the institutions participating in the present project are a matter of some interest. Understanding of these changes helps in gaining an insight into how lifelong education may be implemented.

INSTRUCTIONAL CHANGES

One area in which colleges succeeded in making a number of substantial changes was that of instructional procedures. Some of the changes have already been discussed in Chapter 5 in the context of teaching and learning processes. This earlier discussion will be recapitulated and further developed in the present context.

Changes in teaching and learning strategies

Instructors oriented towards the concept of lifelong education would modify their teaching and learning strategies, for example placing emphasis on individual work by students, encouraging learning from other students, sponsoring research projects, and so on. Some of the ways in which such changes were made are outlined below.

Alternative forms of teaching. Several of the colleges
made serious efforts to develop alternatives to traditional
teaching methods. At Szeged alternative activities such as
project reports were integrated into the more traditional
lecture structure, for example by basing lectures on independent
study, by inserting individual assignments into the structure
of lectures, or by concluding lectures with independent activities. Some ingenious alternative organizational forms for
correlating formal lectures and other kinds of activities were
developed at Torrens: these will be discussed in more detail
in a later section (see p. 137). At Gandhi Shikshan Bhavan and
H. J. College, as well as the other colleges, great emphasis
was placed on teaching through seminars, tutorials and workshops. In addition, vigorous discussion among students was encouraged as a medium of instruction. These forms of instruction
were preferred to traditional lecture methods and to approaches
centering on the instructor as a dominant authority figure.

Practical work. One kind of learning experience stressed
in the colleges was student research projects requiring the investigation of some topic of interest. These included studies
of community educative agencies, studies of the society itself,
studies of schools and schooling, and similar projects. Their
aim was to develop in the students an inquiring attitude to
their profession, and a willingness to ask questions and pursue
answers. They made use of what was referred to at Torrens as
"investigation based" learning. A second kind of practical activity embraced surveys of schools, including interviews with
principals and teachers (Gandhi Shikshan Bhavan and Singapore),
visits to families of low socio-economic status (Gandhi Shikshan
Bhavan and H. J. College), interviews with parents (Torrens),
and similar activities.

Independent learning. All the colleges stressed independent learning as especially important. At Trier and Szeged, for
example, lectures were coordinated to independent reading assignments. At Torrens and Singapore self-directed learning and the
use of learning resources such as libraries were emphasized,
while at H. J. College and Gandhi Shikshan Bhavan the college
instructors made conscious and systematic efforts to foster in
the students independent study and use of a wide variety of
learning resources.

Group learning. Despite the importance attached to independent learning, the ability to learn in groups and to learn from other people was also stressed. All of the colleges involved students in group discussions, group planning, group problem solving and similar activities. In such settings students had the opportunity of learning to state a point of view, of listening to what others thought, of sharing decision-making activities and so on. They also had the chance of learning from others and, at the same time, of acting as learning resources for others.

Alternative forms of communication. Among the teaching and learning processes employed in the participating colleges was the use of methods of communication other than formal written assignments. At Szeged, for example, students gave verbal reports to their classes, at Gandhi Shikshan Bhavan they made verbal presentations to assemblies of the staff and students, and at both Indian colleges they became involved in activities like writing reports in the form of newspaper articles suitable for inclusion in student publications. At Torrens in particular, an attempt was made to foster use of modes of communication which did not involve words at all, especially valuable, although not confined to students whose verbal skills were not well developed. It was done through, for example, presentation of project reports with the aid of videotape, audiotape, film, coloured slides and even cartoons.

Use of microteaching. One teacher-training technique employed at several of the colleges was microteaching (e.g., H. J. College, Trier, Singapore). This technique is one of the most widely used new approaches to teacher training. Conventionally it is used to develop high levels of proficiency in specific skills such as effective use of questions, prompting, clarification of difficulties, avoidance of repetition of pupils' answers, reduction of frequency of one-word responses from pupils, and so on. However, in the present context, an attempt was made to use microteaching for purposes more consistent with the role of the teacher as it is conceptualized in lifelong education. At Trier, for example, it was used to demonstrate the extent to which the goal of interaction between student teacher and pupil had been achieved, and at H. J. College to develop students' skills in fostering self-directed learning and similar lifelong education goals.

Use of media. Alternative means of presenting instructional content were also used in some colleges. At Singapore, for example, instructors had access to transparencies and films, audio and videotapes, art media, carpentry resources, and so on. At Trier videotape was extensively used, for example for analysis of simulated lessons. At Torrens media such as film were frequently employed during formal classroom presentations, as an alternative way of presenting information. In general, media were used wherever possible in all the institutions.

Changes in the role of instructors

Lifelong education implies a new role for the teacher, as has already been pointed out. Instructors in teacher-training institutions are themselves teachers and students are in the position of pupils, allowing for age differences and similar factors. Thus, the implications of lifelong education for the teacher's role apply also to instructors' relationships with students. The guidelines taught become guidelines for teaching. As a result, the function of the college instructors in relation to their students would change.

"Energizers". In all of the colleges, there was a reduction in the amount of formal lecturing, and attempts were made to develop other kinds of instructor-student interactions. At Szeged, independent work was encouraged during lectures in a variety of ways. For example the instructors tried to foster independent activity by introducing problems into their lectures so that students could solve them by individual or group work. At Trier, the structure of classroom activities was developed as a joint project of instructors and students. One of the tasks of the instructors was to make the goals of the class transparent to students, so that it became a joint seeking of commonly agreed-upon goals, not a task imposed by external authority. Free expression of opinions and asking of questions were emphasized at Singapore, Torrens, Gandhi Shikshan Bhavan and H.J. College. The instructors tried to function as introducers of problems, generators of discussion, and guides for the solving of problems. The instructors' role was to energize learning in a variety of forms.

Resource persons. The participating colleges placed a good deal of emphasis on the conduct of independent work by

students. However, the instructors' role was not confined to
judging the end results. In addition to their teaching loads,
they acted as consultants and resource persons to students engaged in research projects. They helped in planning and assembling information, gave advice on practical and theoretical
matters, helped with administrative questions, and so on. In
this way, instructors and students became almost collaborators
in students' independent work.

Co-learners. In the course of working on activities such
as research projects, for example at Singapore, instructors
not uncommonly found themselves on unfamiliar ground, where students had learned more in the course of their research than instructors knew. In this setting, the instructors became co-
learners with the students, developing their own knowledge of
a topic as a result of their collaboration with the students.
Sometimes, in order to be able to make a worthwhile contribution to the project, it was necessary for the instructors to
undertake new learning, either independently or with the help
of colleagues more expert in the particular area involved, or
even with the help of the student collaborators. Instructors
thus became learners, and students became teachers. At Gandhi
Shikshan Bhavan some instructors deliberately sought the role
of co-learner, by undertaking to teach in areas that lay outside their expertise or by swapping teaching assignments with
other instructors, so that it was necessary for them to seek
out new learning in order to be able to fulfil their duties.
At Torrens and H. J. College, too, student-oriented group presentations, research reports and joint participation in learning activities emphasized the role of the instructors as co-
learners.

Members of a community. Informal intercommunications between instructors and students were commonly emphasized in the
colleges. At Torrens, each staff member was assigned responsibility for acting as adviser to a group of students. At Singapore, too, associations between instructors and students in
out-of-the-lecture-theatre activities such as sport were encouraged, to the point where it sometimes became difficult in
certain settings to tell who was an instructor and who a student. This development of a common community was most clearly
seen at H. J. College and Gandhi Shikshan Bhavan, where the
entire staffs participated in the project. Instructors acted
as faculty advisors, providing students with guidance and as-

sistance beyond merely classroom instruction. Free and informal relationships between instructors and students were encouraged. They shared in daily prayers, celebrated national festivals together, and took part together in recreational activities such as the staging of plays, holding of picnics, and participation in sports. At Gandhi Shikshan Bhavan students and instructors shared many of the day-to-day duties of the college such as cleaning the premises, washing dishes and rearranging furniture. In this way, the joint role of instructors and students as equal participants was stressed.

Changes in evaluation procedures

In an institution in which the lifelong education principle has taken firm hold, special forms and purposes of evaluation exist. For example, evaluation serves formative ends, providing information about current status and helping to determine what the next step should be, rather than deciding that a person had passed or failed. Diagnostic evaluation helps to select the path or branch to be followed from the present point for best progress in the future. Responsibility for making evaluative judgments largely rests with the individual involved (self-evaluation), while peers serve as a source of evaluative information. Individuals, peers and authorities join in making cooperative evaluative statements. In fact, a number of changes along these lines were achieved in the colleges participating in the project.

Self-evaluation. At Torrens, students assigned a grade to their own project reports. This process of self-evaluation was at first greeted with some suspicion by students, but eventually was judged to have been successful. Another kind of self-assessment was seen when students were expected to make judgments about their own suitability for the teaching profession on the basis of their teaching practice experiences. Emphasis was on encouraging students to evaluate their own knowledge, skills and techniques. Self-evaluation was also the heart of the assessment procedures at Gandhi Shikshan Bhavan and H. J. College, where students carried out numerous self-assessments using questionnaires specifically prepared for that purpose. In addition, in these colleges self-evaluation was extended to instructors, who were asked to assess themselves on the extent to which they had engaged in lifelong education practices in their own lives and had introduced them into their teaching.

Group evaluation. Evaluation of individuals by groups of
peers, and evaluation of groups by themselves was also practised in the participating institutions. At Torrens, for example, self-assessments were supplemented by group assessments.
At H.J. College and Gandhi Shikshan Bhavan not only did students evaluate each other and instructors, but some student
groups, such as the Student Council, had special responsibility
for providing evaluative information to their peers. At Torrens,
peer evaluation was regarded as sufficiently important for the
recommendation to be made that a peer group advisory system be
established in order to provide peer-based evaluation.

Continuous evaluation and feedback. In order to make the
purposes of evaluation more clearly diagnostic and formative, a
system of continuous evaluation accompanied by feedback of results is required. In all of the colleges, evaluation was organized in such a way that evaluative information was available
during the semester and not merely at the end, although this
was achieved in several different ways. At Torrens, Szeged and
Singapore student activities were spaced throughout the semester
and evaluative feedback was given at frequent intervals, so that
students could assess their strengths and weaknesses and make
plans to improve. At H.J. College, too, evaluative experiences
occurred frequently. Possibly the most thorough implementation
of continuous evaluation was carried out at Gandhi Shikshan
Bhavan. Grasp of the theory of lifelong education was evaluated
by self-ratings and instructor-ratings and feedback provided
throughout the year by faculty advisors. Practice teaching activities were evaluated by supervisors in the schools, by pupils
and by students themselves, again with feedback and guidance.
Participation in celebrations and activities was evaluated by
instructors and students themselves, and feedback provided
through the Students' Council, and finally, participation in
social work in a slum area and work experience were evaluated
by both students and instructors, and feedback provided through
persons in charge of these activities.

Evaluation of instructors. In keeping with the expectation that instructors would themselves become involved in a
process of lifelong learning, and that the learning environment
would itself be evaluated, students were not the only people to
be evaluated. At several of the colleges instructors too were
evaluated either by their students, by other instructors, by
themselves, or by all of these. At Singapore, for example,

students evaluated their classes from the point of view of content, method, use of aids, assignments, classroom climate, and so on. At H. J. College and Gandhi Shikshan Bhavan instructors experienced group evaluation, in the form of evaluation by both their students and their peers (other instructors). An extension of evaluation of instructors was also seen when pupils in the schools at which practice teaching had been carried out evaluated the students who had temporarily become teachers. At Szeged this process was reversed, with student teachers evaluating their teaching practice experiences. Thus, it is apparent that evaluation was greatly extended from being merely evaluation of students by instructors.

ORGANIZATIONAL CHANGES

In developing institutions functioning in ways consistent with the principles of lifelong education, numbers of changes were made that can be referred to as organizational in nature. They included changes in programming and scheduling, changes in relationships with outside-the-college bodies, and other kinds. Some of the more striking changes attempted at the various colleges are outlined in the following sections.

Planning and scheduling

In order to permit a variety of learning modes in the classroom, to foster self- and group-evaluation, to stress the relationship of learning and life, and similar goals, some deviation from traditional organization of contacts between instructors and students was necessary. As has already been pointed out, this included greater emphasis on seminars, tutorials and workshops, presentation of research reports by students, introduction of non-professional people into lecture theatres, and similar activities. It also involved changes in the scheduling of classes, variation from the conventional organization of hour-long meetings at the same time on set days, and so on.

Allocation of class time. One ingenious organizational expedient through which utilization of varied forms and modes of learning could be achieved was seen at Torrens. Both courses introduced there departed considerably from conventional organization of classroom time, in order to foster varied learn-

ing processes. The course for further education students (depicted in Figure 2) was a one-year course extending over 28
weeks of lecture periods broken down into four blocks of seven
weeks each, each block involving a particular theme for study,
as can be seen in the first row of the figure. In each week of
lectures, the class met for three hours of instruction. These
three hours were jointed together into a single three-hour period of time. Within each of the four seven-week blocks, a similar pattern was followed. The first three weeks were devoted
to one hour of lectures and two hours of seminars in which
lifelong education concepts were presented and discussed. The
fourth week involved lectures on research methods, including
how to find information for oneself (self-learning), the fifth
and sixth weeks were free of lectures and were spent in self-
learning and group-learning), and the seventh week was a plenary
session in which all students met together and reported to each
other what they had learned in the previous two weeks (i.e.,
group-learning). The presentation of these reports was, in
each case, the responsibility of a group of students.

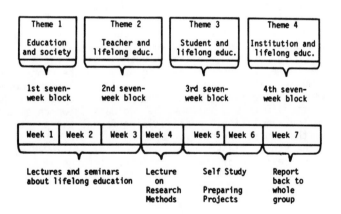

Figure 2: Schematic outline of teaching organization
for further education students at Torrens.

In the case of the one-semester elective course, a special organization was developed for the three hours of class time (see Figure 3). The class met for one three-hour period each week. This period was divided into three components. The first was a period of about half an hour spent discussing "important growth events" that had occurred in the previous week. The second consisted of about 90 minutes in which formal reports on research reports were presented. The final hour consisted of group work spent preparing research projects for which the class was divided into groups.

Duration	about 30 minutes	about 90 minutes	about 60 minutes
Content	Important Growth Events	Formal Instruction	Group Research Project

Figure 3: Schematic breakdown of a three-hour
class session at Torrens.

At Trier, the course was run as a block course of 10 days duration, instructors and students meeting for several hours a day, every day. To permit this, the course was re-scheduled for the between-term period. About four weeks in advance texts were distributed for reading, so that students would have the opportunity for some guided self-learning prior to the commencement of the course. The course started with discussion and more profound study of the texts, continuing for four days. This period of theoretical work was followed by two days in which students prepared the simulation exercises which formed the practical phase of the course. Finally, for the last four days, simulation of the school classroom was carried out, followed by discussion and revision of the simulations. Throughout this period, emphasis was on discussion and joint planning by instructors and students.

Planning of courses. At H. J. College a novel procedure was adopted with the development of "Think Tank" meetings of the college's instructors. Initially, available literature on the topic of lifelong education was distributed among the members of the college staff in order to familiarize instructors with the basic ideas underlying the concept. Subsequently,

Think Tank meetings were held every week so that members of the
college faculty could thrash out details of the concept itself
and its significance for the institution's participation in
the project. The purpose of the meetings was to orient instructors concerning the concept of lifelong education, to discuss the implementation of the project at H. J. College, to
plan the details of the project and such aspects as the research
tools that needed to be constructed, and to discuss any problems
or misconceptions that might have arisen. Eventually, a large
number of committees were formed to carry out special planning
and report back to the Think Tank. They included among others,
one committee to prepare a research design, one to plan sub-
stitutes for traditional teaching methods (such as seminars,
workshops, discussion groups, and so on), one to develop and
foster library work, and 17 special committees to study the implementation of the concept of lifelong education in the teaching of specific subject areas. This Think Tank was the agency
through which the concept of lifelong education was diffused
throughout the teaching and learning processes of the whole
college.

At Szeged, the project was put into effect by means of a
series of meetings of the instructors which had some similarities to the Think Tank procedures adopted at H. J. College.
Members of the Institute of Pedagogy, lecturers on didactics,
and principals of the schools in which students were to do
practice teaching met to review the project. Staff members
then carried out reviews of the literature on lifelong education. This was done initially by independent study, followed
by three meetings for joint discussion of problems and issues
in the area. As a result, the content of the pedagogy lectures was modified, as was that of the didactics programme.
In addition, compulsory observation of real-life classrooms
was organized, along with opportunities for educational exercises in non-classroom settings such as halls of residence.
The method employed required individual work in the intial
stages. Those responsible for the development of new programmes then submitted their proposals to the members of the
Pedagogical Institute for collective discussion and improvement. Thus, planning at Szeged was both an individual and a
group activity.

Assemblies. At Gandhi Shikshan Bhavan, an interesting
innovation was the introduction of a daily assembly, at which

a variety of different learning experiences took place. For example, members of the public who were not professional educators but who had extensive knowledge of some important topic gave talks to the instructors and students, who learned together from the visitors' real-life experiences. Visiting professional educators also gave talks to the members of the college at these assemblies. Even more important, students themselves made presentations at the assemblies. For some of them this was the first time that they had ever made a public appearance of this kind. The topics of student presentations were mainly based on important current events, social problems and issues in India, festivals or celebrations in the life of the masses of the Indian population, or articles from local newspapers. Thus, the assemblies were an important tool for linking life and learning.

Age range of students. A major belief in the area of lifelong education is that education should not be restricted to certain groups chosen because of age, since it is seen as a process that goes on at all age levels. Consequently, a teacher-training institution committed to adoption of lifelong education as a guiding principle would make its programme available to people of all ages, rather than restricting them to those of immediate post-secondary or post-first-degree age level. At Singapore, several measures consistent with this view have been adopted as part of the college's institutional structure. For example, a number of students have been admitted who are of mature age and have served several years in other professions. This was also true of the further education students at Torrens, all of whom were already qualified in a trade, craft or technological field. As a result of this, plus the fact that the college conducts a large number of in-service courses where students are often people well advanced in their field (these will be discussed in more detail in a later section -- see page 148), it is quite common at Singapore to see students of ages beyond those during which initial education is normally obtained, including some who can count members of the instructional staff among their own former pupils! In addition, the age range at Singapore has been extended downwards. For example, students who are participating in remedial reading programmes and therapeutic play groups are about ten years old. Finally, the idea of opening a kindergarten and creche has been discussed at the college, so that in the future persons from about five to fifty-five may possibly be seen participating in the various programmes of the college.

Guidance and individualization of courses

One organizational feature that was seen in various forms in the participating colleges was that of providing individualized programmes for students. This took the form of provision in some colleges of a course structure which made it possible for students to select classes partly according to their own individual needs and interest (e.g., Torrens, Singapore), or of provision of systems of individual feedback (diagnostic evaluation) during the term (e.g., Gandhi Shikshan Bhavan, H. J. College, Trier, Szeged). Organizational measures along this line were also seen at Torrens. In addition to machinery permitting selection of elective classes in order to develop a course suited to a particular student's interests and abilities, it was recommended that instructors be assigned to serve as advisors to groups of students. A second measure was the establishment of a system of peer advisers through whom students could receive feedback from other students rather than from instructors. This expedient of peer guidance was also seen at Gandhi Shikshan Bhavan, in the form of feedback through the Students Council. Other recommendations at Torrens included establishment of a counselling unit and a health service, and appointment of a welfare officer.

At Singapore, a number of courses especially intended to increase "self actualization" were included in the programme. Students could choose from courses like swimming, folk dancing, music or creative writing in order to foster their own "personal growth". A second option which the organizational structure at Singapore permitted students was whether they took their examinations at the end of the second or of the third semester, and in which semester various components of the programme could be studied. Individual counselling was provided to those students who had difficulty in making such choices.

Feedback was provided by a number of channels at Gandhi Shikshan Bhavan. In the area of knowledge of the theory of lifelong education, faculty advisors provided feedback in a programme of continuous evaluation. Similar information concerning students' participation in celebrations and activities was provided through the Students' Council. The persons in charge of social work and work experiences provided feedback to individual students concerning their work in these areas, while counselling was also provided in connection with practice teaching. Thus the evaluative structure of the college was organized in such a way as to provide continuous, diagnostic evaluation to students, in keeping with the concepts of lifelong education.

An aspect of the traditional classroom that was stressed at Trier is that the organization and purpose of the activities going on in the classroom are usually not apparent to students, but are simply determined and imposed by teachers. According to the concept of interaction upon which the Trier procedure was based, one important goal of lifelong education-oriented teaching would be to make the structure and purpose of classroom activities transparent to pupils. This principle was adhered to in the aspects of instruction at Trier with which the present project was concerned. Thus, an attempt was made to develop improvement plans as a result of reflection upon earlier activities.

Students at Szeged spent one teaching day observing school classrooms in action, twice a semester. These observations were structured in a manner aimed at helping the students to make the connection between the content of their lectures in the college and the realities of real-life teaching. This was achieved by providing students with duplicated statements concerning the subjects and aspects of study for the lesson about to be observed. These included, among other things, information on the importance of the material to be taught within the discipline concerned, the aims of the lesson, its structure, and the didactic methods to be employed. This information was provided by the teachers actually teaching the lessons, who were informed well in advance. Students then spent one hour being briefed about the lesson, one hour attending a class, and a third hour meeting in a group to analyze what they had seen. The analyses were structured by specifying in advance what aspects of teaching behaviour were to be discussed. Subsequently, a second lesson was observed and analyzed in the same way. This structure was to promote active individual participation as well as group learning during the after-lesson discussions, while giving students the opportunity of systematically observing the real-life teaching situation.

An important organizational aspect of the programme at H. J. College was the provision of a series of orientation sessions aimed at fostering self-learning in students. They included a lecture on the use of library resources, with particular emphasis on finding information and tracking down sources, and an introduction to tutorial and essay work, as well as an introduction to group discussions, seminars and workshops. This latter introduction included provision of copies of a "question bank", which had been prepared in the Think Tank, to guide self-learning both by individuals and by groups. Finally, students were given instruction in a self-learning technique entitled "SQ3R" (Surveying, Questioning, Reading, Recalling, Reviewing), to help them organize their own self-learning processes. Thus students entered the lifelong education oriented programme already armed with information and skills calculated to help them carry on a process of self-learning, rather than being left, as it were to sink or swim.

Linking college learning to real life

An important notion in lifelong education is that learning is a natural and normal part of life itself, not something that is confined to institutional settings and to a particular period of time in life. Consequently one of the organizational changes seen in the participating colleges was attempts to integrate learning activities within the colleges to the real life of the society of which they were part. This linkage emerged clearly at Gandhi Shikshan Bhavan in a number of ways. For example, a large number of people from the community came to the college and took part as speakers in the daily assemblies. They were either formally-qualified experts such as visiting professors or professional educators, or else people with expertise developed as a result of their life and work, such as, say, farmers who can be considered experts on the raising of crops, even though they may have had no formal, school-centered training. In their case life itself has been the school in which knowledge has been gained.

Close links with the real life of the Indian society were also emphasized by formal celebration of the special days of various religious groups or of national festivals such as Independence Day, Republic Day, Gandhi's Birthday, and by the preparation by students of papers on various aspects of the life of the community. In each case, the goal was to foster learning about and through life itself, and to co-ordinate this learning with the formal learning carried on in classroom settings.

The link between the life of the society and the formal learning of the college was also stressed at both H. J. College and Gandhi Shikshan Bhavan by the addition to the curriculum of work experience as an integral part of the programme. Students spent about 50 hours a year on a regular weekly basis in developing practical manual work skills such as carpentry, bookbinding, gardening and needlework. Participation in these activities was systematically organized and was subjected to the same process of diagnostic evaluation and feedback as were other activities in the colleges.

A further linking of college activities with real life was achieved at Gandhi Shikshan Bhavan and H. J. College through the programmes of social work with residents of slum areas in the community surrounding the colleges. Students visited the slums and carried out surveys of the inhabitants. They attempted to identify their special problems and to help solve them through developing basic hygiene, habits of rudimentary health care, elementary knowledge of nutrition, and through provision of remedial teaching to the deprived children of the slum communities. Again, as with the work experience, these activities were formally organized and integrated into the programme of teacher training on the basis of regular participation on an organized basis.

An interesting attempt to relate learning experiences within the college to life itself was made at Torrens. In the elective course, the first half hour or so of each weekly meeting was devoted to verbal presentations by students in which they related any "significant growth events" that had occurred in their own out-of-the-college lives in the week since the last meeting. These experiences might be seeing a movie or reading a book, being involved in an incident of some kind, meeting someone, or any similar event which proved, even though without deliberate design, to have value as an educative experience for the person reporting it. In this way, the importance of informal, "incidental" learning experiences in real life, and their application to the formal experiences of the college, were emphasized.

An important educational agency in the community is the mass media. This was recognized formally at Singapore and Gandhi Shikshan Bhavan, and learning from newspapers was incorporated into the colleges' teaching and learning processes. At Singapore a collection was put together of newspaper clippings which dealt with learning beyond school age and in non-school settings. These clippings formed a kind of real-life textbook demonstrating the reality of lifelong learning in the lives of members of the public. Clippings included extracts from local newspapers and from international papers, and contained stories

such as "How a blind grandpa got his law degree", "A graduate
at 80", "It's never too late to learn", "White hair college"
and "Back to school with their children". At Gandhi Shikshan
Bhavan, a programme of reading of daily papers was organized.
Students selected various topics of educational or social importance and presented summaries of newspaper or journal articles about them. In this setting, instructors and other students became co-learners and the students making the presentation became teachers.

At Szeged an important out-of-school activity was involvement in the work of youth groups. One of the chief aims of
students' practical activities at the college was to learn about
educational possibilities in after-school hours. As many students as possible were directed into various youth activities
such as Communist Youth Units, hobby groups and troops of Pioneers. As a result, about one quarter of the student body at
Szeged was able to take part in youth activities each year. Experience in the college suggests that a period of half a year
spent in youth work under the auspices of the college is sufficient to establish an interest in such activities among many
students, who then make further contributions on their own in-
itiative. The kinds of activities in which the students participated included giving political lectures, working on various
committees, taking part in the planning of work, and becoming
familiar with the organizational activities of the youth groups.
Often students organized excursions and trips, supervised club
events, formed debating and similar groups, and prepared pupils
for competitions and contests.

RELATIONSHIPS WITH OTHER INSTITUTIONS

One of the basic principles of lifelong education is the
stress placed upon the importance of community educative agencies other than schools. It is argued that such agencies should
be identified and given appropriate recognition as important
centres of learning. School and non-school agencies should be
linked together through a common educational role, and school
learning should prepare students to learn in non-school as well
as school settings. From the standpoint of lifelong education,
this union of school and other community institutions of an educative kind is referred to as "horizontal integration" of
learning experiences. As a consequence of emphasis on horizontal integration, including both institutions engaged in formal
education and those not engaged in it, one major institutional

change in the participating colleges concerned their relationships with other community agencies in which learning could
occur. These included schools, school-linked institutions and
non-school resources.

Relationships with schools

     The first group of community agencies with which teachers'
colleges have horizontal ties are schools. As has already been
pointed out, achieving changes in the classroom teaching behaviour of students when they eventually become teachers in the
official sense, cannot be effected without changes in schools
themselves. This is because the influence of colleagues, superiors and administrators probably plays a much more important
role in the behaviour of beginning teachers than the admonitions
of their former college lecturers, especially as the college experiences become more remote in time. For this reason, the
working practices of schools and, in particular the attitudes
and values of supervisors and such people as inspectors, would
play a key role in determining whether lifelong education-oriented attitudes in beginning teachers survived the transition
from the college to the school setting. As a consequence, a
highly desirable step in teachers colleges would be that of establishing a new kind of relationship with schools themselves.

     This approach was seen very clearly at Szeged. During the
planning stage directors of the schools in which practice teaching was to be done participated in the planning meetings.
Sharing of planning was extended to the actual teachers whose
lessons were to be observed by students during the periods spent
in schools. The teachers were briefed concerning the kind of
things the students were being alerted to watch for, and themselves prepared analyses of the lessons to be observed, emphasizing the goals and methods of the planned lessons. The
students strengthened ties with the schools by participating in
their non-classroom activities, acting as supervisors of youth
groups and participating in clubs and hobby groups, as well as
providing remedial teaching for backward children and special
coaching for children of high ability.

     Schools were also heavily involved in the planning stages
at Gandhi Shikshan Bhavan. During the development of the project, the headmasters of the 20 co-operating schools took part
in meetings with the college staff. One of the steps achieved
was development of procedures for fostering individual learning

among pupils, a plan worked out by the headmasters in conjunction with instructors. At H. J. College, too, a series of meetings with headmasters of co-operating schools was held. In the course of three or four meetings with them, instructors discussed what the schools were expected to do as part of the project, what time and effort they would be expected to expend, and what benefits might accrue to the schools as a result. One aspect of the project, once it was under way, was dissemination of the concepts of lifelong education among teachers in the schools. At H. J. College, instructors sought to communicate the key ideas by means of informal discussions with teachers, through formal talks, through a poster campaign, and in other ways.

The necessity for a close relationship between colleges and schools was also emphasized in an interesting way at Singapore and Torrens. At both these institutions it was accepted, at least in principle, that college instructors ought to spend a period of each year actually engaging in classroom teaching at the school level, so that they would not experience an "Ivory Tower" effect becoming remote from the day-to-day experiences of teachers actually engaged in schoolteaching. This goal was pursued by attempting to develop effective mechanisms for the release of college staff for periods of teaching in schools, or even by requiring such periods. Both these colleges also stressed the importance of instructors and students carrying out programmes of active inquiry and research on the practical problems of schools. Examples of such projects at Singapore included research on the effects of enrichment activities in the attainment of science concepts, English language proficiency among Chinese secondary school students, and difficulties arising from the learning of mathematics in the second language. The role of the colleges in conducting research into questions of interest to the schools was also stressed at Gandhi Shikshan Bhavan and H. J. College.

An additional way in which contact with schools was fostered was through the provision of in-service training to practising schoolteachers. Such courses were mounted at Gandhi Shikshan Bhavan and Singapore, for example. At Torrens, the course for further education students, developed as part of the present project, was in effect an in-service course, since all of the students already possessed trade or technical qualifications, and were already engaged in teaching in schools. They came to the college for only part of each week to gain formal teaching qualifications while actually "on the job", as it were. These students thus provide a particularly interesting example of the link between the participating colleges and the schools through the medium of in-service training. They are an interesting group for a second reason. When they entered the college they had already obtained other qualifications and had spent varying periods engaged in working at a trade before deciding to enter teaching and acquire new professional and intellectual skills. As a result, they may be regarded as practical examples of people engaged in lifelong education, carrying out a formal study of the process in which they are actually engaged.

Relationships with institutions other than schools

In addition to schools, society has a number of other institutions and organizations of an education-related kind. These too would be expected to be involved in the horizontal integration of educational facilities which is part of lifelong education. Some of these bodies are special kinds of school, some have primarily educational functions or are closely linked to schools although not actually schools themselves, while others are not typically regarded as educational agencies at all. In the present project, links were established with all kinds.

Education-related agencies. One step in this direction was taken at Singapore, where widespread contacts were established with bodies such as the Ministry of Education, teachers' unions, and the Adult Education Board. These contacts included dissemination of lifelong education concepts, for example through translation of documents about lifelong education from English to both Chinese and Malay and subsequent publication in a journal published by the college itself and in other sources, such as the newsletter of a teachers' union. The college's intention was to disseminate information as widely as possible among other education-related institutions. Students in the lifelong education elective at Singapore also engaged in fieldwork in educational agencies in the community, such as the school for spastic children, the American School, the school for the blind, a creche and kindergarten, and similar institutions. Projects were also planned on the YMCA, the extra-mural studies programme of the university, libraries, and other such bodies.

In a similar way, links with education-oriented agencies in the community were established at some of the other colleges.

At Torrens, for example, the university radio station, an educational TV studio, and a community centre were visited. At
Szeged students worked in halls of residence in which some
pupils lived, and also participated in cultural, scientific and
recreational clubs and organizations. At both Indian colleges
students took part in excursions and educational visits to appropriate institutions in the community. Thus, it is apparent
that the development of horizontal connections with educative
elements of the societies in which the colleges were situated
was one of the lifelong education oriented activities that was
implemented.

   "Non-Educational" institutions. In addition to schools
and closely education-related agencies, societies have many institutions, groups and organizations which, while not "official-
ly" or formally engaged in education, have substantial educational functions. These agencies include businesses and factories, trade unions, political parties, churches, cultural organizations, clubs and societies, and many more. They are the
scene of much learning, and their importance as informal educational institutions should not be overlooked. However, they
are frequently not adequately acknowledged, and greater understanding of their educational role is needed. In keeping with
this view, some of the participating colleges established links
with such community institutions through visits, in-service
training programmes and research projects. At Singapore, for
example, a number of institutions not connected with the formal
education system and not involved in educating children, established in-service training courses in co-operation with the
college. Such institutions included the Telecommunications
Authority of Singapore and the Port of Singapore Authority.
Another way of forming relationships with such institutions was
through fieldwork. This included visits to a home for the aged
and a community centre as well as contacts with the media
through visits to radio and TV stations. Other community agencies of a relatively unacknowledged educational potential were
visited and studied, including the aquarium, the zoo, the botanical gardens, a bird park, museums, an observatory, and a
science centre.

   Similar contacts with these kinds of agency were established at other colleges. At Torrens, for example, not only
were a union headquarters and a community centre visited, but
also an "alternative" culture, in an attempt to study a group

with an undoubted educational role, but one which had consciously rejected the conventional, established forms of societal organization. As has been mentioned previously, students in both Indian colleges engaged in social work with slum
communities near the colleges, participating in health and
nutrition programmes, as well as in educational programmes aimed for example at raising the educational standards of people
living in the slums. In the case of Szeged, students worked
with youth organizations such as the Young Pioneers, and also
participated in the educative activities of Young Communist
groups and of other political work or cultural organizations.
It is thus apparent that there was recognition at several of
the colleges that a variety of locations, methods and forms of
learning exist outside the formal educational system.

SUMMARY

Institutions adopting lifelong education as an organizing
principle would make a number of changes in their own way of
functioning. Such changes would affect teaching and learning
activities within the colleges, instructors' role and their
relations with students, evaluation procedures, and similar aspects of the teaching and learning processes. Such institutions would also make a number of changes in their own internal organization, for example in the planning and scheduling
of courses, the provision of support services for lifelong education-oriented activities, and similar aspects. Finally,
they would change their relationships with other community organizations and structures, in an integration of college activities with those of other learning agencies. The basic aim
of these changes would be to make the institutions themselves
function as examples of the principles of lifelong education in
action.

A number of such changes were made in the colleges involved
in the present study. They included ways of teaching differing
from the traditional lecture method, emphasis on practical
work and independent learning, opportunities for group work,
and use of self-evaluation, group evaluation and continuous
evaluation. They also included emphasis on the role of instructors as resource persons, co-learners and "energizers" of
learning.

In the area of organizational change, scheduling of courses was made more flexible and alternative forms were adopted,

group planning of courses was seen in some colleges, and other changes such as admission of students outside the conventional age range were effected. Attempts were also made to introduce more individualized selection of courses, and to provide feedback on the effects of various kinds of activity.

Finally, integration of teaching and learning activities within the colleges with learning activities and processes in the community was achieved through visits, research projects, excursions, and the like, encompassing schools, community agencies clearly connected with education such as museums or educational media, and other organizations and institutions with a significant, but often unrecognized educational function, such as trade unions, political parties, youth groups and similar bodies.

CHAPTER 8

EVALUATION OF OUTCOMES

METHODOLOGICAL DIFFICULTIES

Although most of the colleges reached some conclusions about the outcomes of the programmes they had implemented, there were substantial methodological differences in the ways in which conclusions were reached and in the extensiveness and nature of the evaluation procedures. In some cases evaluation was based on formal procedures and used rating scales, check lists and questionnaires, with quantification of data, statistical tests, and drawing of conclusions on a relatively "scientific" basis. Such procedures yielded what may be called "quantitative" findings. However, some of the investigations involved only formulation of impressions and opinions, and the making of subjective judgments. These less formal findings (referred to here as "qualitative" findings) were to be found in all of the reports.

One of the reasons for the frequent lack of adherence to strict research practice was the absence of a single research design, largely because of the widely differing purposes, motives, rights and duties of the participating institutions. In this sense, the variability in the forms of the project was a disadvantage, although it also had advantages, as has already been pointed out. A second reason for the lack of experimental strictness was the feeling among some of the participants that insistence on formal and standardized methods could well obscure important findings. The Trier report, for example, includes an extensive discussion of the use of evaluation in projects like the present one. Two basic kinds of approach to evaluation are described. The first is the formal approach involving establishment of clearcut criteria, operationalization of goals, specification of treatment, and numerical measurement of results. However, it is argued that such an approach would not necessarily be capable of obtaining some of the most important data. Indeed, it might make measurement or even manifestation of the traits in question impossible, for example if an attempt were made to measure flexibility through the use of methods precluding flexible behaviour. The alternative is a less rigid and formal approach, with greater comprehensiveness and more qualitative forms of assessment.

For some readers the frequent deviations from strict research methodology will detract seriously from the convincingness of the findings and conclusions. Certainly there is considerable variation from report to report, and even between the different parts of individual reports, in the ways in which findings were obtained, the rigour with which the validity of purported findings was tested, and the kinds of data on which conclusions were based. This variability is reflected in the presentation of findings in the present chapter. No contempt for rigorous research practice is intended, however, nor a cavalier attitude to empirical evidence. It is hoped, on the contrary, that a helpful and valid assembling of findings of various kinds has been achieved, through an acceptable combination of qualitative and quantitative approaches.

QUANTITATIVE INVESTIGATIONS

Procedures in the various colleges

Three colleges carried out quantitative evaluations which were linked by being relatively formal, systematic and numerical. However, they varied considerably in a number of details, including the nature of the instruments developed, the respondents to whom they were administered, the methods of data analysis, and similar aspects. For this reason, the quantitative investigations in the three colleges are described separately.

Szeged. The first group studied at Szeged consisted of 280 teachers already working in schools. They were tested in order to ascertain whether the principles of lifelong education were already well known among Hungarian teachers, and whether students at the end of their exposure to the lifelong education-oriented teachers' college curriculum showed greater knowledge about or interest in lifelong education than teachers.

If they did not, the effectiveness of the newly adopted curriculum would obviously come into question. The second and third groups consisted respectively of 257 students tested at the beginning of the third year of studies, and 210 tested at the end of the year. These last two groups were drawn from the same set of people, and thus provided an opportunity for comparing the responses of students before the programme with those at its end. The same questionnaires were administered (see the following paragraph for a description of these instruments), so that a test-retest study can be said to have been carried out.

The instruments used for assessing the teachers' and students' knowledge and attitudes in the area of lifelong education consisted of five questionnaires especially developed for the purposes of the project, and listed in full in the Szeged report. In this institution the major purpose of orienting teacher training in terms of lifelong education was not to transmit factual knowledge, but to modify attitudes to schooling and teaching and eventually to change teaching behaviours. Consequently the Szeged questionnaires concentrated on opinions about the educational process, attitudes to school and learning, and similar areas of interest. The instruments developed did not refer overtly to lifelong education, but each gave respondents opportunities to express lifelong education-oriented attitudes and opinions. For the most part, lifelong education-related statements were embedded among masking items involving education but not explicitly referring to lifelong education.

The first questionnaire contained a list of 100 positive human characteristics, including 15 thought by the experimenters to be especially related to lifelong education. The respondents were asked to rate each of these on a five-point scale ranging from "Unimportant" to "Essential", according to how important they thought it was for future teachers. The second instrument made use of the same 100 items, but this time the respondents were asked to say how important they thought it was for each trait to be developed in pupils (the "rising generation"). The third test was concerned with the purpose of education. Again it involved 100 items divided into 20 blocks of 5. In 12 of the blocks, one of the items referred to learning, while the other four referred to other pedagogical issues. The purpose of the questionnaire was to study attitudes to learning; the learning-oriented items in these 12 blocks were the key measures.

The fourth test most nearly approached a test of knowledge about lifelong education. It consisted of 35 questions for each of which the respondents had to select the best answer from among four alternatives provided. Of these questions, 18 were related to lifelong education. The fifth test asked respondents to list the 10 most important tasks for the modernization of the Hungarian educational system. This was an open-ended test to which the students and teachers responded in their own words. A summary of the five tests, including some examples from each, is to be found in Table 16.

The five questionnaires were administered once only to the 280 teachers, whereas in the case of the students they were administered both at the beginning and at the end of the 3rd year of teacher training (the year re-oriented in terms of lifelong education). Subjects were not told that the tests were concerned with lifelong education, but merely that the Unesco Institute was interested in their opinions. The first three tests were scored by recording the percentage of the people in each of the three groups who rated each of the lifelong education-oriented items as "Essential". Subsequently, comparisons were made among the groups in order to ascertain whether there were differences in the importance they attached to the items. In the case of the fourth test, respondents were scored correct or incorrect according to which alternative they chose. Finally, in the case of the open-ended test on priorities for Hungarian education, suggestions were rated by judges according to whether or not they were lifelong education-related, and the percentage of lifelong education-oriented suggestions given various priorities was calculated for each of the three groups of respondents. Subsequently, comparisons were made between the three groups in terms of their scores on the various questionnaires. Findings based on these instruments are summarized in the results section.

H. J. College. Subjects for the formal evaluation of outcomes at H. J. College were drawn from two sources. The first source was the college itself, from which the "experimental" group of 154 students enrolled in the 1974-75 academic year was obtained. This group of people was further subdivided into 78 students who participated in an internship programme which took place in the co-operating schools associated with the college (referred to as "Internees"), and 76 students who paid only brief visits to the schools and taught only occasional or "stray" lessons (referred to as "Non-internees"). The second group of subjects came from another College of Education into which the

Table 16

Instruments Used at Szeged

Instrument	Nature	No of Items	Examples	
1. Desirable Properties of Future Teachers	Rating Scale ranging from "Unimportant" (rating of 1) to "Essential" (rating of 5)	100	**Property**	**Rating**
			i) Critical attitude	....
			ii) Desire for knowledge	....
			iii) Sensitivity to problems	....
			iv) Inclination to make innovations	....
2. Desirable Properties of the Rising Generation	Rating Scale ranging from "Unimportant" to "Essential"	100	Same as above	
3. Desirable Properties of a Progressive Education System	Rating Scale assigning each property a score from 1 (lowest) to 5 (highest)	100	i) Mastery of learning methods	....
			ii) Developing a desire to acquire knowledge	....
			iii) Fostering readiness to learn	....
			iv) Developing the habit of learning	....
4. Opinions about Education	Multiple Choice items with one "correct" answer	100	Where should adult education be practised?	
			A. At every type of school, course, or cultural institution, and in independent individual learning activities	
			B. In organized adult education	
			C. In cultural institutions	
			D. In individual, independent learning	
5. Tasks for the Development of Education	Open ended, essay-type test	....	List of 10 tasks, in order of priority, that you regard as important from the point of view of Hungarian public education	

concept of lifelong education had not been formally introduced. This college was very similar to H.J. College in that it was affiliated to the University of Bombay, followed the same syllabus prescribed by the university, drew students from similar communities of India, admitted students of similar socio-economic status, and used the same criteria as did H.J. College for the admission of students. This group comprised 86 students, and was referred to as the "control" group.

A number of instruments were developed specifically for the project. They included attitude scales, questionnaires, a checklist, and interviews. Examples of this material are given in Table 17. In addition, standard tests of intelligence and personality were administered to the Internees and Non-Internees, in order to make sure that they were matched on these dimensions.

There were two attitude scales, both concerned with attitudes to learning. The first scale (*Scale A*) was administered to the experimental group as a pre-test and also as a post-test, and was also administered to the control group on one occasion only (at the end of their course). It consisted of 25 items to which subjects responded on a five-point scale. The second scale (*Scale B*) was administered to both experimental and control groups immediately after the internship programme. It consisted of 17 items with multiple-choice answers, and required the selection of reasons why a given learning activity should be pursued.

There were also two questionnaires (*Questionnaire A* and *Questionnaire B*) concerned with evaluating the impact of the project on the students on the one hand, and with students' orientation towards continued learning and the means of such learning on the other. A third, *Open-Ended Questionnaire* was administered after completion of the internship programme, in order to study the extent to which the principles of lifelong education had been internalized by students, and how effective they thought their dissemination of the concepts to pupils and schoolteachers had been.

Two interviews were also conducted, the first before the commencement of the programme and the second after its conclusion, in order to ascertain whether any changes had taken place in students in the areas of reading interests, co-curricular interests, attempts at self-improvement, willingness to share experiences, and finally, outlook on education.

Table 17

Instruments Developed at H. J. College

Instruments	Nature	No of Items	Examples
1. Attitudes to Lifelong Education (Referred to as _Scale A_)	A list of statements to which students responded using a 5-point rating scale ranging from "Strongly Agree" to "Strongly Disagree"	25	i) "I would only join a course of further study if I had to" Strongly Agree / Agree / Don't Know / Disagree / Strongly Disagree
2. Reasons for Pursuing a Learning Activity (Referred to as _Scale B_)	Multiple choice test with three alternatives for each item	17	i) People should learn throughout their lives a) if they have money b) if they have time c) if they want to improve their quality of life
3. Evaluation of the College and its Staff (Referred to as _Questionnaire A_)	A mixture of open-ended items requiring numerical estimates, opinions or suggestions (examples i) and ii), plus 14 items requiring a statement of agreement or disagreement on a 5-point scale (example iii)	25	i) What percentage of the instructors are lifelong learners? ii) What subjects in the college syllabus give most scope for introduction of lifelong education? iii) Staff members have developed the attitude of co-learners. Strongly Agree / Agree / Don't Know / Disagree / Strongly Disagree

Instruments	Nature	No of Items	Examples
4. Future Plans (Referred to as Questionnaire B)	Six open-ended items concerning further study plans, suggested changes in the college, etc. (examples i) and ii), plus 16 "True-False" items containing statements reflecting attitudes, especially towards their own future behaviour (example iii)	22	i) How do you plan to carry on further studies after leaving the college? ii) What new features should be added to the BEd course? iii) I would like to emphasize lifelong learning. Yes / No
5. Internalization of Lifelong Education (Referred to as Open-Ended Questionnaire)	Four items requiring free responses in which students described or listed actions (examples i) and ii), plus four items on which they rated the attitudes of pupils and fellow teachers on a three-point scale (example iii)	8	i) What is the role of the student teacher in practice teaching sessions? ii) What was the main approach you adopted to teaching? iii) The pupils' attitude towards you was Positive / Indifferent / Negative
6. Practice Teaching Activities Check List (Referred to as Checklist cum Rating Scale)	A list of activities on which students indicated how often an activity had been used, on a 5-point rating scale ranging from "Always" to "Never"	22	i) During practice teaching I undertook diagnostic measures Always / Often / Sometimes / Occasionally / Never ii) During practice teaching I disseminated lifelong education concepts in the school community through informal discussions Always / Often / Sometimes / Occasionally / Never

As was the case at Szeged, emphasis was placed at H. J. College on the fact that the major purpose of the project was to develop teachers who behaved in the classroom in ways consistent with the principles of lifelong education. Consequently, a major part of the evaluation of outcomes was assessment of the programme's effects on practice teaching behaviour. For this reason, a *checklist cum rating scale* of all the activities and practices carried out during practice teaching was prepared for each student. This checklist included activities connected with planning and evaluation, diffusion of lifelong education concepts through content of lessons and teaching methods, practising of lifelong education principles, and participation in school and community activities.

The battery of instruments just described was administered to the three groups of subjects at various times in the 1974-75 academic year; at the beginning of the year (tests of intelligence and of personality), both at the beginning and at the end of the year (*Scale A, Scale B* and the interviews), immediately after the completion of practice teaching (*Checklist cum Rating Scale* and *Open-Ended Questionnaire*), and at the end of the year (*Questionnaire A* and *Questionnaire B*). The tests were scored in the appropriate ways, and subsequently various comparisons among the three groups of subjects were made (e.g., internees versus non-internees, experimental group versus control group, or pre-test versus post-test).

Gandhi Shikshan Bhavan. Two basic groups of subjects were involved in the evaluation study at Gandhi Shikshan Bhavan. The first consisted of 83 students enrolled in the college in the 1974-75 academic year. This group was sometimes further subdivided into two sub-groups comprising 38 students (46%) who had already had some teaching experience prior to entering the college, and 45 students (54%) without prior experience. The second group of subjects consisted of approximately 80 students who had been enrolled in the 1973-74 academic year. These people had not been exposed to the lifelong education-facilitating curriculum introduced for the purposes of the present study, and as a result were able to serve as a kind of control group. The 1973-74 group (the control group) was rated and assessed only at the end of the academic year in which they had been enrolled; however, most of the ratings and assessments of the 1974-75 group (the experimental group) were carried out on two occasions, either during both the first and second terms, or else both at the commencement of the project and its end. Consequently, two kinds of comparisons were possible - experimental-group versus control-group comparisons and pre-test versus post-test comparisons.

A variety of instruments and procedures were developed for the empirical study. Much of the evaluation derived from ratings of students' behaviour in certain areas, both by instructors and by students themselves. As a first step in this process, eight aspects of teaching behaviour were identified as the key ones in which attitudes to lifelong education would be manifested. These aspects are listed in Table 18. The first phase of the quantitative evaluation at the college centered on ratings of the students on these eight aspects of attitude by their instructors, by their peers, and by themselves. The ratings involved several areas of students' behaviour including their work in class, their participation in social work activities, and their behaviour during college life.

Table 18

Key Aspects of Attitude to Lifelong Education

1. Attitude to pupils.

2. Attitude to colleagues.

3. Attitude to superiors.

4. Attitude to learning.

5. Attitude to schoolwork and difficulties with it.

6. Attitude to society.

7. Attitude to aesthetics.

8. Attitude to professional values.

The first area in which ratings were carried out was concerned with behaviour in seminars and discussion groups, and with the papers students presented. It concentrated upon their knowledge of the implications of lifelong education. The eight aspects of attitude already mentioned were assessed on a five-point scale, ranging from "Not Satisfactory" to "Very Good".

This rating was carried out in both terms of the 1974-75 academic year. The second area studied was social work and participation in community life. Again eight aspects of attitude were rated both by instructors and by students themselves, using a five-point scale ranging from "Not Satisfactory" (or sometimes "Poor") to "Very Good". Finally, a sociometric procedure based on anecdotes about students' behaviour was used for assessing the eight key aspects of attitude. The behaviours described in the anecdotes were rated on a five-point scale from "1" (least favourable rating) to "5" (most favourable), in the first instance by instructors. Subsequently, in a process of group evaluation, students selected five other students whom they knew well, and rated each of them on the eight attitudinal dimensions. The procedures just described were also carried out in both terms of the academic year.

A second approach to assessing attitudes involved the use of a questionnaire describing 25 hypothetical situations from the lives of imaginary teachers. Having described the situation, each item asked a question about the events described. In answering the questions, students revealed their own attitudes. These attitudes were then rated by instructors on a five-point scale ranging from "Highly Desirable" to "Undesirable". This questionnaire was administered both as a pretest and also as a post-test, in order to permit comparisons of students' attitudes before and after exposure to the lifelong education-oriented curriculum. Some details of this test, and of the practice teaching self-evaluation questionnaire discussed in the next paragraph, are given in Table 19.

A third form of evaluation was concerned with practice-teaching behaviours. In both terms instructors analyzed remarks sheets filled in by supervisors of practice teaching, as well as students' lesson files, in order to assess the use or non-use of such lifelong education-oriented practices as self-study, group-study, activity lessons, dramatization, use of media, use of pupils to teach other pupils, introduction of members of the society (parents, experts, other adults) as instructors, and celebration of national festivals. In addition, self-evaluation of practice teaching was carried out through the use of a self-evaluation questionnaire, in which students indicated things like the extent to which they had used various kinds of instructional materials, their use of seating arrangements to facilitate learning, involvement of pupils in planning, fostering of self-directed learning, fostering of co-learning, and similar activities. This questionnaire was administered as

Table 19

Questionnaires Developed at Gandhi Shikshan Bhavan

Instrument	Nature	No of Items	Examples
1. Attitudes to Teaching	Imaginary situations involving teachers are described. Students write open-ended answers to questions about the situations.	25	i) Shri Taneja is a very busy man. His work as a teacher along with his duties as a parent take up a lot of time. But every day for half an hour before he goes to bed, he reads something concerning his subject. Q. What do you admire in Shri Taneja? ii) "I don't like working in a school close to my house", says Shri Swarma, "One has to be careful every moment, even after school hours." Q. Do you agree with Shri Swarma? Why? iii) During the course of a language lesson, a pupil suddenly asked "What is Theosophy?" Q. What would be your reaction?
2. Practice Teaching Self-Evaluation Questionnaire	A series of questions are asked. Students respond by selecting an appropriate response such as "Always / Often / Sometimes", "Yes / No", or "Very Good / Good / Fair / Unsatisfactory"	11	i) Did you attend prayers? Always / Often / Sometimes ii) How would you evaluate your classroom preparation for the lesson? Very Good / Good / Fair / Unsatisfactory iii) Were other student teachers' remarks about you Helpful? / Annoying?

part of the post-test. Finally, pupils were brought into the
evaluative process by being interviewed by instructors at the
end of the year, in order to obtain their assessments of the
teaching ability of students.

Results of quantitative studies

Basically there were three areas in which findings were
obtained in the three quantitative investigations outlined
above. These included findings about the level of knowledge
concerning lifelong education, about students' attitudes to
learning, teaching and schooling, and finally about the adoption of behaviours consistent with the principles of lifelong
education during practice teaching. Findings about all three
of these areas will be presented in the present section. They
are based on data given in the various national reports. However, they do not necessarily exhaust all information contained
in the reports, since some selecting has been done for the purposes of the present book. The reporting of results in the
present section thus involves a summary and synthesis; more
complete details may be obtained by consulting individual
national reports. In general, conclusions made by the national
teams on the basis of their data and listed in the national reports as findings have been accepted at face value - for example if a finding was said to be significant in the national
report, this conclusion was accepted in compiling the present
section, even if appropriate statistical tests or other such
procedures were not given.

Knowledge about lifelong education. At Szeged the fourth
test was concerned with "the level of knowledge in connection
with lifelong education" (Part G, p. 30). For some items as
many as 95% of the respondents were reported to have selected
the "correct" alternative in the case of both students and
teachers. These figures were so high that no detailed analysis
of this test was subsequently carried out. This reported finding may indicate that there is an extraordinarily high level of
knowledge of the principles of lifelong education among teachers and students. However, it is also true that the fundamental
theses of lifelong education are highly plausible and attractive
statements that are likely to be approved of when presented to
educators, even in the absence of knowledge of lifelong education. Although they may be surrounded by distractors, they are
easily picked out as statements of desirable educational goals,

even for persons who would not normally have generated the statements for themselves, and who may not have encountered them before.

Thus, the general problem arises that many respondents may have been able to guess what answers were desired and to have responded accordingly, introducing a strong social desirability bias. This problem would not be confined to the investigation of knowledge about lifelong education, of course, and it should be borne in mind when considering all of the findings reported here. It was in an attempt to deal with such problems that the methods of "hidden" key items embedded in distractors as well as use of open-ended questionnaires not directly referring to lifelong education were adopted in some of the institutions. In any case, the data in the Szeged report indicated that subjects seemed to possess a high level of knowledge about the concept of lifelong education, even before they had experienced the lifelong education-oriented curriculum. It is not clear whether this reflected a genuinely high level of knowledge or the operation of social desirability effects. The problem might perhaps be avoided by asking simply "What is lifelong education?", but this kind of question has other disadvantages in that, for example, it does not lend itself easily to objective scoring, requiring content analysis or similar techniques.

According to the Gandhi Shikshan Bhavan report, assessment of knowledge about lifelong education showed that relatively small but consistent increases occurred from the first term to the second in the proportions of students judged to have shown "Very Good" knowledge about the concept, while the proportion of students judged to have shown only "Satisfactory" or "Fair" knowledge had decreased correspondingly, both in paper readings and also in discussions and seminars (see p. 195 of the college's report). For example, an increase from 32% to 48% in the "Very Good" category was reported for knowledge in discussions and seminars. An increase in the reported level of knowledge about lifelong education was also seen in the self-ratings. However, although there were increases during the course of the year, they were much smaller in this case, mainly because students rated themselves highly even during the first term. For example, 85% of students reported that they possessed "Very Good" or "Good" knowledge even at the first assessment.

Attitudes to lifelong education. Although knowledge of
the basic principles of lifelong education is undoubtedly an
important first step in teacher training, a second important
element is students' intentions, values, opinions and beliefs.
Consequently, a major issue in evaluating the effects of the
curriculum oriented towards lifelong education is the attitudes
of the students. Indeed, as will become apparent shortly, the
bulk of the findings bore upon the affective domain.

At *Szeged* all three groups of respondents were reported to
have given the highest ratings to openmindedness, sensitivity
to problems, and flexibility in the broad area of personal attitudes, both for future teachers and for the rising generation.
Students rated these properties more highly at the post-test.
Interestingly, practising teachers rated them lower than students, on both occasions. Thus, even students with no formal
training in the area of lifelong education seemed to be more
positively oriented towards it than experienced teachers, and
this positive evaluation increased during the exposure to the
lifelong education curriculum. In the area of learning, all
three groups rated desire for knowledge as the most important
trait, although there was no significant difference on the pre-
and post-tests. Practising teachers gave desire for knowledge
the lowest rating, whereas they rated knowledge of learning
processes highest. Interest in permanent self-education was
highly rated by students, and significant differences between
pre-test and post-test scores were reported in the rating of
disposition for experimenting, in inclination for making innovations, and in impatience with conservative attitudes. The
percentages of members of each group rating the various traits
as "Essential" are shown in Table 20.

When attention turned to the functions of a progressive
system of education, moderately high ratings were reported for
all three groups for the importance of schooling as a way of
establishing learning in adulthood and developing learning abilities. About 25% of respondents rated these two goals as most
important, suggesting that a considerable transformation of
traditional goals for schooling has already occurred in Hungary.
However, the rating of these goals was not significantly higher
on the post-test. By contrast, developing readiness to learn
was rated more highly at the post-test than the pre-test, as
was fostering good learning habits. In the area of evaluation,
development of measures of educability was highly rated by students, especially at the post-test. Table 21 contains a summary of the percentages of members of each group who rated the

Table 20

Percentages of Respondents at Szeged
Rating Various Properties as "Essential" for
Future Teachers and for the Rising Generation

| | Future Teachers | | | Rising Generation | | |
| | Students | | Teachers | Students | | Teachers |
Property	Pre-Test	Post-Test		Pre-Test	Post-Test	
Open-Mindedness	23	32	17	23	33	15
Flexibility	17	22	11	11	16	6
Sensitivity to Problems	18	25	14	15	26	8
Desire for Knowledge	44	42	33	54	47	37
Desire for Learning	24	18	15	33	31	22
Ability to Learn	10	16	9	14	16	13
Knowledge of Learning Processes	24	23	34	8	12	11
Interest in the Profession	54	47	56	28	26	36
Permanent Self-Education	49	46	36	35	43	22
Detailed Knowledge	11	11	19	8	9	11
Impatience with Conservative Attitudes	8	9	6	13	19	8
Critical Attitude	11	8	11	10	8	7
Inclination to make Innovations	7	9	3	8	13	5
Disposition for Experimenting	6	6	5	5	9	4
Thinking Ability	31	41	24	27	28	23

Table 21

Percentages of Respondents at Szeged Rating Various
Properties as "Essential" for Progressive Education

Property	Students		Teachers
	Pre-Test	Post-Test	
Establishing Adult Learning Ability	24	25	22
Establishing Self-Educational Ability	18	22	18
The Learning Methods Offered by the Curriculum	12	16	6
Developing Desire for Knowledge of Subject Matter	18	25	6
Fostering Readiness to Learn	36	39	38
Fostering Ability to Learn	26	29	24
Encouraging Demand for Learning	15	18	21
Establishing the Habit of Learning	30	34	4
Guiding the Learning Process	18	16	9
Testing Educability	25	35	9
Diagnosis and Treatment	27	26	49
Fostering Self-Evaluation	12	10	14

various traits as "Essential" for progressive schooling. Taking
the results for this test of the perceived purposes of schooling
as a whole, it was concluded that lifelong education concepts
were more highly rated by students than by practising teachers,
and that there were changes in the lifelong education-oriented
direction from the pre-test to the post-test.

The last instrument used at Szeged to measure students' and
teachers' attitudes to education and schooling was the open-
ended questionnaire, in which they listed the 10 tasks they regarded as the most important for Hungarian education. The responses were item-analyzed by judges, according to what aspects
of education they referred to. In the teachers' group, about
18% of the suggestions were concerned with lifelong education,
either directly or indirectly, while among students the pre-
test figure was 41% rising to 48% at the end of the year. Once
again students, even before exposure to the curriculum oriented
towards lifelong education, placed greater emphasis on its pre-
cepts. This emphasis seemed to have been strengthened during
the year's programme.

In order to permit further comparison of the level of understanding of lifelong education and the degree of acceptance of
its principles among the three groups, further analyses were
carried out of the first three questionnaires referred to above.
In each case, this comparison was done by defining as "standard"
or "perfect" a pattern of responses in which the lifelong education-oriented responses were all checked as highly important.
Subsequently, individual questionnaires were scored according
to how closely they resembled this idealized pattern, a score
of 100 indicating perfect agreement between a student or teacher's responses and the ideal. It was then possible to calcul-
ate the average resemblance for each group, and to carry out
statistical tests to determine whether there were significant
differences among them. The means of the three groups on the
three tests are shown in Table 22.

Results showed that, on all three tests, there was a significant difference between the mean pre-test score and the
mean post-test score obtained by the students. In each case,
the reported post-test means were numerically higher, indicating on average, a better approximation to the "perfect" pattern of responses among the students who had completed the
lifelong education programme. On two of the three questionnaires, practising teachers were reported to have obtained
significantly lower scores than the students' post-test scores.

Table 22

Mean Levels of Correspondence at
Szeged Between Beliefs and the Ideal

Area	Students		Teachers
	Pre-Test	Post-Test	
Properties of Teachers	26.0	30.0 *	27.0
Properties of the Rising Generation	27.0	31.0 *	25.0 **
Properties of a Progressive Education System	23.0	26.0 *	21.0 **

* Significantly different from the pre-test mean (p < .05)

** Significantly different from the post-test mean (p < .05)

No significant differences were reported between teachers'
scores and those of students at the pre-test. The conclusions
drawn from these findings were that Hungarian students and
teachers are already well informed about the theory of lifelong
education, but that this knowledge and interest was successfully
enhanced by the experimental curriculum.

At *Gandhi Shikshan Bhavan* comparisons were made in the
eight areas listed in Table 18 between attitudes at the commencement of the course and at its end, and also between students exposed to the modified curriculum during the 1974-75
academic year (the experimental group) and those following the
conventional curriculum during the 1973-74 year (the control
group). The percentages of students in each of these groups
obtaining ratings of either "Highly Desirable" or "Undesirable"

are shown in Table 23. In the case of the experimental group,
the proportion of students whose attitudes were rated as
"Highly Desirable" was reported to have increased in all eight
attitude categories, while there was said to have been a corresponding fall in the proportion of students rated as showing
"Undesirable" attitudes. In the comparisons between the experimental group and the control group, a higher proportion of
experimentals was rated as showing "Highly Desirable" attitudes,
and a slightly lower proportion as showing "Undesirable" ones.
In addition to the data just discussed, attitudes were also
assessed through the use of anecdotal records collected by instructors, as well as through descriptions of students by their
peers. In this case, it was concluded that students who had
experienced the lifelong education curriculum were more helpful,
co-operative and friendly than those who had not.

Table 23

Percentages of Students Showing Desirable and
Undesirable Attitudes at Gandhi Shikshan Bhavan

| Attitude To | Experimental Group | | | | Control Group | |
| | Pre-Test | | Post-Test | | | |
	Highly Desirable	Un- Desirable	Highly Desirable	Un- Desirable	Highly Desirable	Un- Desirable
Pupils	20	10	35	2	30	3
Colleagues	27	11	38	7	20	10
Superiors	31	9	40	3	24	4
Learning	25	8	36	1	31	5
Work and Difficulties	26	9	34	7	30	7
Society	20	13	40	4	23	10
Aesthetics	20	7	29	2	21	7
Professional Values	20	20	36	11	35	6

At *H.J. College* it was reported that there were statistic-
ally significant differences between experimentals and controls
on items of *Scale A* and *Scale B* such as those involving desire
to participate in further study courses (X^2 = 9.67, df = 2,
p <.01), desire to carry out further study through reading
books and journals (X^2 = 15.72, df = 2, p <.01), desire to continue studies for self improvement (X^2 = 17.00, df = 2, p <.01),
and desire to continue learning even after retirement (X^2 =
26.37, df = 4, p <.01). There were also significant differences
in items involving factors such as desire to motivate others to
learn (X^2 = 11.57, df = 2, p <.01), desire to teach students the
skills of learning (X^2 = 9.84, df = 2, p <.01), and desire to
discuss problems of education with pupils (X^2 = 13.81, df = 4,
p <.01). Thus, it could be said that students who had been exposed to the lifelong education-oriented curriculum showed
greater desire to continue their own learning, and to improve
their own knowledge and professional competence. They were, in
fact, significantly more interested in being lifelong learners
themselves. In addition, they were more concerned about arous-
ing motivation for continued learning in pupils, and were more
committed to fostering skills in the domain of "learning to
learn".

When attention was turned to comparisons of the pre-test
and post-test scores of the experimental group, rather than to
comparisons between experimental and control groups, a number
of significant differences between scores at the beginning of
the course and at its end were reported. For example, on *Scale
A* there were significant differences in items concerned with
desire to participate in courses of further study (X^2 = 10.10,
df = 4, p <.05), desire to increase professional efficiency
through further study (X^2 = 10.60, df = 4, p <.05), desire to
undertake research in education (X^2 = 25.58, df = 4, p <.01),
and desire to continue learning even after retirement (X^2 =
56.27, df = 4, p <.01). Changes in attitudes during the course
of the year were also seen in the ratings derived from the interviews conducted at the beginning and the end of the programme.
Again, these mainly involved increases in students' rated interest in self-improvement, their willingness to share learning
experiences, and their understanding of the purpose of education. Table 24 lists mean ratings of students by instructors
on several aspects of attitude to education and learning.

Thus, not only did the students who had been exposed to the
lifelong education-oriented curriculum show a number of sig-
nigicant differences from those who had not, as has been pointed

out in the previous paragraph, but there were also significant changes in their attitudes during the course of the year, as the comparisons between pre-test and post-test scores indicate. These changes were mainly concerned with students' desire to become lifelong learners themselves.

Table 24

Attitudes to Education and Learning at H. J. College

Area	Pre-Test Mean	Post-Test Mean
Reading Interest	42.50	48.25
Co-curricular Interests	52.00	57.00
Self-improvement	27.00	53.00
Willingness to Share Experiences	39.00	53.25
Outlook on Education	39.00	61.00

Teaching Behaviours. At Gandhi Shikshan Bhavan instructors analyzed the lesson files of students at the end of each term, and assessed the extent to which teaching methods had included activities consistent with the principles of lifelong education. The frequency data indicated that substantial increases occurred from the first to the second term in the use of certain practices such as group methods and self-study. Among inexperienced students (those with no previous teaching experience), the proportion using lifelong education-oriented procedures was reported to have increased sharply for self-study methods (42% to 84%), group study (48% to 88%), activity lessons (26% to 84%), and dramatization(13% to 44%). There was also said to have been some development of the practice of pupils teaching other pupils and of use of adults other than teachers as instructors. Similar increases were reported among students who had already had some experience of teaching in schools, except that the frequency with which this kind of activity was employed by students with teaching experience was

lower in all cases, a finding which again raises a point mentioned in connection with findings at Szeged. Students seem
to be more receptive to lifelong education ideas than do experienced teachers, suggesting that the school setting is not
as supportive of the concept of lifelong education (or of other
novel education principles) as a teacher-training institution.

It was also possible to compare the classroom-teaching behaviour of the experimental group with that of students enrolled
in the college in the year before the commencement of the lifelong education curriculum. A total of 70% of the 1974-75 group
were judged to have used "modern strategies" (i.e., project
methods, self-directed learning, group evaluation, etc.), whereas only 43% of the 1973-74 group were judged to have done so.
A second set of data was available in the form of students' responses to a questionnaire in which they described their own use
of various classroom procedures consistent with the principles
of lifelong education. According to these instruments, there
was greater success in the experimental group in the use of
teaching aids and instructional materials specially prepared
by students themselves or by pupils, use of variable seating
arrangements, involvement of pupils in planning lessons, promotion of self-learning, fostering of co-learning, relating
learning to pupils' own interests, and development of systems
of continuous evaluation. Possibly as a result, more than 80%
of the experimental group reported that they had gained "very
much" from practice teaching, whereas only 26% of the controls
did so.

Finally, data were obtained from a relatively neglected
source: not only the schools, but the pupils too, were polled
for their reactions to the methods and procedures introduced
by the students. Their responses indicated that there was a
highly positive reaction to things like the introduction of
self-study and group-study methods, activity lessons, dramatizations and similar procedures. In all cases the reported
proportion of schools responding positively was in excess of
85%.

At H. J. College it was concluded that students made substantial use of integrative planning of their lessons, provided
diagnostic feedback to their pupils, participated in non-classroom activities, dealt individually with the particular needs
of special children such as bright children, slow learners or
problem children, adopted a problem-solving and project approach,

made use of participatory and self-directed evaluation, and involved pupils in planning and organizing social and cultural activities. Internees were found to be significantly better at these kinds of activities than were non-internees, suggesting that the opportunity for systematic and integrated practice teaching experience in which there is, for example, continuity from one lesson to another, provides better opportunities for student teachers to adopt innovative methods.

QUALITATIVE FINDINGS

In addition to findings derived from formal investigations of the kind just described, a number of conclusions were drawn in the various local projects on the basis of more subjective sources of information. These included informal observations, conversations with colleagues and students, impressions gained during participation in the projects, and similar sources. Such findings were not usually supported by data or statistics, and are sometimes little more than speculations. Nonetheless, they provide many useful insights into the outcomes of the projects in the various colleges.

At Torrens, data were gathered which lay mid-way between the kinds referred to earlier as "quantitative" and the kinds of impressions, feelings and speculations referred to as "qualitative". This was achieved by having a "participant observer" take part in the course for students in further education in both 1974 and 1975. The observer attended all lectures and one of the seminar groups in both years, just as if he were a student enrolled in the course. He talked with other students and made his own private observation of the courses. In addition, the observer prepared and administered a questionnaire to his fellow students in both years. His findings, both on the basis of his subjective observations and also those deriving from his analysis of the questionnaires, were subsequently presented in four formal written reports centering on three key questions about the course: What was its relevance to the needs of the students enrolled in it? What influence did it have on the students? How could it be improved? This method of data collection seems to be an example of the second kind of "more comprehensive" and "less rigid" approach referred to in the Trier report.

One important finding was that the students found the ap-

proach stimulating. In particular, according to the observer,
they appreciated the opportunities for informal contacts with
instructors, and for both self-learning and group-learning,
for example through interactions in seminars. These latter
kinds of learning included student-to-student contacts and
also student-instructor contacts. In this kind of setting, it
was found that bluffing was very difficult, so that the students tended to be well-prepared for their seminars. As a result of the experience of guided and self-learning and interaction with groups of learners, many of the students were able
to develop their own reporting techniques to a high level of
efficiency. They also became acutely aware of the fact that
they were learning all the time, and that lifelong education is
a process of obtaining information and using it to the best advantage. Overall, the observer concluded that the students, as
a result of their participation in the lifelong education-oriented course, had become aware of their role in fostering
"further education", had developed an inquiring attitude to education, were aware of the dangers of rigid thinking, were able
to apply some of the principles of lifelong education to their
own specialist teaching areas, and hoped to develop an inquiring
attitude in their own pupils, thus preparing them for lifelong
education.

The second lifelong education-oriented course at Torrens
was a one-semester option available to all students in the third
year of their programme, in both 1974 and 1975. Evaluation was
carried out in two ways. The first involved filling out a questionnaire by the students, while the second consisted of a number
of questions about the course, to which the students responded
together as a group and also individually in interviews with
the instructor. A number of broad, general conclusions were
reached (some of these have already been mentioned in Chapters
5, 6 and 7). Students were said to have been initially reluc-
tant to accept innovations such as self-evaluation or the use
of media as alternatives to traditional practices. In a similar
way, they were ill at ease developing a self-growth plan, although they found it worthwhile afterwards. Alternative methods of presenting papers (such as through the use of film or
audiotapes) were found to have been greatly appreciated by
those students who found difficulty in verbal expression. Similarly, visits to real-life educational agencies outside the
schools were regarded as the most valuable parts of the course
according to the Torrens report, involving as they did contact
with practical affairs rather than theory. Students were said

to have become more involved with the community and with such practical agencies, with an increase in contacts with scouts, youth clubs, professional associations and similar bodies. Finally, they were reported to have enjoyed the sense of controlling their own learning experiences, to have developed more confidence in their ability to express themselves and to use information sources both inside and outside the college, and to have made considerable use of papers prepared by their peers, in a process of interlearning.

An anecdote illustrating some of these findings concerns a student who was an Italian immigrant and had been experiencing some difficulties because of his imperfect mastery of the English language. Some weeks after the commencement of the course he was observed leaving the library with a pile of seven books under his arm, whereas previously he had avoided textbooks because of the difficulty in reading them. Subsequently, he enthusiastically quoted facts and statistics from the relevant literature to support his point of view, both in class and during coffee-break discussions. A similar anecdote involves an instructor who met a former student who was a professional hairdresser. This student was now making a study of such phenomena as the chemistry of hair and soap in her after-work hours, and reported that she was achieving a whole new outlook on her trade.

At Szeged it was observed that opportunities for self-learning seemed to arouse positive motivation in students. In the case of instructors the experience of functioning as a co-learner made it possible for them to "get closer to the students", and as a result to make better plans and design more effective lectures. However, co-learning and the fostering of self-learning both require that instructors be well-prepared: as was pointed out in the Torrens report, learning situations of this kind make bluffing very difficult. Independent learning is also greatly facilitated by the provision by the institution of a supportive infra-structure which includes sophisticated tools such as audio-visual equipment.

It was also observed at Szeged that students were able to make a valuable contribution to practice teaching in the extended form adopted there. It was concluded that they participated willingly, and particularly enjoyed tutoring backward children or those with special learning problems. Even a short period of only six months spent in working with such children

or with youth clubs, study groups and other out-of-school activities was reported to be long enough to instil lasting interest in them. However, an important factor in the value of
the practice teaching activities to the students was found to
be the attitude of the supervising teachers. Where they took
the students' participation seriously, it was concluded that
students did well and gained much from the experience.

Data of the less formal, more comprehensive kind were obtained at Gandhi Shikshan Bhavan by asking both students and
also pupils in the schools in which the students did their
practice teaching to write down subjective impressions of various
aspects of the programme. Pupils were asked to comment on the
performance of the students as teachers during the 1974-75
academic year. The favourable comments mentioned in the college's report stressed the opportunities the students gave to
pupils to engage in independent thinking and learning, the appreciation by the pupils of co-learning experiences, the use
of alternative methods such as dramatization, and the linking
of the classroom to real-life problems. These comments led to
the conclusion that the students, in the role of teachers, had
promoted self-direction among the pupils, had understood the
role of the teacher in lifelong education, and had developed
skill in using various strategies of learning.

In order to obtain a qualitative appraisal of college life,
students in the 1974-75 batch were asked to write down any two
incidents and experiences from the year which struck them as
memorable. These experiences were then rated by judges as
falling into the cognitive domain (concerned with facts, knowledge and learning), or into the affective domain (concerned
with feelings, values and attitudes). About 70% of the anecdotes were rated as referring to the affective domain, suggesting that the greatest impact of the programme had been in the
area of opinions, values, attitudes and the like, rather than
in increased knowledge.

At H. J. College quantitative data already reported were
supplemented by asking students to write down their personal
reactions to the lifelong education curriculum. These subjective reactions were then read through, and a number selected
and reported verbatim. This procedure was adopted in order to
fill gaps that might have been left by the other techniques.
On the basis of these comments, it was concluded that the students had reacted positively to the concept of lifelong education. The aspects of the programme they found most useful were

internships, group-learning procedures such as tutorials, seminars and group discussions, and self-study activities such as library projects and library reading. In broader terms, it was concluded that the incorporation of the concept of lifelong education into the teaching programme had led to radical changes in the college, centering on self-study, formative evaluation and remedial teaching. This had in turn promoted self-learning as an institutional norm.

FINDINGS CONCERNING INSTRUCTORS

At H. J. College, the quantitative investigation was extended by administering a number of instruments not only to students, but to instructors as well. As a result, a number of findings were made about the effects of the lifelong education programme on the instructors.

The first of these findings concerned the identification of lifelong learners among the instructors. Both instructors and students were asked to name, in order of merit, five staff members whom they considered to be lifelong learners. When this was done, it was found that there was a high level of agreement in the persons rated by the two groups. When the ratings were compared by calculating the rank-order correlation between the two sets of data, the correlation coefficient was found to be .66, indicating that the two groups had achieved a substantial degree of agreement concerning the identities of lifelong learners among the instructors. This agreement was found to result from emphasis in both groups on adaptive and innovative behaviour, as well as on the importance of co-learner attitudes. In a similar way, when students and instructors were asked to rate students as lifelong learners, 24 names were mentioned by both instructors and students, the same student being given the highest ranking as a lifelong learner by both groups.

Instructors were also asked to rank the five subjects in the curriculum through which the concepts of lifelong education had most effectively been disseminated during the project. Students carried out the same task and there was a correlation of .93 between the rankings of the two groups. Highest ranked were sociology, philosophy and psychology, although all subjects were regarded as having helped in the dissemination of lifelong education concepts. When respondents were asked to indicate which subjects they thought had the highest potential for dis-

semination of lifelong education a similar ranking emerged,
with sociology, philosophy and psychology again receiving the
highest ratings.

The final scale completed by instructors was a so-called
"project evaluation form" containing 16 statements about the
place of lifelong education in the curriculum and its effects
on the college. Instructors were asked to indicate the degree
of their agreement or disagreement on a five-point scale rating
from "Strongly Agree" to "Strongly Disagree". Analysis of
these responses was reported to have indicated that the instructors did not think that a separate class on lifelong education is required as part of the lifelong education-oriented
curriculum. They were said to have agreed that the concept can
be introduced by its diffusion through the existing curriculum.
It was also reported that they saw lifelong education as mainly
an attitude that is practised, not as a set of facts that are
known.

According to the H. J. College report, the instructors
agreed that lifelong education had satisfactorily been diffused
through the existing syllabus, that the students had shown
lifelong education attitudes in tutorials, seminars and practice
teaching, and that self-learning had been promoted as a result
of the project. They were also reported to have agreed that
the introduction of the concept of lifelong education had improved teaching in the college. In the case of instructors
themselves, it was agreed that they had often displayed lifelong education-oriented behaviours, and that the introduction
of the concept into the college had promoted self-learning
among them. All in all, the project was said to have been positively rated by most instructors, and was felt to have been
successful in its goals.

At Gandhi Shikshan Bhavan too, part of the evaluation phase
of the project involved assessing the outcome of the programme
in terms of behaviour changes in the instructors. How such
changes could be defined and measured was a major problem, especially in view of the fact that a small group of only 13 persons was involved. Eventually it was decided to compare the
behaviour of the instructors before and after the lifelong education curriculum had been established and taught in the college. Conclusions were based on observation of changes in the
instructors' work in the college, on their attitudes as they
were revealed in their planning, by their responses to a spec-

ially developed proforma, and by analysis of their responses
to a request to describe two personal experiences they had
undergone during the year. In the first two cases, data were
collected by four senior staff members who maintained a day-to-
day diary of the instructors' work.

The results, as outlined in the Gandhi Shikshan Bhavan report, showed that instructors were actively involved in a process of professional inquiry, with the establishment of a
number of research projects concerning schools, teachers and
teaching. They were also involved in professional growth activities, for example through the reading of books and journals
about education. They had organized a number of in-service programmes for teachers in the Bombay area, and had organized activities based on the principles of lifelong education in the
course of these in-service projects. All 13 reported that they
had made use of self-study and group-study methods, and that
they entered into discussions with members of the community
brought into the college as guest speakers. Overall, it was
concluded that the instructors had experienced a change in
their attitudes to learning, and also in the approaches they
employed in fostering learning in their students.

SUMMARY

Findings outlined in the various reports are basically of
two kinds; those derived from relatively formal, objective
methods, and those mainly based on less formal, subjective impressions and conclusions. Although data yielded by objective
techniques yield more "scientific" findings, they can be supplemented in a valuable way by more subjective information,
thus giving a more comprehensive picture of the effects of the
lifelong education-oriented curriculum.

At Szeged, Gandhi Shikshan Bhavan and H. J. College, bat-
teries of instruments were developed and administered to various
groups including pupils, students, instructors and teachers, in
order to assess the effects of the curriculum on their knowledge,
attitudes and behaviour. In general it was reported that there
was already a substantial degree of endorsement of lifelong education principles among both students and teachers, and that
this increased during the course oriented towards lifelong education. In the attitudinal domain, increases were reported,
for example, in interest in self-improvement and continued

learning, in open-mindedness and flexibility, and in acceptance
of the importance of educability. Finally, in practice teaching, increases were reported in the use of self-study methods,
in group work, and in the use of methods such as projects,
self-evaluation, and so on. Actual teaching experience in
schools seemed, if anything, to reduce acceptance of lifelong
education, raising the question of whether schools may tend to
be resistant to change.

In the case of more qualitative findings, methods employed
included the use of a participant observer who kept notes, administered questionnaires, and prepared written reports. Observations of this kind, and also in the form of anecdotes,
diaries, group discussions and similar techniques, were interpreted as indicating that students accepted the lifelong education orientation as valid and worthwhile, that they began to
make greater use of self-learning, group-evaluation, planning,
and similar procedures, and that they became more inquiring
and aware of problems of inflexibility and rigidity. Experiences centering on involvement in the community were found
to be valuable and informative, and there were suggestions that
interest in such activities persisted beyond the life of the
courses. In the classroom, data gathered from pupils, and
from other sources such as supervising teachers' reports and
notes, suggested that students gave emphasis to self-direction
among pupils, employed a variety of learning strategies, and
adopted teachers' roles consistent with the principles of lifelong education.

A final set of findings concerned instructors. It was concluded that instructors developed different relationships with
students, that they adopted teaching and learning methods more
consistent with lifelong education and that, in their personal
and professional lives, they participated in a number of growth
activities such as conducting research projects, reading books
and journals, and disseminating the concepts of lifelong education to colleagues and friends.

Three broad and general findings were reported in the
various local studies. It was concluded that the effects of
the lifelong education orientation were most marked in the attitudinal domain, that students readily accepted the ideas of
lifelong education and succeeded in adopting methods and procedures consistent with its principles, and that the lifelong
education orientation seemed to transfer to activities outside
college lecture theatres. It was also concluded that the gen-

eral principles of lifelong education can be given practical
expression in a variety of settings under differing socio-political conditions. This is hopeful evidence for its practicability as a set of working guidelines.

CHAPTER 9

IMPLICATIONS FOR CHANGE

The present chapter attempts to synthesize the national studies. Its aim is to develop a number of generalizations concerning the problems, necessary preconditions, facilitating and inhibiting factors, difficulties, and similar issues in implementing lifelong education, and to outline some of the probable results and effects of adopting a lifelong education-oriented programme. The chapter is thus concerned with generalizations about the practical implications of the present project. In addition, it has a second purpose, arising from the fact that it became apparent during the study that much information about how to implement lifelong education is still lacking. For example some of the generalizations developed state that certain measures "should" be adopted, but details of how they could be put into practice are not clear. Consequently, the chapter also outlines some of the broad empirical questions which remain to be answered. Hopefully this may suggest areas of action not only for planners, administrators and innovators, but also for researchers.

It has not been possible to develop a single set of definitive statements concerning the ways in which all teacher training institutions could be re-organized in keeping with the principles of lifelong education. As has already been mentioned, the colleges faced different demands from the educational, social and political systems of which they were part. Structures, organizations and procedures differed from system to system, roles, rights, privileges and duties of staff and administrators varied widely, the kinds and extent of external supervision were different in differing countries, and many similar factors existed. As a result, it was impossible to develop a formula or blueprint to be followed by all institutions. In any case, narrow prescriptive statements were not contemplated when the pro-

ject was being developed. The intention was to suggest, stimulate, and offer examples and guidelines, not to make definitive rulings. In keeping with this goal, broad outlines only
are identified here, usually illustrated by references to the
colleges which took part in the project. It is not claimed
that all possible generalizations have been made. The national
reports have been treated as data and a set of findings based
on these data have been identified. These are thought to represent a useful treatment of the material, although they undoubtedly reflect the judgment of the authors, and other approaches certainly exist.

INSTITUTIONAL IMPLICATIONS OF THE STUDY

The role of lifelong education in guiding change

Lifelong education has been criticized because it does not
contain any fundamentally new ideas. It is true that most of
its main arguments have been put forward before, even in writings going back to antiquity. It has also been criticized by
some writers because it is so broad and general that it encompasses all educational practices likely to be widely accepted
as worthwhile. However, as Cropley (1977) has pointed out,
there is novelty and value in bringing together a scattered set
of reform-oriented ideas. Identifying, organizing and label-
ling these ideas, whether they are novel or not, and linking
them to felt needs in contemporary life provides a rationale
for the development of innovative educational practices in a
systematic and coherent, rather than piecemeal way. Lifelong
education thus acts as a unifying theme, ideal, or framework
for reform, which focuses and organizes efforts aimed at educational change in an inter-connected and comprehensive way. In
this respect, despite the disadvantages from the point of view
of experimental methodology, the fact that the concept is not
rigidly formalized and is at the same time comprehensive may be
an advantage from the point of view of practical innovators.
The broad framework makes it possible for concrete expression
of the principle to be worked out in local terms, and in ways
consistent with the particular socio-political system involved.
For educational principles which claim to have world-wide application, this may be essential.

The inevitability of institutional change

For purposes of description and analysis, the adoption of

lifelong education in a teachers college was presented in earlier chapters as having three conceptually separate aspects.
These involved dissemination of information about lifelong education, the modification of teaching practice in ways consistent with its principles, and finally the re-organization of
the institutions themselves, so that they functioned as practical examples of lifelong education. The experience of actually
implementing the project made it plain that this division was
conceptually useful, but that it did not work out in practice.
Even relatively minor changes in content were, in all cases,
accompanied by some degree of institutional change, for example
in the organization of classes, the nature of evaluation procedures, or in staff-student relations. Institutional factors
thus assumed considerable importance in evaluating the effects
of adoption of lifelong education.

The structure of changes

The institutional changes in the various colleges can be
analyzed in terms of structural features, such as the magnitude
of the changes, their duration, and similar features. This is
done in the present section.

Large- versus small-scale change. One of the major ways
in which projects differed was the role of the changes introduced: in some colleges the researchers succeeded in introducing
very extensive changes involving the entire organization of the
college (e.g., Gandhi Shikshan Bhavan, H.J. College), whereas
in others the change was limited in scope (e.g., Trier, Singapore). It seems that a conscious decision is needed concerning
whether any changes will be large- or small-scale. Where
changes are to be small in scale the most workable approach
may well involve introduction of a core course on an elective
basis. If larger-scale changes are possible, they may be introduced in the form of a compulsory core course, followed by
re-organization of the foundations of education courses as the
next possible step, and then re-orientation of courses in the
theory of teaching. Only in the final step, where there is
very large-scale change, comes conscious and deliberate adoption of lifelong education as a principle for guiding the organization of the whole college. Nonetheless, although implementation of a core course may be the most convenient way of
introducing lifelong education, there are some doubts concerning
the real necessity of such a course, as will be discussed more

fully in the section after the next.

Duration of change. A second generalization concerns what may be called the "duration" of the changes. Lifelong education material could, for example, be introduced in the form of a short, intensive course which stood alone, as was done at Trier. It could also involve an extended programme running through a semester (Singapore) or a full year (Torrens), but again standing relatively alone. On the other hand, a short introduction to the concepts of lifelong education may be employed, but inter-related to other lifelong education activities, as was done at Szeged and H.J. College. Finally, in the right circumstances, it was also shown that an extended programme continuing throughout the year and closely inter-linked with other activities of the college was practicable (e.g., Gandhi Shikshan Bhavan).

Need for a special course. The findings in the various colleges suggest that, at least where a large-scale change is achieved, as was the case at Gandhi Shikshan Bhavan and H.J. College, a special core course is not necessary. In such circumstances it seems to be possible to achieve the desired goals by infusing the existing curriculum with ideas and practices emanating from the principles of lifelong education, even when there is a high degree of outside control over the content of courses. Where the changes in curriculum are small-scale as was the case at Singapore, a core course may achieve only limited effects. Thus its necessity is again open to question. One reason for this is that where a course is introduced on an elective basis and taught to a handful of students, instructors may simply find themselves preaching to the already converted because of restriction of enrolment to students who already have a commitment to lifelong education (whether consciously or not). Another reason is that a brief exposure to the principles of lifelong education, or an exposure embedded in a larger context not oriented toward lifelong education or possibly even antagonistic to it, may be insufficient to achieve substantial results.

Time factor. In all the colleges involved in the project, a substantial period of time was spent in preparation for the study. This period was required for planning, designing programmes, developing measuring instruments, consulting with colleagues in other departments and institutions, and similar activities. On the basis of the experience of the present group of institutions, it seems that a period of about six months is

needed for this planning and co-ordinating phase. The time-
span of the project has a second aspect too. At the time at
which the national reports were being prepared, most of the
colleges had been actively pursuing lifelong education goals
for only about one year, or at most a little longer. It seems
possible that this period is too short to assess the effects of
the project on the colleges. It is probably too brief for the
attempted changes in institutional functioning to "take hold"
and to begin to have a major influence on the pattern of teacher training in a college. Thus, a longer research period is
called for in evaluation of the project's institutional effects,
including follow-up studies in which students could be contacted
once they had left the colleges, in order to ascertain the extent to which any changes of knowledge, attitudes or behaviours
achieved at the colleges persisted in schools.

Implications for costs. None of the participating colleges carried out cost analyses, and no cost/benefit studies
were done. Nonetheless, some implications for the cost of implementing lifelong education in a college can be obtained from
the various projects. In the main, it seems that large expen-
ditures were not involved. One possible reason for this was
that many learning resources were generated by students themselves. Many other necessary resources were readily available
in the community in the form of newspapers, knowledgeable people, and many others. Resourcefulness along with increased use
of facilities already existing in the community apparently had
favourable consequences as far as costs were concerned. Another
cost advantage of lifelong education is that no large initial
outlay of money, for example for physical plant, is necessary.
It is true that increased cost may be encountered for things
like making the basic literature available, developing supportive systems such as AV/TV facilities, upgrading libraries to
the point at which they can support self-learning, and similar
purposes. However, such changes can be introduced in ways compatible with an institution's financial resources and with
those of the society in which it is located. Furthermore, the
potential cost increases outlined, such as improving libraries,
may be of a kind that are highly acceptable in many societies,
so that the funds may be deemed to have been well spent. All
in all, it seems that costs can be kept to a point at which
they are within the capacity of an institution with the necessary will, especially where ingenuity and personal commitment
are high.

Relations with other institutions. An important question

for teacher-training institutions is the role they are to play
in the broader network of educative agencies in society. The
present project stressed the links between teachers' colleges
and institutions in everyday life such as places of work, trade
unions, community centres and similar agencies. Practices
adopted in the various participating institutions have suggested some ways in which these links can be effected, for example
through visits, research projects, the use of personnel from
other institutions as instructors in the colleges, and through
in-service training both of professional teachers and of other
teachers.

Relations with schools would be expected to change too.
For example, achieving lifelong education goals in the schools
cannot be managed by teacher-training institutions alone. The
involvement of school personnel, key administrators and supervisors, planners, and even politicians, is necessary. One way
in which the colleges could possibly forge closer ties with the
schools, and at the same time disseminate the ideas of lifelong
education, would be through the provision of in-service training programmes. These programmes would make it possible to introduce practising teachers to the principles of lifelong education. They could also foster the development of positive, supportive attitudes in teachers, administrators, supervisors and
planners.

Preparatory steps. Adoption of lifelong education in a
teacher training institution requires endorsement by instructors. This necessitates understanding of what it implies and
acceptance of its principles. Consequently, a period of preparation is necessary. In most of the participating colleges
this was achieved through the collection and distribution of
relevant materials and through meetings and discussions, in
which a clearer understanding was obtained of the basic ideas
implied by lifelong education and of the implications of its
adoption for teaching and learning strategies, college organization, instructors' workloads, and similar factors. At H.J.
College this involved the establishment of a "Think Tank" which
met regularly and tried both to crystallize the ideas of lifelong education and also, largely through the work of a series
of sub-committees, to work out the operational details of the
project as it was to be carried out in the college. In all of
the colleges the preparatory steps included the collection of
materials which clarified the basic principles of lifelong education and gave examples of methods and procedures consistent
with them. At Singapore these materials included newspaper

cuttings giving examples of lifelong learning in real life, so
that it is apparent that the collection of materials need not
be conceptualized merely in terms of library acquisitions and
the like. Even materials such as those collected at Singapore
can, if they are lodged in some central place such as the college library, provide a basic stock of reference materials and
a valuable source of ideas.

Necessary pre-conditions

Certain features of the structure, organization and leadership of a college seem to be important in determining whether
or not lifelong education can successfully be implemented as an
organizing principle. Some understanding of these features is
needed for facilitating its adoption in teacher training, since
they appear to provide necessary pre-conditions for the adoption
of a lifelong education-oriented programme.

Autonomy. One important condition is freedom from external
pressure to conform to norms or standards prescribed from outside the institution. Examples include the imposition of a curriculum by an external agency, as was seen at Gandhi Shikshan
Bhavan and H.J. College, where the curriculum is set down by
Bombay University. Even here, however, expedients such as the
"lifelong education-supplemented curriculum" can be worked out.
While a certain degree of autonomy is needed, a problem also
arises when the level of independence reaches the point at which
there is little or no co-ordinated effort among instructors.
This is the problem of making changes on a scale large enough
for any significant or worthwhile effects to be achieved. As
has already been mentioned, in practice it was not feasible to
think of changes as isolated; they tended to interact with each
other and to support each other, with curricular changes necessitating changes in scheduling, evaluation, instructor-student
relations, and so on. As a result it seems to be very difficult for a small group of instructors working in isolation from
their colleagues to achieve change of a sufficient magnitude.
In this respect, the role of the head of the institution may be
a key one. Where the college's director or principal goes beyond merely tolerating the project, but lends it active support,
its prospects seem likely to be greatly enhanced.

Readiness for change. One major determinant of what could
be achieved was found to be the readiness of the college to accept change, and especially change along the lines suggested by

lifelong education. Where there is a state of readiness for
change, acceptance of lifelong education would be expected to
be rapid. However, where the need for change is not felt, or
where there is even commitment to principles at variance with
those of lifelong education, little success can be expected.
At Torrens, for example, a change in the curriculum for further
education students had already been planned, and the lifelong
education principles were closely related to the college's existing philosophy. Consequently, they were accepted willingly
by certain instructors and students because they provided a set
of guiding principles helpful in planning the necessary changes.
By contrast, at Singapore a new curriculum had only recently
been adopted, so that there was less readiness to make further
large-scale changes. The project was not actively opposed in
any of the colleges, but in some it was regarded as the exclu-
sive business of the small group of people directly involved.
In these settings, less sweeping changes were achieved, and the
effects of the programme were much more modest.

The role of the college's size. As the size of an institution increases, involvement of all or most of the instructors
becomes more difficult, particularly when they enjoy high levels of independence and autonomy. Thus, especially where the
college's leaders are not strongly involved, it seems unlikely
that substantial re-organizations of the institution's *modus
vivendi* will be achieved. This raises the possibility of changes
on a scale too small to have any substantial effect, and consequently suggests that small size may be a necessary or at least
helpful pre-condition, or conversely that large size may be an
obstacle. On the other hand, it is also possible that the negative consequences of large size can be overcome by expedients
such as focusing changes on a single year in a multi-year programme, including only part of the student body in the programme, or applying the principles of lifelong education to only
part of the college's curriculum, such as, say, practice teaching. Thus, institutional size appears to be a factor with implications for the adoption of lifelong education-oriented
changes, but one which can be coped with if treated in appropriate ways.

EFFECTS ON INSTRUCTORS

A second major aspect of the changes was concerned with
their effects on teaching personnel within the colleges. Clearly the instructors would play a key role in adoption of a life-

long education-oriented curriculum, so that specific considera-
tion of its implication for them is called for.

Instructors' workload

A commitment to lifelong education on the part of a teacher-training institution is very largely a matter of questions
such as the way in which teaching is organized, the kinds of
assignments instructors set, the style and purpose of evaluation, the relationships between instructors and students, and
similar matters. These do not necessarily involve increased
monetary expenditure, as has already been pointed out. However,
the question arises of whether or not a change in instructors'
workloads is implied. At Torrens, for example, it was reported
that, if anything, there was a reduction in workload, as the
nature of work shifted from formal lecturing to advising, leading, guiding and energizing. The Szeged report made the point
that more was expected of the instructors, in the sense not of
increased hours of work, but of increased flexibility of methods, familiarity with a wider range of learning modes, willingness to adopt different procedures, and so on. Only at Gandhi
Shikshan Bhavan and H.J. College was it reported that the actual workload of instructors increased. A possible generalization linking these apparently differing findings is that adoption of lifelong education in a teachers' college results in a
qualitative change in the workload of the instructors which may
or may not involve them in a corresponding *quantitative* change --
the kind of work definitely changes, but the amount of work may
or may not change. It should also be borne in mind that perception of workload is largely a subjective phenomenon, so that
reported changes in this area could, to some extent at least,
reflect changes in instructors' attitudes to their work.

Instructors' motivation

Even though two of the colleges reported an increase in
workload for their instructors, they did not report that the
people involved complained about this. On the contrary, the
increased workload was largely self-imposed, and was uncomplain-
ingly accepted. One possible reason for this is that acceptance
of the concept of lifelong education has a positive effect on
the motivation of instructors. Having accepted the role implied
for them by lifelong education, and having begun the process of
sweeping change in teaching methods, evaluation processes, and
so on, instructors seemed to experience strong positive motiva-

tion to foster independent learning in students, to co-ordinate learning activities to real life, and to implement the other aspects of lifelong education. This phenomenon of high levels of intrinsic motivation is also seen in students. The principle of lifelong education seems to capture their interest and to give a sense of purpose and meaning to their studies, with a resultant increase in motivation. Thus, one of the effects of adoption of lifelong education seems to be the development of a positive motivational climate affecting both instructors and students.

Need for insight

An important thing about the implementation of lifelong education in a teachers' college is that it is chiefly a matter of changes in teaching methods, evaluation procedures, relations between instructors and students, and so on. However, carrying out the necessary changes requires expenditure of time, effort and ingenuity on the part of instructors. The changes also have implications for the basic role, or even institutional identity, of instructors. As a result, a substantial level of commitment is required on their part, along with insight into the implications of lifelong education for their job.

EFFECTS OF LIFELONG EDUCATION ON STUDENTS

The major purpose of adopting lifelong education in teacher training is presumably to affect the students involved. Consequently, the question of how they responded to the changes made in the colleges participating in the present study is of considerable interest.

High level of pre-existing knowledge

Evaluation of the level of knowledge of lifelong concepts, for example at Szeged and Singapore, indicated that both practising teachers and college students already possessed a good deal of knowledge of the basic principles, even without special instruction in the area. Although this could be interpreted as indicating that the basic ideas of lifelong education have already been successfully disseminated among teachers and students, it is also possible that it simply indicates the ability of both groups to recognize desirable educational goals and principles when they see them. This interpretation is strengthened by the fact that many of the basic ideas dealt with in the context of lifelong education clearly involve desirable goals, regardless of whether or not the observer is interested in lifelong education or even knows anything about it. The tendency to react positively to such recognizably "good" principles would be reinforced by the desire of teachers to espouse desirable goals, and that of students to please their instructors. Attempts were made to deal with this problem, for example by embedding key statements in lists of material not directly related to lifelong education, as was done at Szeged. However, in general even those without special training in lifelong education scored well on knowledge-oriented tests.

Greater amenability of students

Where students who had neither received any special training in connection with lifelong education nor had any prior teaching experience were compared with experienced teachers, it was found, for example at Szeged and Gandhi Shikshan Bhavan, that the inexperienced people tended to obtain higher scores for knowledge about lifelong education and attitudes towards it than did those with teaching experience. This raises the question of the apparently more favourable orientation to lifelong education of people without teaching experience. It may indicate a stronger interest in innovation, democratization and the like in newcomers to the teaching profession than among those who have had experience "in the field". This in turn raises the question of whether factors in schools may, in some countries at least, discourage the acceptance of lifelong education attitudes, or for that matter, innovative practices in general. These inhibiting factors include structural features such as inertia in the school system, lack of support for innovation, and similar factors, and also process features such as the socialization of newcomers into a prevailing conservative mould, despite their initially innovative attitudes.

Central role of affective factors

The main effects of the lifelong education-oriented curriculum on the students seemed to be in the affective domain. Even where fairly specific behaviour changes were seen, such as increased use of self-directed learning, or adoption of different seating arrangements during practice teaching, the practices and methods seemed to interact with attitudinal and motivational factors, resulting in improved morale, greater interest, or

higher levels of enthusiasm. Similarly, students showed increased feelings of responsibility for themselves and keener
interest in fostering lifelong learning in their pupils. They
became aware of themselves as lifelong learners, and developed
attitudes likely to encourage continued professional development, personal updating, habits of inquiry and innovation, and
similar properties.

The avalanche effect. One encouraging observation was that
innovations in the direction of lifelong education seemed to
foster development of a more receptive climate. In this sense,
an avalanche effect was seen. For instance, inviting members
of the community to give talks in the colleges increased knowledge about the community and awareness of its relationship to
the colleges. This fostered greater interest in the social context of education, desire for more contacts, and so on. In the
same way, as students took more responsibility for their own
learning they became more capable of such responsibility and
sought it more, so that self-evaluation, self-directed learning
and similar activities seemed to develop a dynamism of their
own, which made them self-sustaining or even expanding in their
effects.

Build-up of motivation. The various activities such as
self-directed learning, and the broadening of the sources of
learning, built up in students a feeling that their learning
was under their own control and that it was closely linked to
their own needs. As a result, there was an increase in their
motivation, as well as an improvement in the skill with which
they made learning choices for themselves or carried out other
lifelong education-oriented activities. Similarly, with increasing experience they became more confident of their own
ability to make use of a wide variety of information sources,
and to express themselves when communicating their independent
findings to other people. They also began to seek more information from non-college sources and, as was shown with the anecdotes from Torrens about the immigrant and about the hairdresser, to apply learning to their real lives.

Acceptance of self-evaluation. At first students did not
really believe that self-evaluation was to be taken seriously.
As a result they were initially hesitant about using it and
doubtful of its value. At Torrens, for example, they were very
ill at ease over developing personal growth plans, although
they eventually found that the procedure was worthwhile, and
self-evaluation was increasingly accepted as a normal activity.

Again, as in the two previous paragraphs, an increase or build-up occurred.

Effects on morale. The idea of lifelong education was found to be readily acceptable to students. It "made sense" to them. It helped them to understand their role as teachers, and also helped them to get a new perspective on the pupils' position in the educational process. The idea of lifelong education made their own teachers college programmes seem relevant and practical, and gave them a different attitude to their own learning, which seemed to be related to their own real-life needs rather than a formal barrier to be endured and overcome. This phenomenon extended to social life and self-concept, too. Students developed a feeling of being different from people who did not think in lifelong education terms. There was thus a build-up in their morale, as a result of developing the sense that they were actively involved in a worthwhile process from which they could expect to gain considerable benefit.

Orientation to the external world. Participation in learning activities in the world outside the college seemed to last longer than was strictly required by the college programmes. Familiarity with the community as a source of learning turned students to the social, cultural and vocational worlds for learning experiences, so that there was increased heterogeneity of experience and a wider range of learning activities. The lifelong education programme helped to develop an orientation to the external world, and thus to break the isolation of the colleges from their communities.

IMPLICATIONS FOR PRACTICE TEACHING

One important aspect of the preparation of future teachers is the provision of practical experiences in which they practise the skills of teaching, get the feel of the classroom, experience the teacher's role, and learn to interact with people in the process of deliberate and systematic learning. These are, of course, the experiences of practice teaching. In the present project an attempt was made to infuse the practical activities with the principles of lifelong education, with a certain degree of success as has been reported already. At this point, some generalizations can be made.

Broader concept of practice teaching

Acceptance by students.   A broadened conceptualization of
practice teaching was adopted in several of the colleges. As a
result, students carried out their practice teaching activities
not merely in schools, but in a number of other settings, including clubs and youth groups, as well as holiday camps, slums
and similar locations. The participation of the students
in a much wider range of activities such as those just mentioned was found to be feasible. It was evaluated by students as
providing a valuable source of learning about the practical
business of teaching, in its broadest sense. They were enthu-
siastic, even inspired, by the opportunity of teaching and
learning in a much wider range of situations than those encompassed by traditional practice teaching.

Need for preparation.   However, the modifications made in
the conduct of practice teaching required a good deal of careful preliminary preparation, especially where the activities
concerned were conducted in schools but outside classrooms (for
example through participation in school clubs, tutoring of backward or bright children, and so on). In the case of experiences
in the classroom setting, planning of methods and specification
of goals was also required, in order to enhance the worthwhile-
ness of the practice teaching experiences. At several of the
colleges meetings were held with heads and/or staff members of
schools involved in practice teaching, in order to clarify the
goals of the project with them and enlist their aid and active
support. At Szeged, for example, classroom activities were analyzed and specified in lifelong education-oriented terms, and
check lists or structured observation schedules were distributed
in advance.

Integrated experiences.   Practice teaching may take the
form of relatively disjointed experiences, for example involving
a short period spent in contact with learners on a regular basis
such as, say, half a day a week. On the other hand, it may also involve a lengthy period such as several consecutive weeks,
in which students may take responsibility for the planning and
co-ordination of an on-going set of activities, observe the effects of their efforts, provide feedback to pupils and receive
it themselves, and so on. At the same time, supervisory personnel such as co-operating teachers may be incorporated into
the planning of practice teaching so that it becomes a joint
venture between instructors, students and practising teachers.
Experiences of this "integrated" kind were found to be more pos-

itively rated by students, and to lead to more positive change
in students' behaviour as teachers.

Effects of school factors

Both teaching practice and actual teaching are, of course,
primarily carried on in schools, despite the emphasis given
in earlier sections to the role of learning agencies outside
schools and to teaching activities outside the classroom, or
even outside schools altogether. Thus, the school itself is an
important element in the implementation of lifelong education.
For this reason, it is necessary to consider the role of the
climate of opinion in schools, the willingness of schools and
teachers to accept change, and similar factors, when evaluating
projects aimed at fostering the acceptance of lifelong education as a principle for the organization of education.

Inertia in the system. Especially at Szeged and Gandhi
Shikshan Bhavan, it was found that teaching experience seemed
to result in reduced willingness to accept the ideas of lifelong education. Experience in schools apparently militates
against acceptance of lifelong education or, quite possibly,
against acceptance of innovation in general. This means that
the principles of lifelong education may be very difficult to
implement through an approach based primarily on changes in
teachers college curricula. Initially as pupils, later during
practice teaching, and eventually as qualified teachers, students such as those involved in the present project may spend
much of their time in learning environments little affected by
lifelong education, at least antipathetic but possibly even
resistant to it. In all probability this does not result from
active hostility to change, but from the problem of sheer inertia in the complex system represented by schools and the socio-political forces whose action they reflect. Support systems, promotion procedures, methods of curriculum development,
and similar factors, may not be geared to fostering change but,
if anything, to impeding or even resisting it. A simple example may be seen in the effects of changing the seating arrangements in a classroom, for instance to encourage group work. Moving the furniture may run contrary to established traditions for
the conduct of classes in a school (other teachers, for example
may want to return the desks to their original positions, and no
mechanisms may exist for quickly moving them around), while established work patterns for janitorial staff may not include
sweeping around desks arranged in some unusual configuration.

Patterns of reinforcement in schools. Once they have left the teachers college, students are exposed to the socializing influences of their peers in the schools (i.e., to the expectations and sanctions of other teachers). As a result, they come under strong pressure to conform to the norms of the school, and are rewarded or punished according to how thoroughly they succeed in doing so. These pressures may be expected to exert a more powerful influence than the earlier exhortations of their instructors in the teachers college which they have now left. Furthermore, the data of the various studies have suggested that, in some settings at least, the principles of lifelong education were not widely accepted by practising teachers. Thus, although students may have been exposed to practices and procedures arising from lifelong education during their college training, these kinds of behaviours may not be encouraged in the school setting, and may therefore be difficult to maintain and may soon disappear. This point reinforces the idea mentioned earlier that reform of teacher training along the lines of lifelong education may not be possible unless it is accompanied by changes in schools.

Role of key personnel. Although peers (i.e., other teachers) clearly exert an important influence on young teachers and on each other, there is a second major group of people in the school setting whose influence is of considerable importance. This group includes supervisors, such as senior teachers, leaders at the school level such as school directors or principals, other supervisory personnel such as inspectors of schools (where they exist), and administrators at the level of local authorities, school boards, state departments of education, and the like. Where these people communicate to teachers expectations which are highly inconsistent with those of lifelong education, demonstrate such negative behaviours in their own practices, reward procedures and methods which are oriented away from the goals of lifelong education, and provide structures which make adoption of lifelong education difficult, the practices of classroom teachers must be expected to follow suit. On the other hand, where they give concrete and moral support, lifelong education-oriented practices will persist. Thus, an important factor in the emergence of lifelong education as a working principle in real-life teaching, rather than as an ideal bandied about in teachers colleges but ignored in practice, will be the fostering of lifelong education orientations in key educational personnel. This point of view emphasizes once again the importance of consultation and joint planning between teachers colleges and other agencies of the educational system. It

also suggests that expedients like in-service training with a
lifelong education orientation would be an important function
of teachers colleges attempting to foster acceptance of lifelong education in schools.

Effects on pupils. Presumably, the ultimate purpose of
adopting lifelong education would be to affect the knowledge,
skills, attitudes, habits and values of pupils, although teacher training in the context of lifelong education is also seen
as serving the students, for example by fostering in them habits of lifelong learning. As a result, one major way of inves-
tigating the effects and the value of a lifelong education-oriented programme of teacher training would be by examining its
effects on pupils. To some extent this was done, at least at
Szeged, Gandhi Shikshan Bhavan and H.J. College. Especially at
the latter two colleges, systematic data were collected concerning the behaviour of the students during practice teaching,
with particular reference to the kinds of activities they encouraged in pupils.

In addition, in the two Indian colleges pupils actually
rated students in various ways, and also indicated their reaction to the lifelong education practices. Comments made to a
free-response instrument filled out by pupils at Gandhi Shikshan
Bhavan (see p. 212 of the original report) included statements
such as "The teacher did not act as a compelling authority",
"We arrived at our own conclusions", "We planned and prepared
work together, and so we came to know each other better", indicating that students had succeeded at least to some extent in
adopting the teacher's role outlined in Chapter 2. In addition,
comments went on to add statements like "Why should teachers in
schools tell us everything? Give us a chance to discuss and
talk among ourselves; we can do so much on our own", and "After
knowing people's problems...we felt like doing something for
them", which suggest that pupils had, in at least some cases,
begun to endorse the idea of self-directed learning, and to see
the relationship between schooling and problems of real life.
Thus, there are some grounds for concluding that short-term effects on pupils can be achieved, even in a programme of only
one year's duration. However, much more extensive studies in
this area are called for, including both follow-up studies of
the behaviour of the students once they become practising teachers, and also longer-term studies of both students and pupils.

IMPLICATIONS FOR FURTHER WORK

Improved research methodology

All six institutions involved in the present project made reference to the question of developing an appropriate methodology and suitable evaluative procedures. However, not all succeeded in putting into practice objective, rigorous programmes when judged from the point of view of research methodology, rather than from that of modifying curriculum. Nonetheless, a number of valuable and even ingenious techniques were suggested or implemented, including the use of a participant observer, check lists and rating scales, structured interviews, free-response instruments which could be scored on the basis of predetermined criteria, diaries, and several more.

However, a number of problems arose. One was that many of the data were obtained in situations in which the people being rated were at least partially, if not fully, aware of the purpose of the assessment. As a result, data could be biased by respondents' desire to display their belief that innovation is a good thing, that humanistic stances are more laudable, and similar beliefs, as well as by the quite understandable wish to give answers which would be pleasing to instructors who had revealed their point of view in lectures and discussions. In addition, where data were based on ratings by instructors who were aware of the purpose of the ratings and of the hoped-for results, the problem of wishful thinking on the part of judges arises. Finally, there is the problem that the devices employed for assessing certain aspects of behaviour may themselves change the frequency of appearance or quality of the behaviours in question.

These kinds of problem were not ignored by the various researchers, and a number of expedients were adopted in order to avoid or reduce their effects. Nonetheless, it is clear that there is need for refinement of research methods in studies of the present kind, as well as for development of measurement techniques that permit unbiased evaluation of outcomes. In this latter respect, unobtrusive measures of behaviour somewhat resembling the participant-observer approach adopted at Torrens seem to offer promise. Also needed are more objective methodologies, the development of instruments whose purposes are not so obvious and which are less likely to be affected by desirability effects, use of judges who are naive with regard to the identity of subjects (i.e., whether they are

members of control or experimental groups), scoring of pre- and
post-test instruments not only by "blind" judges, but also at
the same point in time, with the additional refinement that rat-
ers are unaware whether it is pre- or post-test material they
are assessing, and many more such improvements of methodology
and procedure. On the other hand, it is not clear whether many
institutions would be willing to participate in studies adopting a rigorous methodology, and there certainly seems to be a
danger that the research demands would be irreconcilable with
the educational demands. Nevertheless, effecting this recon-
ciliation is probably a crucial further task in the area of
methodology.

Long-term studies

Evaluation of any curricular changes, whether adopted in
the name of lifelong education or not, can be only imperfectly
achieved through short-term studies such as those reported here.
The lifelong education-oriented curriculum was partly aimed at
achieving changes which would be seen not only in school settings, but out of school too, and not only during the period of
teacher training, but in the future, since it was hoped that
the students would become lifelong learners. This means that
evidence of the success or failure of some of the goals of the
programme would not exist until at least several years had
passed. In a similar way, hoped-for effects on pupils would
not be fully observable after only a few weeks, or even months,
of being taught in accordance with the principles of lifelong
education, because some of the effects of lifelong education-
oriented teaching would involve peoples' behaviours, attitudes
and values when they became adults.

What this means is that the effects of a lifelong education-oriented curriculum cannot adequately be evaluated by
short-term studies. Positive results after perhaps one year
cannot demonstrate that lifelong habits have resulted from exposure to a lifelong education-oriented curriculum, either in
students or in pupils. For this reason, the crucial experiment
to test the effects of instruction in accordance with the principles of lifelong education would have to be a long-term study,
covering a good proportion of the lifespan of the people concerned. Such an experiment is, of course, beyond the capacity
of most institutions. It would present many practical difficulties such as cost, attrition (loss of subjects through
death, refusal to co-operate, disappearance without for-

warding address, and similar causes), and unwillingness of researchers to wait a lifetime for results. To call for a study of this magnitude is thus probably unrealistic. However, the present findings may be interpreted as sufficiently suggestive to justify further research not only employing improved research techniques, as was urged in the previous section, but also of longer-term design.

Analysis of college features

It was found that various aspects of a particular college, such as methods, philosophy or perception of the need for change, affected the extent to which changes in line with the principles of lifelong education could be implemented. Thus, it was concluded that the *modus operandi* of a teachers college is one of the factors determining whether or not lifelong education can be established there. However, it does not seem likely that, in practice there are some conditions which are entirely favourable to lifelong education, others which are entirely unfavourable. It is more probable that there are certain aspects of institutions which make the adoption of lifelong education easier, others which make it more difficult, that there are some preconditions which are helpful others which are not, that there are some aspects of curriculum in which lifelong education is harder to implement, others in which it is less difficult, and so on.

Some tentative suggestions in this area have been made in earlier sections of the present chapter. However, there is now need for a research programme which concentrates on identifying the supportive features in a college, determining which are crucial and which merely helpful, identifying inhibiting aspects and determining which if any are fatal to lifelong education, and similar topics. At the same time, there is also need for research showing which aspects of lifelong education are crucial for achieving worthwhile change in a teachers college, which are most acceptable to colleges, which are unattainable, and similar findings, bearing in mind the probability that the answers will differ from society to society.

Analysis of the role of schools

It has already been stressed in other sections that schools may not provide an environment favourable to the survival of lifelong education skills, attitudes and values once students

have completed their college training. However, it seems
unlikely that all aspects of schools are inimical to lifelong education. Thus, one research task is to identify those
aspects of school as we currently know it which most inhibit or
block the adoption of lifelong education. Perhaps more impor-
tantly, there is also need to identify those aspects which are
most favourable to its implementation. Conversely, it seems
probable that some of the complex of principles, goals and ideals referred to as "lifelong education" will have greater survival power than others in the school setting, for example because they more closely resemble currently-accepted notions,
are less threatening to teachers or administrators, or because
they appear to meet felt needs for change. This suggests that
there is likely to be an interaction between school curriculum
on the one hand, and aspects of lifelong education on the
other. Those aspects of lifelong education which are most acceptable, and which affect the most amenable elements of school
would have the highest likelihood of acceptance. Within each
society, identification of the most acceptable aspects of lifelong education and of the most supportive aspects of existing
school curriculum would thus be a research task of considerable
value.

Determination of basic qualifications

The role of the teacher within a lifelong education orientation and the kinds of things teachers should be skilled at
have been discussed in earlier chapters. Many of the findings
reported earlier also concerned changes in learning skills or
in attitudes and values. However, it is not clear whether
these various cognitive and affective properties are all equal-
ly important. For example, more knowledge is needed concerning
what constitutes the crucial basic skills that teachers should
possess if lifelong education is to be implemented. It is also
unclear whether everybody with an interest in teaching as a
career (whether because of a genuine sense of vocation or for
other reasons) can develop the necessary skills and values,
once they have been defined. Thus, the question of selection
criteria arises. Many highly-developed countries are currently
experiencing surpluses of trained teachers, so that they have
the opportunity of selecting among applicants for entry to the
teaching profession. Alternatively, procedures could be developed
for helping teacher-trainees evaluate their own suitability for
the profession and make appropriate decisions about whether to
continue in it.

A number of researchable questions may therefore be asked. What are the core skills that lifelong education teachers should possess? What are the indispensable attitudes and values they require? Who is capable of developing these cognitive and affective properties? Could appropriate selection procedures be designed? What kinds of instruments would be needed for self-assessment of either a summative or formative kind in this area? What kinds of follow-up or in-service experiences would foster the necessary skills and attitudes? Again, as has been mentioned repeatedly, answers may differ from society to society, while the possibility must be faced that answers to some of the questions are impossible, for example because the matter of precisely what constitutes a "good" teacher has so far defied unequivocal research-based answers.

How to maintain skills?

Students commencing their careers as practising teachers will usually work in settings not consciously oriented towards lifelong education, and quite possibly resistant or even hostile to it. The problem of socialization of young teachers into the ways of the majority, and their tendency to adopt the norms of established colleagues, supervisors and administrators, has already been discussed. The system may not provide any support for lifelong education-oriented values and skills, even if it is not actually hostile to them, and there is thus a great danger that they will quickly disappear once the teachers college has been left behind. In this climate, an important research question is that of how to support, maintain and even foster the lifelong education orientation among novice teachers. It is also important to know how to initiate interest among experienced teachers. In the latter case, in-service training suggests itself, and the question then arises of how to provide such training, how to motivate teachers to take it, how to reward them for having done so, and so on. At the same time, there is need for investigation of the kinds of ongoing, day-to-day support services which are called for. They could take the form of visiting or peripatetic teachers, "trouble-shooter" services, in-school seminars or staff colloquia, continuous self- and group-assessment, and other such expedients.

FUTURE PROSPECTS

It seems fitting to end the book with a brief comment on what the future may bring, as far as the adoption of lifelong

education is concerned. Innovations in educational thought and
practice seem to follow a broadly similar developmental path,
and lifelong education will probably move in the same way. The
first step after the initial theoretical developments is the
popularization and widespread dissemination of the ideas underlying the innovation, whatever it involves. At this stage, for
example, it appears in the lectures of progressive teachers-col-
lege instructors as an important new idea. The second step is
the adoption of the idea in the statements of administrators,
leaders of teachers organizations, policy makers and similar
people, and the emergence of attempts by progressive teachers
to implement it at the classroom level. The third stage is
that of re-appraisal, when critical writers expose some of the
weaknesses of the idea. Finally, remnants of the innovation
survive in the educational system, largely in the form of altered goals, modified methods, changed attitudes, and so on.
The system remains more or less intact, having incorporated the
main ideas of the innovation in forms compatible with its main
structure as it existed before, through the process of "dynamic
conservatism" (Duke, 1976, p. 87).

Something similar is probably in store for lifelong education. The concept has now passed through the first stage, and
is well into the second, with the third also under way. The
first flush of enthusiasm is fading, and the time has arrived
for the down-to-earth practical thinking. As Duke has said, it
now seems unlikely that the ideas of lifelong education will
reform the educational world either overnight, or by taking it
by storm. In countries with well-established educational traditions and solidly-entrenched educational establishments, proponents of lifelong education will probably have to be content
to make their gains by fostering and supporting changes of direction and emphasis in line with the principles of lifelong education, rather than by fiat or revolution. On the other hand,
where a felt need exists for radical transformation of educational practices, such as is the case in many less-developed
nations, it seems possible that lifelong education could be
adopted on a large-scale basis. Thus, its effects may conceiv-
ably be more profound in some of these countries than in more
highly-developed ones.

Although referring to Australia, Duke (1976) has discerned
a number of trends in educational thinking which probably also
apply to many other countries, and which suggest that many of
the principles of lifelong education are finding acceptance.
Among these trends are the increasing emergence of values em-

phasizing pluralism, diversity, democratization and improved quality of life, de-emphasis of schools as the sole source of education, de-bureaucratization of schooling with associated democratization and diversification, recognition of work and life experiences as important job credentials, and the integration of school experiences with work and the everyday life of the community. However, he sees these changes as gaining impetus over the next 25 years. Thus, the prospects for lifelong education may be favourable, but it will probably be necessary for its proponents to be patient.

APPENDIX A

FULL POSTAL ADDRESSES OF
PARTICIPATING INSTITUTIONS

Australia (Torrens)

Torrens College of Advanced Education
Holbrooks Road
Underdale, South Australia 5032

Australia

Federal Republic of Germany (Trier)

Fachbereich I - Pädagogik
Universität Trier
Postfach 3825
5500 Trier

Federal Republic of Germany

Hungary (Szeged)

József Attila Tudományegyetem
Pedagógiai Tanszék
Szeged
Táncsics Mihály u. 2

Hungary

India (Gandhi Shikshan Bhavan and H.J. College)

Gandhi Shikshan Bhavan
Juhu, Bombay 400 054

India

Hansraj Jivandas College of Education
Samshodan Sadan
South Avenue
Khar, Bombay 52 (AS)

India

Singapore

Institute of Education
Paterson Road
Singapore 9

Republic of Singapore

APPENDIX B

KEY PARTICIPANTS IN EACH INSTITUTION

The people whose names are listed here are those who made substantial contributions to the local phases of the project, for example through their involvement in planning, executing and evaluating the procedures adopted. Their names are listed in alphabetical order, with no seniority or priority implied. The UIE is indebted to these people for their assistance.

Australia (Torrens)

G.G.R. Dick
L. Hayes
G.A. Ramsey
A.A. Sandery
B. Tyler

Federal Republic of Germany (Trier)

M. Gebauer
A. Gilles
U. Holefleisch
H. Larson
J. Losch
P. Losch
H. Merkens
M. Nießen
H. Seiler
U. Werthmanns
R. Zimmermann

Hungary (Szeged)

Ảgoston György
Kẽkes-Szabõ Mihály
Nagy Istvánné
Nagy József
Török László

India

Gandhi Shikshan Bhavan

S. Ankolvi
K. Chandana
M. Chawla
V. Dave
L. Gharpure
A. Kalla
M. Katdare
S. Khanolkar
M. Krishnaraj
V. Melina
S.R. Pandya
B. Patel
L. Patel
V. Patel
D.N. Rai
M. Shekhar
S. Shukla
K. Thakar

H.J. College

C. Abros
J.R. Bhamaria
K.K. Bhatt
S.S. Boyce
W.L. Dhopatkar
C.G. D'lima
N.V. Gayatonde
S.N. Gayatonde
N.A. Karnataki
N.S. Marker
L.V. Nayampalla
D.N. Samant
V.B. Sampat
N.N. Shukla

Singapore

Fathol Rahman
Ho Wah Kam
Seng Seok Hoon
Tan Wee Kiat
R. Wong

APPENDIX C

TABLES OF CONTENTS OF THE FINAL LOCAL REPORTS

Australia (Torrens)

DEVELOPING A TEACHER EDUCATION CURRICULUM
USING THE CONCEPTS OF LIFELONG EDUCATION

Appendices

SECTION II - History and Development of the New
Course for Further Education Students

Appendices

Federal Republic of Germany (Trier)

TEACHER TRAINING IN ACCORDANCE WITH THE PRINCIPLES
OF LIFELONG EDUCATION - INTERACTIONIST VARIANT

Hungary (Szeged)

TEACHER PREPARATION IN THE PERSPECTIVE
OF LIFELONG EDUCATION

Introduction (Part A)

Modification of Pedagogical Program According
to the Demands of Lifelong Education (Part B)

Realization of Principles of Lifelong Education
in Modernizing the Didactic Program (Part C)

Methodological Reforms in Pedagogical Training
(Part D)

Analytical Survey of Pedagogical Observations of
3rd Year Arts Students in Grammar Schools (Part E)

Experiences with Pedagogical Exercises of 3rd
Year Students (Part F)

Comparative Study on Attitudes of Teachers and
Would-Be Teachers Toward Lifelong Education (Part G)

India

Gandhi Shikshan Bhavan

CURRICULUM OF TEACHER PREPARATION FACILITATING
LIFELONG EDUCATION (Published as Volume 12, whole
Number 4 of *Quest in Education*)

H.J. College

DEVELOPMENT OF CURRICULUM FACILITATING TEACHER-
EDUCATION ON THE BASIS OF THE PRINCIPLES OF
LIFELONG EDUCATION

Singapore

TEACHER PREPARATION IN ACCORDANCE WITH THE
PRINCIPLES OF LIFELONG EDUCATION

REFERENCES

Agoston, G. La communauté en tant qu'éducateur. *Acta Universitatis Szegediensis de Attila Jôszef Nominatae Sectio Paedagogica et Psychologica*, 1975, 18, 5-15.

Anderson, D.S. The development of student teachers: A comparative study of professional socialization. In *New patterns of teacher education and tasks*. Paris: OECD, 1974.

Aujaleu, E. Medicine of the future. *World Health*, 1973 (April), 23-29.

Bär, S., and Slomma, R. *Initial and further training of teachers in the GDR*. Berlin: Ministry of Education of the GDR and UNESCO Commission of the GDR, 1973.

Batyshev, S.I. The revolution in science and technology and the problem of training skilled workers in the USSR. *Soviet Education*, 1972, 14, 7-29.

Bengtsson, J. Recurrent education and manpower training. *Adult Training*, 1975, 2, 7-9.

Coleman, J.S. How do the young become adults? *Review of Educational Research*, 1972, 42, 431-439.

Coles, E.K.T. Universities and adult education. *International Review of Education*, 1972, 18, 172-182.

Coombs, P.H. *New paths to learning*. New York: International Council for Educational Development, 1973.

Council of Europe, Notes of the Council of Europe on permanent education. *Convergence*, 1968, 1 (14), 50-53.

Cropley, A.J. Lifelong education: A panacea for all educational ills? *Australian Journal of Education*, 1974, 18, 1-15.

Cropley, A.J. Some psychological reflections on lifelong education. In R.H. Dave (Ed.), *Foundations of lifelong education*. Oxford: Pergamon, 1976.

Cropley, A.J. *Lifelong education: A psychological analysis*. Oxford: Pergamon, 1977.

Dauber, H., Fritsch, H., Liegle, L., Sachs, W., Scheilke, C.T., and Spiekermann, M. Lebenslanges Lernen -- lebenslängliche Schule? Analyse and Kritik des OECD-Berichts "Recurrent Education". *Zeitschrift für Pädagogik*, 1975, 21, 173-192.

Dave, R.H. Lifelong education and school curriculum. *UIE Monographs*, 1973 (Whole No. 1).

Dave, R.H. (Ed.), Reflections on lifelong education and the school. *UIE Monographs*, 1975 (Whole No. 3).

Dave, R.H. (Ed.), *Foundations of lifelong education*. Oxford: Pergamon, 1976.

DE'Ath, C. Anthropological and ecological foundations of lifelong education. In R.H. Dave (Ed.), *Foundations of lifelong education*. Oxford: Pergamon, 1976.

Delker, P.V. Governmental roles in lifelong education. *Journal of Research and Development in Education*, 1974, 7, 24-34.

Dubin, S.S. The psychology of lifelong learning. New developments in the professions. *International Review of Applied Psychology*, 1974, 23, 17-31.

Duke, C. Australian perspectives on lifelong education. *Australian Education Review*, 1976 (Whole No. 6).

Dumazedier, J. (with others), *The school and continuing education*. Paris: UNESCO, 1972.

Dumazedier, J., and de Gisors, H. Education permanente et auto-formation par le livre. *Education Permanente*, 1973, 20, 17-51.

Durkheim, E. *Sociologie de l'éducation*. Paris: Presses Universitaires de France, 1961.

Faure, E. (with others), *Learning to be: The world of education today and tomorrow*. Paris and London: UNESCO and Harrap, 1972.

Frese, H.H. Permanent education -- dream or nightmare? *Education and Culture*, 1972, 19, 9-13.

Hicter, M. Education for a changing world. *Prospects: Quarterly Review of Education*, 1972, 2, 298-312.

Hiemstra, R. Community adult education in lifelong learning. *Journal of Research and Development in Education*, 1974, 7, 34-43.

Horn, J.L., and Donaldson, G. On the myth of intellectual decline in adulthood. *American Psychologist*, 1976, 31, 701-719.

IBE, Final Report of the International Conference on Education, 35th Session, Geneva, August 27th - September 4th, 1975. Geneva: IBE, 1975.

Jacks, M.L. *Total education; a plea for synthesis*. London: Paul, Trench, Trubner, 1946.

James, Lord (with others), *Teacher education and training*. London: HMSO, 1972.

Janne, H. Theoretical foundations of lifelong education: A sociological perspective. In R.H. Dave (Ed.), *Foundations of lifelong education*. Oxford: Pergamon, 1976.

Kirpal, P.N. Historical studies and the foundations of lifelong education. In R.H. Dave (Ed.), *Foundations of lifelong education*. Oxford: Pergamon, 1976.

Knowles, M.S. Toward a model of lifelong education. In R.H. Dave (Ed.), Reflections on lifelong education and the school. *UIE Monograph*, 1975 (Whole No. 3).

Knowles, M.S. Non-traditional study -- Issues and resolutions. *Adult Leadership*, 1975, 23, 232-235.

Kupisiewicz, C. On some principles of modernizing the school system as a base for adult education. *Convergence*, 1972, 5 (3), 15-19.

Lengrand, P. *An introduction to lifelong education*. Paris:

UNESCO, 1970.

Lynch, J. Lifelong education and the preparation of educational personnel. *UIE Monographs*, 1977 (Whole No. 5).

McClusky, H. Y. The coming of age of lifelong learning. *Journal of Research and Development in Education*, 1974, 7, 97-106.

Ministry of Education, Sweden, Motives for recurrent education. *Convergence*, 1972, 5 (4), 54-62.

Rohwer, W.D. Prime time for education: Early childhood or adolescence? *Harvard Educational Review*, 1971, 41, 316-341.

Schaie, K.W. Translations in gerontology -- from lab to life. Intellectual functioning. *American Psychologist*, 1974, 29, 802-807.

Silva, A. Education for freedom. *Prospects: Quarterly Review of Education*, 1973, 3, 39-45.

Skager, R. *Lifelong education and evaluation practice*. Oxford: Pergamon, 1978 (in press).

Skager R., and Dave, R.H. *Curriculum evaluation for lifelong education*. Oxford: Pergamon, 1977.

Suchodolski, B. Out of school. *Prospects: Quarterly Review of Education*, 1972, 2, 142-154.

Suchodolski, B. Education, between being and having. *Prospects: Quarterly Review of Education*, 1976, 6, 163-180.

Suchodolski, B. Lifelong education -- some philosophical aspects. In R.H. Dave (Ed.), *Foundations of lifelong education*. Oxford: Pergamon, 1976.

Tough, A. *The adult's learning projects*. Toronto: OISE, 1971.

Ulmer, C. Remediation as a lifelong learning activity. *Journal of Research and Development in Education*. 1974, 7, 45-55.

Unesco, Working paper for UNESCO Symposium on the Contribution of Persons other than Teachers to Educational Activities in the Perspective of Lifelong Education, Paris, 13-17 September 1976.

Wlodarski, Z. Biopsychological problems of lifelong education. In Maciaszek, M., Wolczyk, J., and Wroczyński, R. (Eds.), *School and lifelong education.* Warsaw: Polish Scientific Publishers, 1976.

Wolczyk, J. The role, goals and functions of teachers in the perspectives of lifelong education. In Maciaszek, M., Wolczyk, J. and Wroczyński, R. (Eds.), *School and lifelong education.* Warsaw: Polish Scientific Publishers, 1976.

Wroczyński, R. Lifelong education and scientific-technological revolution. *Paideia*, 1973, 3, 149-156.

SELECTED BIBLIOGRAPHY

Prepared with the assistance of Ursula Giere

The lists of reference materials which follow are restricted to publications in the English language. They are also restricted to works which have appeared in book form and which, in almost all cases, have been published by commercial publishers. The exceptions to this rule are mainly reports issued by learned societies, international agencies, and various national bodies. Even here, however, the list has been restricted to materials which are likely to be accessible to interested readers. The result is that many important working papers, internal reports, and other documents of this kind have been omitted. Finally, the sources listed are restricted to works appearing since 1970, with the exception of a few "classics" in their areas.

The books cover three broad areas: writings on lifelong education itself, texts on teacher training (with particular reference to aspects such as change, innovation and linking of learning with work), and finally, curriculum development and innovation. Each of these three areas is the subject of a separate list. The purpose of the lists is to provide a starting point for planners, curriculum developers, administrators, teachers college staff, teachers and students who wish to pursue an area in greater detail. They are not exhaustive, by any means, and may have omitted major works in the various areas covered. However, they provide a useful set of background readings for educators wishing to go more deeply into the study of innovations in teacher training, especially within the context of lifelong education.

Lifelong Education

Ahmed, M. and Coombs, P.H. (Eds.), *Education for rural development. Case studies for planners.* New York: Praeger, 1975.

Asian Institute of Educational Planning and Administration,
Lifelong education. Report of the meeting of experts held at
New Delhi from 10th to 18th August, 1970. New Delhi: Asian
Institute of Educational Planning and Administration, 1970.

Bortner, R.W., Dubin, S.S., Hultsch, D.F. and Withall, J. *Adults
as learners.* Proceedings of a conference. Pennsylvania: The
Pennsylvania State University, 1974.

Brembeck, C.S. and Thompson, T.J. *New strategies for educational development. The cross-cultural search for nonformal alternatives.* Lexington, Mass.: Lexington Books, Heath, 1974
(3rd ed.).

Carnegie Commission on Higher Education, *Toward a learning society. Alternative channels to life, work, and service.* A
report and recommendations by the Carnegie Commission on Higher Education. New York: McGraw-Hill, 1973.

Commission on Non-traditional Study, *Diversity by design.* San
Francisco: Jossey-Bass, 1973.

Coombs, P.H. and Ahmed, M. *Attacking rural poverty. How non-
formal education can help.* A research report for the World
Bank. Prepared by the International Council for Educational
Development. Edited by Barbara Baird Israel. Baltimore:
Johns Hopkins University Press, 1974.

Coombs, P.H., Prosser, R.C., Ahmed, M. and Israel, B.B. (Eds.),
New paths to learning for rural children and youth. New York:
International Council for Educational Development, 1973.

Council of Europe, *Permanent education. The basis and essen-
tials.* Strasbourg: Council for Cultural Co-operation, Council
of Europe, 1973,

Council of Europe, *Permanent education.* A compendium of studies
commissioned by the Council for Cultural Co-operation. A contribution to the United Nations' International Education Year.
Strasbourg: Council of Europe, 1970.

Cropley, A.J. *Lifelong education: A psychological analysis.* Oxford: Pergamon Press, 1977.

Dave, R.H. (Ed.), *Foundations of lifelong education.* Oxford: Pergamon Press, 1976.

Evans, A.A. *Flexibility in working life. Opportunities for individual choice.* Paris: OECD, 1973.

Faure, E., Herrera, F., Kaddoura, A., Lopes, H., Petrovsky, A.V., Rahnema, M. and Ward, F.C. *Learning to be. The world of education today and tomorrow.* Paris: Unesco, 1972.

Hesburgh, T.M., Miller, P.A. and Wharton, C.E. *Patterns for lifelong learning.* San Francisco: Jossey-Bass, 1973.

Holt, J. *Instead of education. Ways to help people do things better.* New York: Dutton, 1976.

Houghton, V. and Richardson, K. *Recurrent education.* London: Ward Lock Educational and The Association for Recurrent Education, 1974.

Houle, C.O. *The design of education.* San Francisco: Jossey-Bass, 1972.

Husén, T. *The learning society.* London: Methuen, 1974.

Hutchins, R.M. *The learning society.* Harmondsworth: Penguin Books, 1970.

Illich, I. *Deschooling society.* New York: Harper and Row, 1970.

Jessup, F.W. (Ed.), *Lifelong learning. A symposium on continuing education.* Oxford: Pergamon Press, 1969.

Kidd, J.R. *How adults learn.* New York: Association Press, 1975 (2nd ed.).

Kidd, J.R. *The implications of continuous learning.* Toronto: Gage, 1966.

Knowles, M. *Self-directed learning.* New York: Association Press, 1975.

Lengrand, P. *An introduction to lifelong education.* London:

Croom Helm, 1975.

Lowe, J. *The education of adults: a world perspective.* Paris: Unesco Press and Toronto: Ontario Institute for Studies in Education, 1975.

Maciaszek, M., Wolczyk, J. and Wroczyński, R. (Eds.), *School and lifelong education.* Warsaw: Polish Scientific Publishers, 1976.

Malassis, L. *The rural world. Education and development.* London: Croom Helm, 1976.

Mann, J. *Learning to be. The education of human potential.* New York: Free Press, 1972.

Richmond, W. *Education and schooling.* London: Methuen, 1975.

Romero Brest, G.L. de, Pain, A. and Brusilowsky, S. *Lifelong education: an alternative strategy for educational planning.* Buenos Aires: Centro de Investigaciones en Ciencias de la Educación, 1972.

Schwartz, B. *Permanent education.* The Hague: Nijhoff, 1974.

Shukla, P.D. *Life-long education.* New Delhi: Orient Longman, 1971.

Stoikov, V. *The economics of recurrent education and training.* Geneva: International Labour Office, 1975.

Toffler, A. (Ed.), *Learning for tomorrow. The role of the future in education.* New York: Random House, 1974.

Unesco, *The school and continuing education. Four studies.* Paris: Unesco, 1972.

Teacher Training

Adams, E. (Ed.), *In-Service education and teachers' centres.* Oxford: Pergamon Press, 1975.

Bolam, R. *Teachers as innovators – The types of environment most likely to favour the active and effective participation of teachers in educational innovation.* Paris: Organization for Economic Co-operation and Development, 1974.

Cane, B. *In-service training*. A study of teachers' views and preferences. Slough: National Foundation for Educational Research in England and Wales, 1969.

Commonwealth Secretariat, *Teacher education in a changing society*. Commonwealth Conference on Teacher Education held in Nairobi, Kenya, 26th April - 11th May 1973. London: Commonwealth Secretariat, 1974.

Dodd, W.A. *Teacher education in the developing countries of the Commonwealth*. London: Commonwealth Secretariat, 1970.

Edelfelt, R.A. and Johnson, M. (Eds.), *Rethinking in-service education*. Washington: National Education Association, 1975.

Eggleston, S.J. Initial and continuing training of teachers - new trends and concepts. In: *New patterns of teacher education and tasks*. *General analyses*. Paris: OECD, 1974.

Erdos, R. and Clark, J.H. (Eds.), *Correspondence courses for in-service teacher training at primary level in developing countries*. Report of a meeting of international experts. Hamburg: Unesco Institute for Education, 1971.

Frey, K. *Federal Republic of Germany: Switzerland*. Paris: OECD, 1976.

Gage, N.L. (Ed.), *Handbook of Research on Teaching*. Chicago: Rand McNally, 1963.

Gage, N.L. *Teacher effectiveness and teacher education - the search for a scientific basis*. Palo Alto, Calif.: Pacific Books, 1972.

Galthrop, K. and Owens, G. (Eds.), *Teachers for tomorrow*. *Diverse and radical views about teacher education*. London: Heinemann, 1971.

Gwyn, R. *Current trends in teacher education: a survey*. Committee for higher education and research. 33rd meeting. Strasbourg: Council of Europe, 1976.

Haberman, M. and Stinnett, T.M. *Teacher education and the new profession of teaching*. Berkeley, Calif.: McCutchan, 1973.

Havelock, R.G. and Havelock, M.C. *Training for change agents.
A guide to the design of training programs in education and
other fields.* Ann Arbor, Mich.: The University of Michigan,
Institute for Social Research, Center for Research on Utilization of Scientific Knowledge, 1973.

Hawes, H.W.R. Lifelong education, schools and curricula in developing countries. *UIE Monographs*, 1975 (Whole No. 4).

International Council on Education for Teaching, *Crisis and
change in teachers education: international perspectives on
theory and practice.* Washington, D.C., 1971.

International Schools Association, *Early training for the un-
known, the unexpected and the possible.* Geneva: International
Schools Association, 1972.

James, L. *Teacher education and training.* London: HMSO, 1972.

Johnston, D.J. *Teachers' in-service education.* Oxford:
Pergamon Press, 1971.

Kaye, B. *Participation in learning. A progress report on some
experiments in the training of teachers.* London: Allen and
Unwin, 1970.

King, E.J. *The education of teachers. A comparative analysis.*
London: Rolt, Rinehart and Winston, 1970.

King, E.J. (Ed.), *The teacher and the needs of society in evolution.* Oxford: Pergamon Press, 1970.

Klassen, F.H., Imig, D.G. and Collier, J.L. *Innovation in
teacher education: an international perspective.* Washington,
D.C.: International Council on Education for Teaching, 1972.

Klassen, F.H. and Collier, J.L. *Innovation now! International
perspectives on innovation in teacher education.* Washington,
D.C.: International Council on Education for Teaching, 1972.

Klassen, F.H. and Imig, D.G. (Eds.), *National and community
needs - the challenge for teacher education: international
perspectives on theory and practice.* Washington, D.C., International Council on Education for Teaching, 1973.

Lynch, J. Lifelong education and the preparation of educational personnel. *UIE Monographs*, 1977 (Whole No. 5).

Lynch, J. and Plunkett, H.D. *Teacher education and cultural change. England, France, West Germany.* London: Allen and Unwin, 1973.

Marklund, S. *Retrospects and prospects in teacher training research.* Stockholm: Research and Development Bureau, National Board of Education, 1973.

Organisation for Economic Co-operation and Development, *New patterns of teacher education and tasks. General analyses.* Paris: Organisation for Economic Co-operation and Development, 1974.

Organisation for Economic Co-operation and Development, *The teacher and educational change. Vol. 1: A new role.* General report. Paris: OECD, 1974

Organisation for Economic Co-operation and Development, *The teacher and educational change. Vol. 2: Recent trends in teacher recruitment.* Paris: OECD, 1974.

Razik, T.A. *Systems approach to teacher training and curriculum development: the case of developing countries.* Paris: Unesco, International Institute for Educational Planning, 1972.

Rubin, L.J. (Ed.), *Improving in-service education: proposals and procedures for change.* Boston, Mass.: Allyn and Bacon, 1971.

Ryan, K. (Ed.), *Teacher education.* Chicago, Ill.: The University of Chicago Press, 1975.

Ryba, R. (Ed.), *Teacher education.* Proceedings of the Comparative Education Society in Europe. Lund: Berlin, 1972.

Silberman, M.L., Allender, J.S. and Yanoff, J.M. (Eds.), *The psychology of open teaching and learning. An inquiry approach.* Boston: Little, Brown, 1972.

Smith, B.O. (Ed.), *Research in teacher education. A symposium.* Englewood Cliffs: Prentice-Hall, 1971.

Smith, B., Cohen, S.B. and Pearl, A. *Teachers for the real*

world. Washington: American Association of Colleges for
Teacher Education, 1969.

Taylor, W. *Society and the education of teachers.* London:
Faber and Faber, 1969.

Thornbury, R.F. (Ed.), *Teachers' centres.* London: Darton,
Longman and Todd, 1973.

Tibble, J.W. (Ed.), *The future of teacher education.* London:
Routledge and Kegan Paul, 1971.

Unesco, *Practical guide to in-service teacher training in
Africa. Establishment, execution and control of training
programmes.* Paris: Unesco, 1970.

Unesco Regional Office for Education in Asia, *Further education
of teachers in service in Asia: A regional survey.* Bangkok:
Unesco Regional Office for Education in Asia, 1973.

World Confederation of Organizations of the Teaching Profession,
The teachers's changing role in the school of the future.
Beirut: Author, 1972.

Yates, A. (Ed.), *Current problems of teacher education.* Hamburg,
Unesco Institute for Education, 1970.

Curriculum Change and Innovation

Beauchamp, A. *Curriculum theory.* Wilmette, Ill.: The Kagg
Press, 1973 (2nd ed.).

Burns, R.W. and Brooks, G.D. (Eds.), *Curriculum design in a
changing society.* Englewood Cliffs, N.J.: Educational Technology Publications, 1970.

Cave, G. *An introduction to curriculum development.* London:
Ward Lock, 1971.

Dahlloef, U. Lundgren, U.P. and Sidöö, M. *Reform implementation
studies as a basis for curriculum theory: three Swedish approaches.* Göteborg: Institute of Education, 1971.

Doll, R.C. *Curriculum improvement. Decision-making and process.* Boston: Allyn and Bacon, 1971 (2nd ed.).

Drumheller, S.J. *Handbook of curriculum design for individual instruction. A systems approach. How to develop curriculum materials for rigorously defined behavioral objectives.* Englewood Cliffs, N.J.: Educational Technology Publishers, 1972.

Eisner, E.W. (Ed.), *Confronting curriculum reform.* Boston: Little, Brown, 1971.

Eisner, E.W. and Vallance, E. (Eds.), *Conflicting conceptions of curriculum.* Berkeley, Calif.: McCutchan, 1974.

English, F.W. and Kaufman, R.A. (Eds.) *Needs assessment: a focus for curriculum development.* Washington: Association for Supervision and Curriculum Development, 1975.

Goodlad, J.I. *School, curriculum, and the individual.* Waltham, Mass.: Blaisdell, 1966.

Grobman, H. *Developmental curriculum projects: decision points and processes. A study of similarities and differences in methods of producing developmental curricula.* Hayward, Calif.: Peacock, 1970.

Hamilton, D. *Curriculum evaluation.* London: Open Books, 1976.

History of Education Society, *The changing curriculum.* London: Methuen, 1971.

Hyman, R.T. (ed.), *Approaches in curriculum.* Englewood Cliffs, N.J.: Prentice-Hall, 1973.

Kopp, O.W. and Zufelt, D.L. *Personalized curriculum: Method and design.* Columbus, Ohio: Merrill, 1971.

Lawler, M.R. (Ed.), *Strategies for planned curricular innovation.* New York: Teachers College Press, 1970.

Lawton, D. *Social change, educational theory and curriculum planning.* London: University of London Press, 1973.

OECD/Centre for Educational Research and Innovation, *Handbook on curriculum development.* Paris: Organisation for Economic Co-operation and Development/Centre for Educational Research and Innovation, 1975.

Payne, D.A. (Ed.), *Curriculum evaluation. Commentaries on purpose, process, product.* Lexington, Mass.: Heath, 1974.

Popham, W.J., Eisner, E.W., Sullivan, H.J. and Tyler, L.L. *Instructional objectives.* Chicago: Rand McNally, 1970.

Popham, W.J and Baker, E.L. *Establishing instructional goals.* Englewood Cliffs, New Jersey: Prentice-Hall, 1970.

Postlethwaite, T.N. *General principles of curriculum development.* Paris: Unesco/International Institute for Educational Planning, 1973.

Razik, T.A. *Systems approach to teacher training and curriculum development: the case of developing countries.* Paris: Unesco/International Institute for Educational Planning, 1972.

Reid, W.A. and Walker, D.F. (Eds.), *Case studies in curriculum change: Great Britain and the United States.* London: Routledge and Kegan Paul, 1975.

Schools Council, *Evaluation in curriculum development: 12 case studies.* London: MacMillan, 1975.

Shipman, M.D., Bolam, D. and Jenkins, D.R. *Inside a curriculum project. A case study in the process of curriculum change.* London: Methuen, 1974.

Skeel, D.J. and Hagen, O.A. *The process of curriculum change.* Pacific Palisades, Calif.: Goodyear Publishing Company, 1971.

Staples, E. (Ed.), *Impact of decentralization on curriculum: Selected viewpoints.* Washington: Association for Supervision and Curriculum Development, 1975.

Stenhouse, L. *An introduction to curriculum research and development.* London: Heinemann, 1975.

Taylor, P.H. and Walton, J. (Eds.), *The curriculum: research, innovation and change.* Preceedings of the inaugural meeting of the Standing Conference on Curriculum Studies. London: Ward Lock, 1973.

Tyler, R.W. *Basic principles of curriculum and instruction.* Chicago: The University of Chicago Press, 1969.

Weiss, J. (Ed.), *Curriculum evaluation: Potentiality and reality.* Toronto: Ontario Institute for Studies in Education, 1972.

Wiseman, S. and Pidgeon, D. *Curriculum evaluation.* Slough, Bucks: NFER, 1972.

Zammit-Mangion, J. *Modernising educational administrations to facilitate the formulation and implementation of curriculum development plans.* Paris: Unesco/International Institute for Educational Planning, 1973.

INDEX